love,
joy,
peace,
patience,
kindness,
goodness,
faithfulness,
gentleness,
self-control

Galatians
five
twenty-two
twenty-three

Against these things there is no law.

DATE:

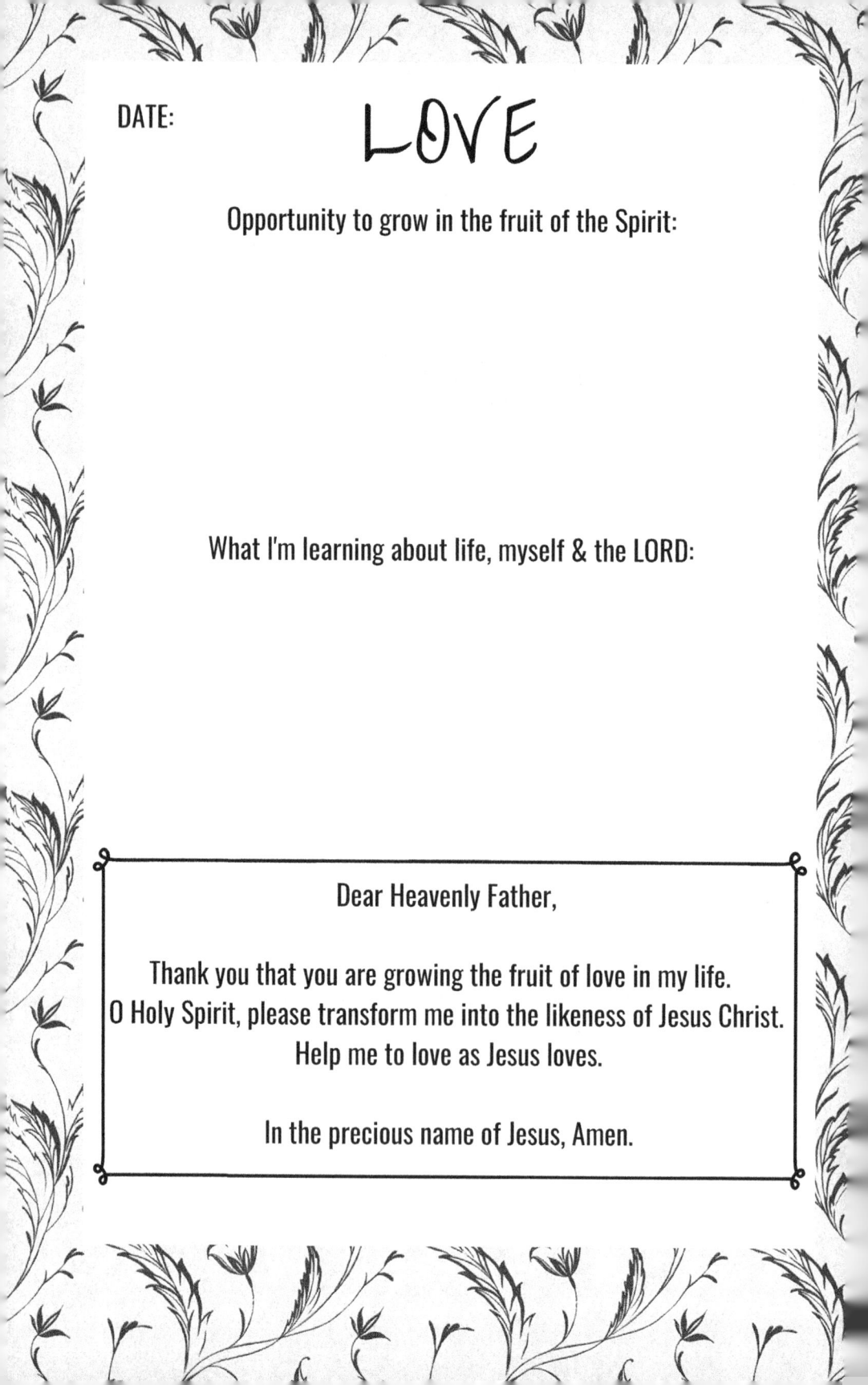

LOVE

Opportunity to grow in the fruit of the Spirit:

What I'm learning about life, myself & the LORD:

Dear Heavenly Father,

Thank you that you are growing the fruit of love in my life.
O Holy Spirit, please transform me into the likeness of Jesus Christ.
Help me to love as Jesus loves.

In the precious name of Jesus, Amen.

DATE:

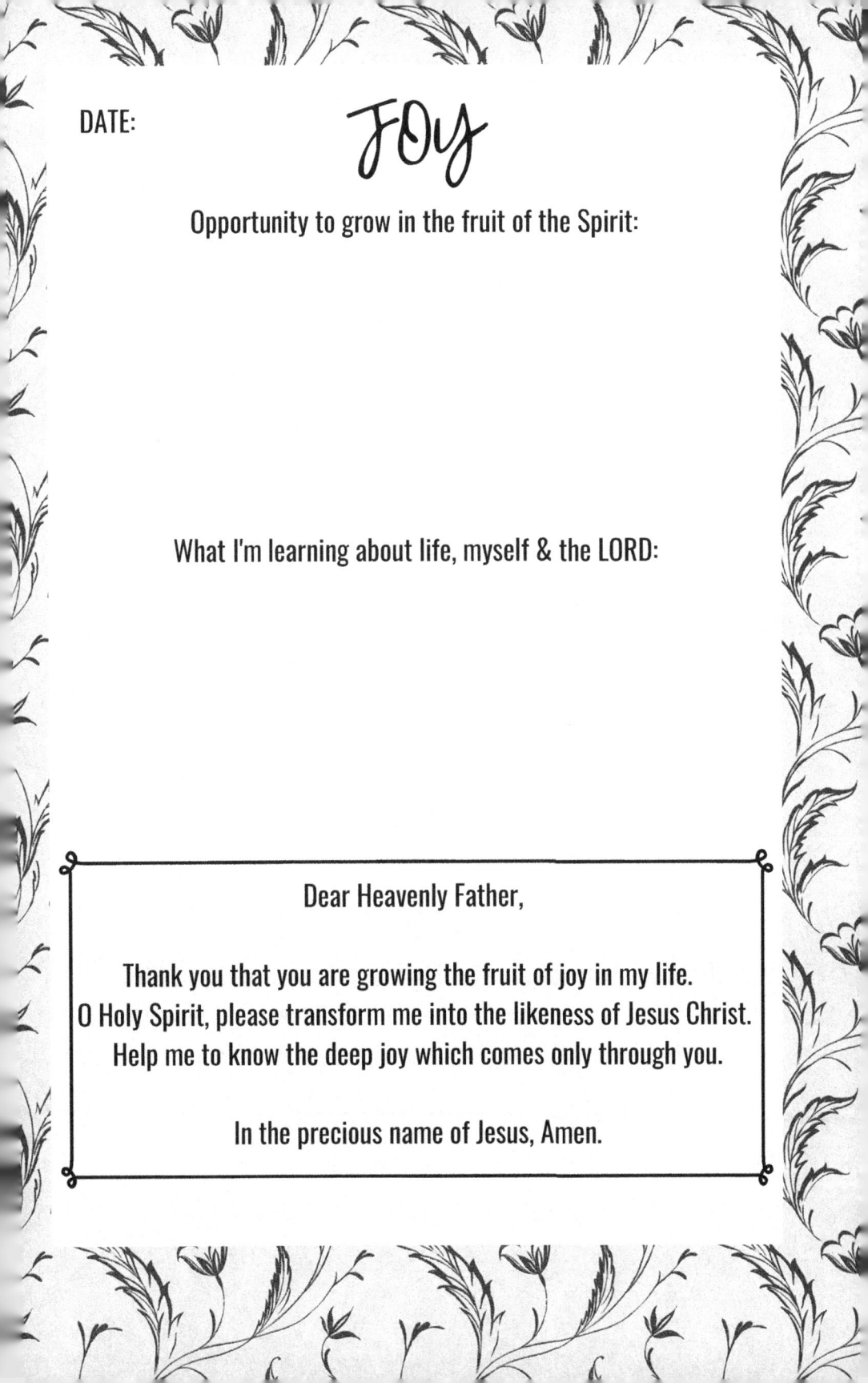

JOY

Opportunity to grow in the fruit of the Spirit:

What I'm learning about life, myself & the LORD:

Dear Heavenly Father,

Thank you that you are growing the fruit of joy in my life.
O Holy Spirit, please transform me into the likeness of Jesus Christ.
Help me to know the deep joy which comes only through you.

In the precious name of Jesus, Amen.

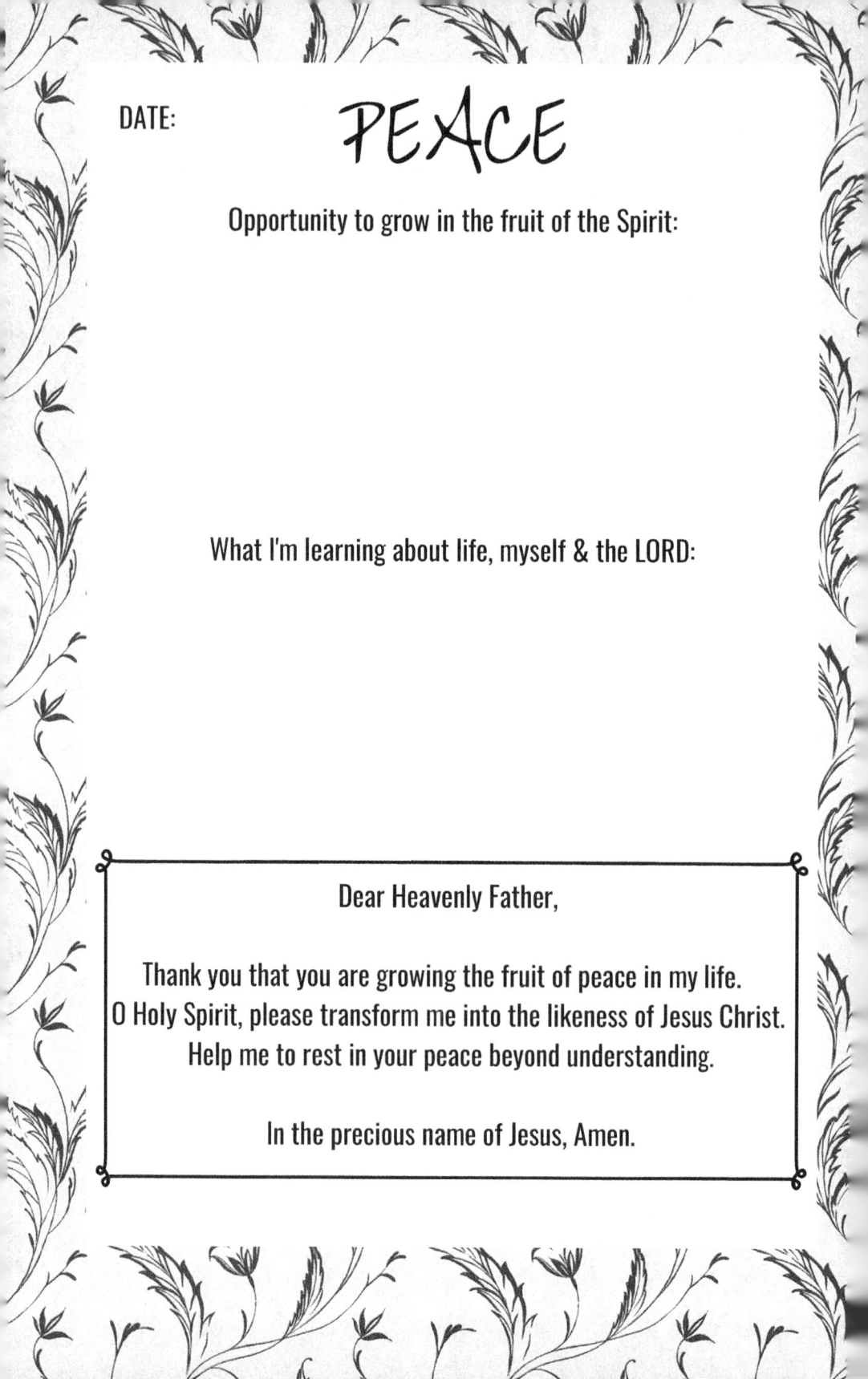

DATE:

PEACE

Opportunity to grow in the fruit of the Spirit:

What I'm learning about life, myself & the LORD:

Dear Heavenly Father,

Thank you that you are growing the fruit of peace in my life.
O Holy Spirit, please transform me into the likeness of Jesus Christ.
Help me to rest in your peace beyond understanding.

In the precious name of Jesus, Amen.

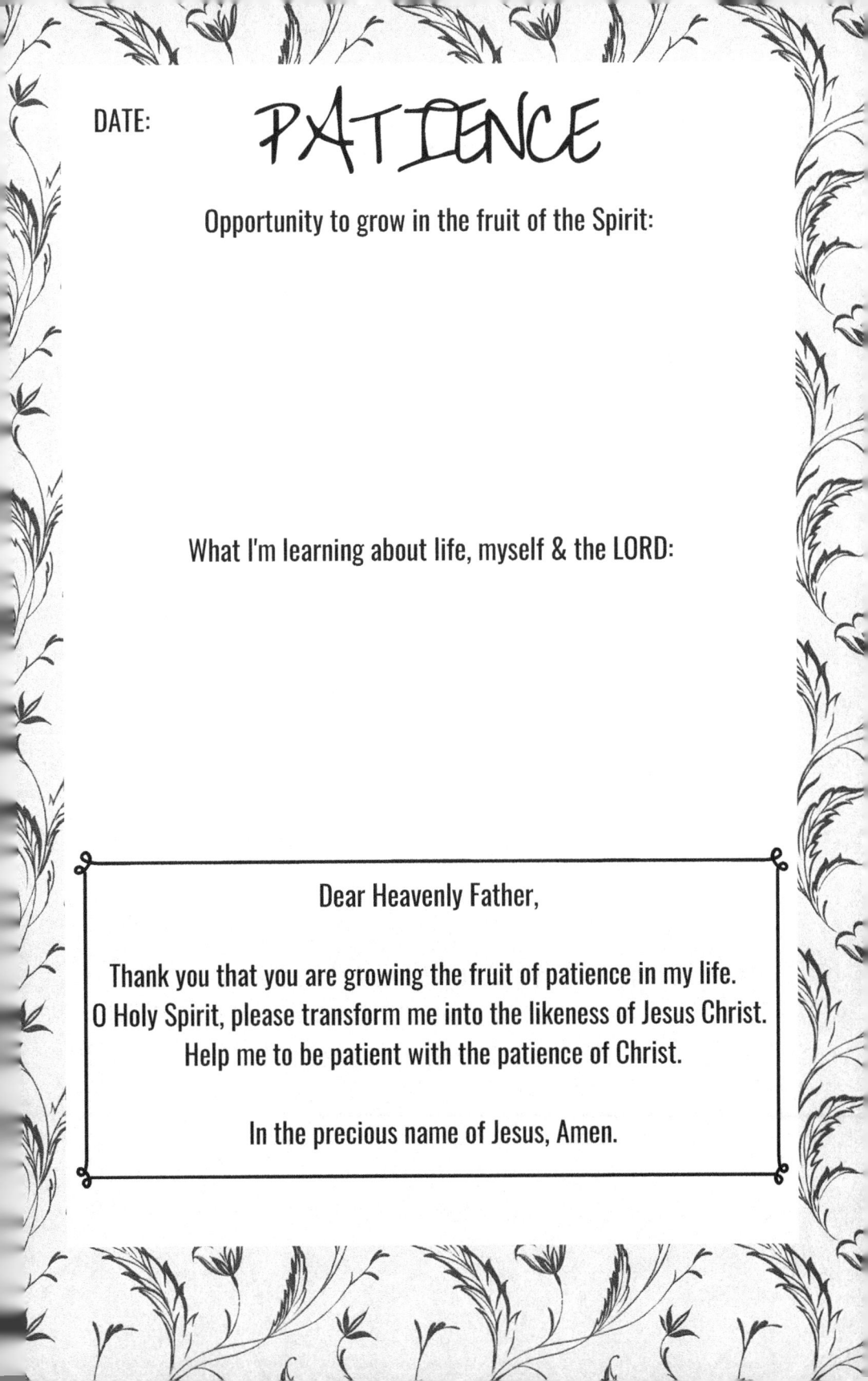

DATE:

PATIENCE

Opportunity to grow in the fruit of the Spirit:

What I'm learning about life, myself & the LORD:

Dear Heavenly Father,

Thank you that you are growing the fruit of patience in my life.
O Holy Spirit, please transform me into the likeness of Jesus Christ.
Help me to be patient with the patience of Christ.

In the precious name of Jesus, Amen.

DATE:

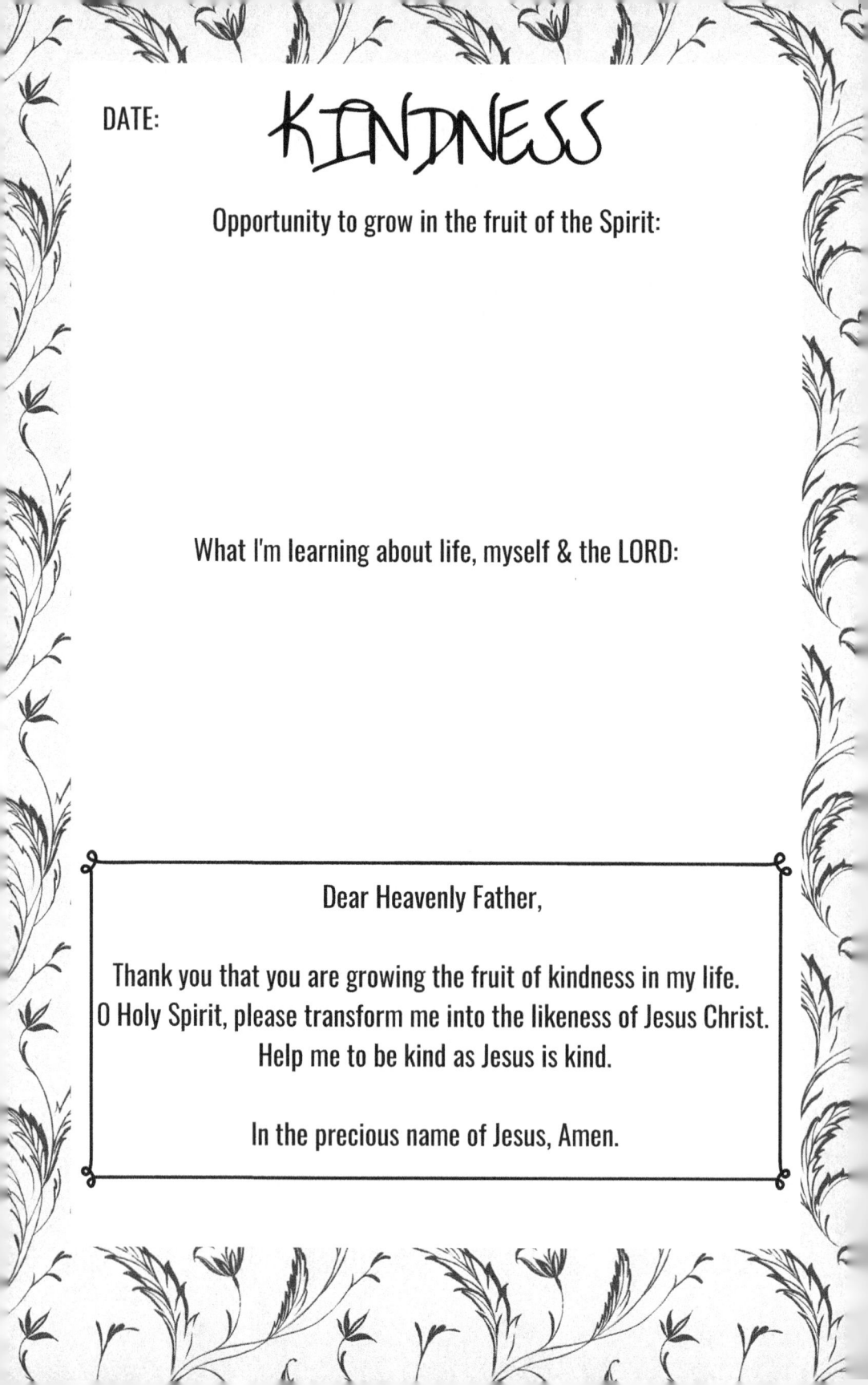

KINDNESS

Opportunity to grow in the fruit of the Spirit:

What I'm learning about life, myself & the LORD:

Dear Heavenly Father,

Thank you that you are growing the fruit of kindness in my life.
O Holy Spirit, please transform me into the likeness of Jesus Christ.
Help me to be kind as Jesus is kind.

In the precious name of Jesus, Amen.

DATE:

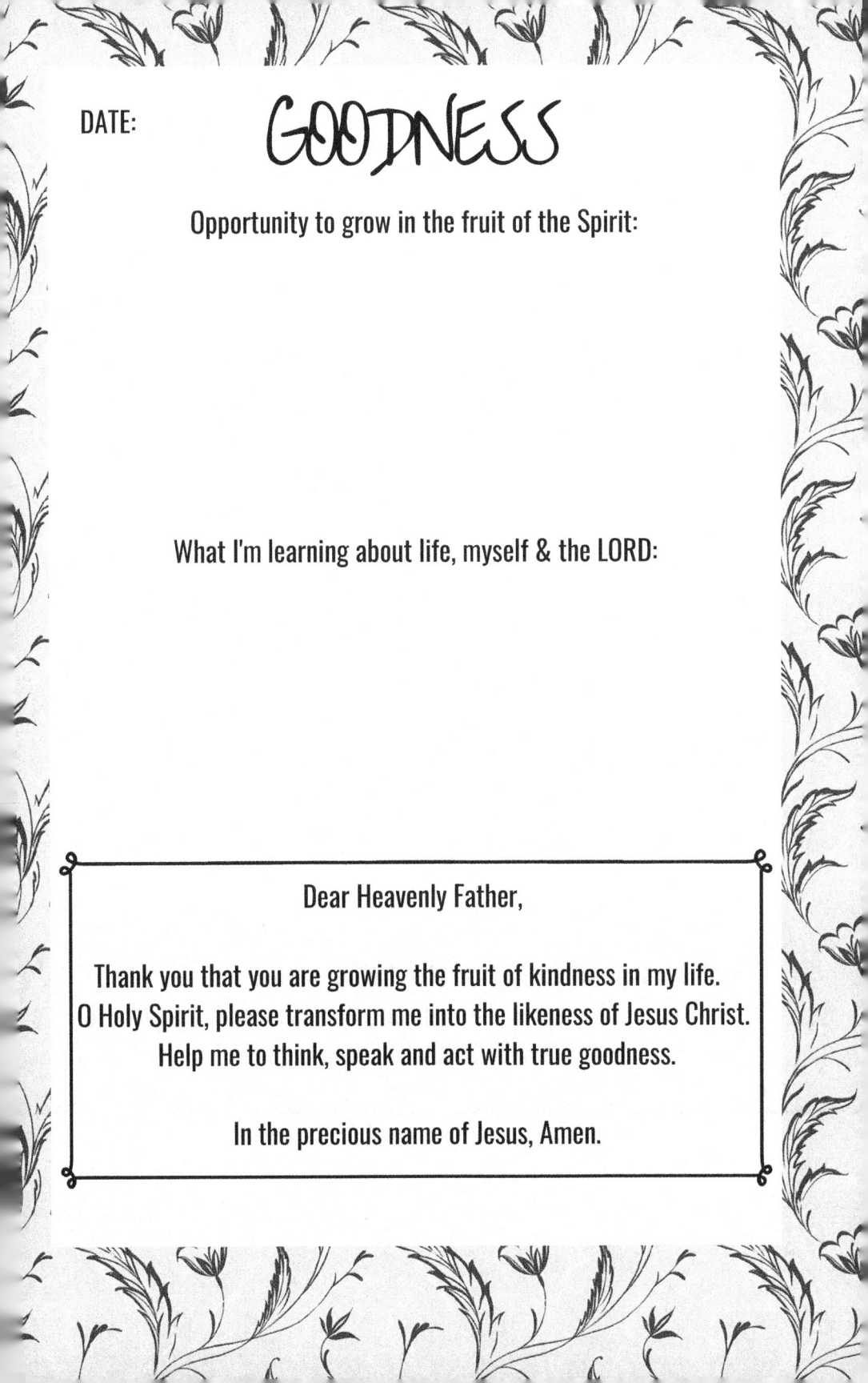

GOODNESS

Opportunity to grow in the fruit of the Spirit:

What I'm learning about life, myself & the LORD:

Dear Heavenly Father,

Thank you that you are growing the fruit of kindness in my life.
O Holy Spirit, please transform me into the likeness of Jesus Christ.
Help me to think, speak and act with true goodness.

In the precious name of Jesus, Amen.

DATE:

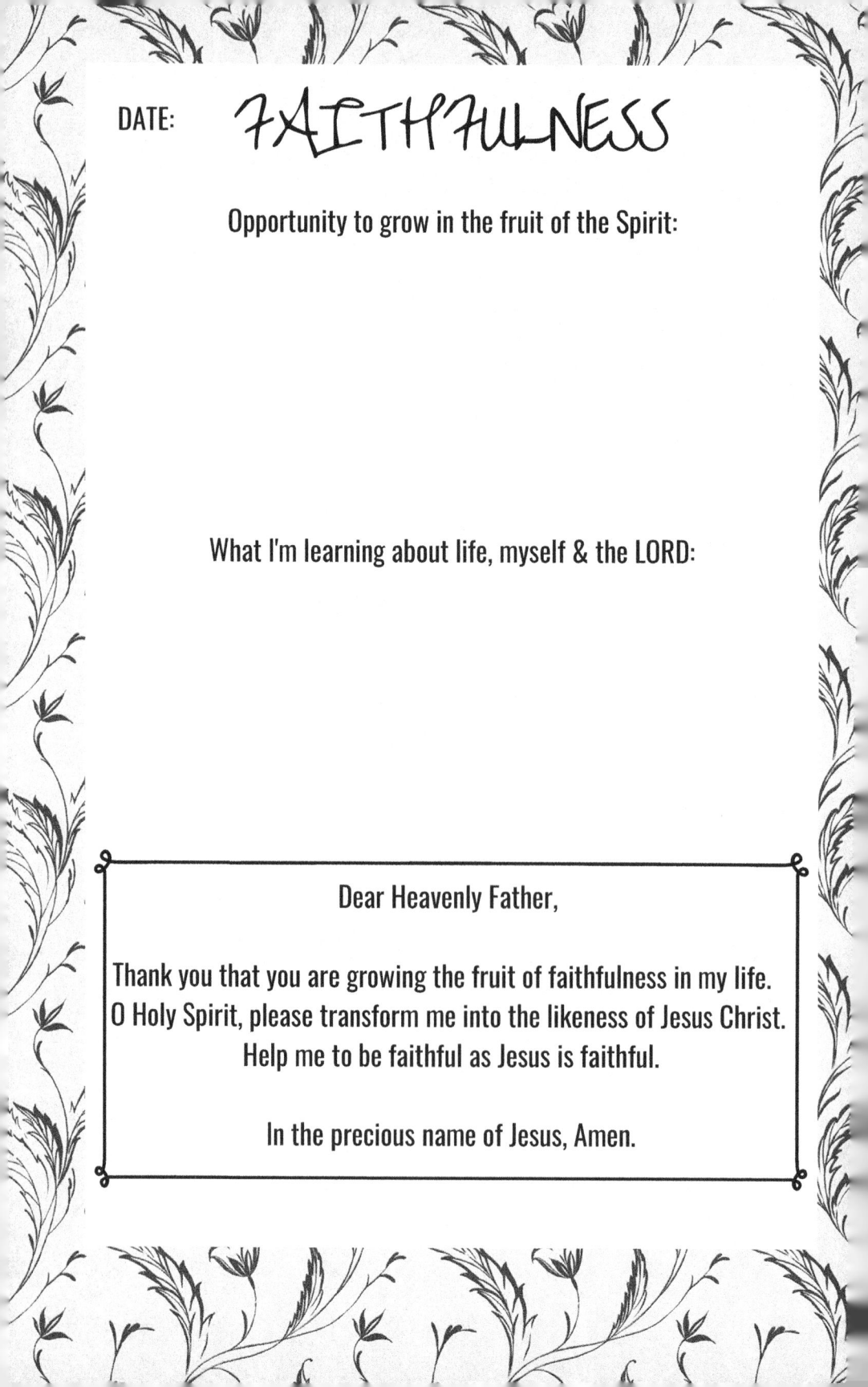

FAITHFULNESS

Opportunity to grow in the fruit of the Spirit:

What I'm learning about life, myself & the LORD:

Dear Heavenly Father,

Thank you that you are growing the fruit of faithfulness in my life. O Holy Spirit, please transform me into the likeness of Jesus Christ. Help me to be faithful as Jesus is faithful.

In the precious name of Jesus, Amen.

DATE:

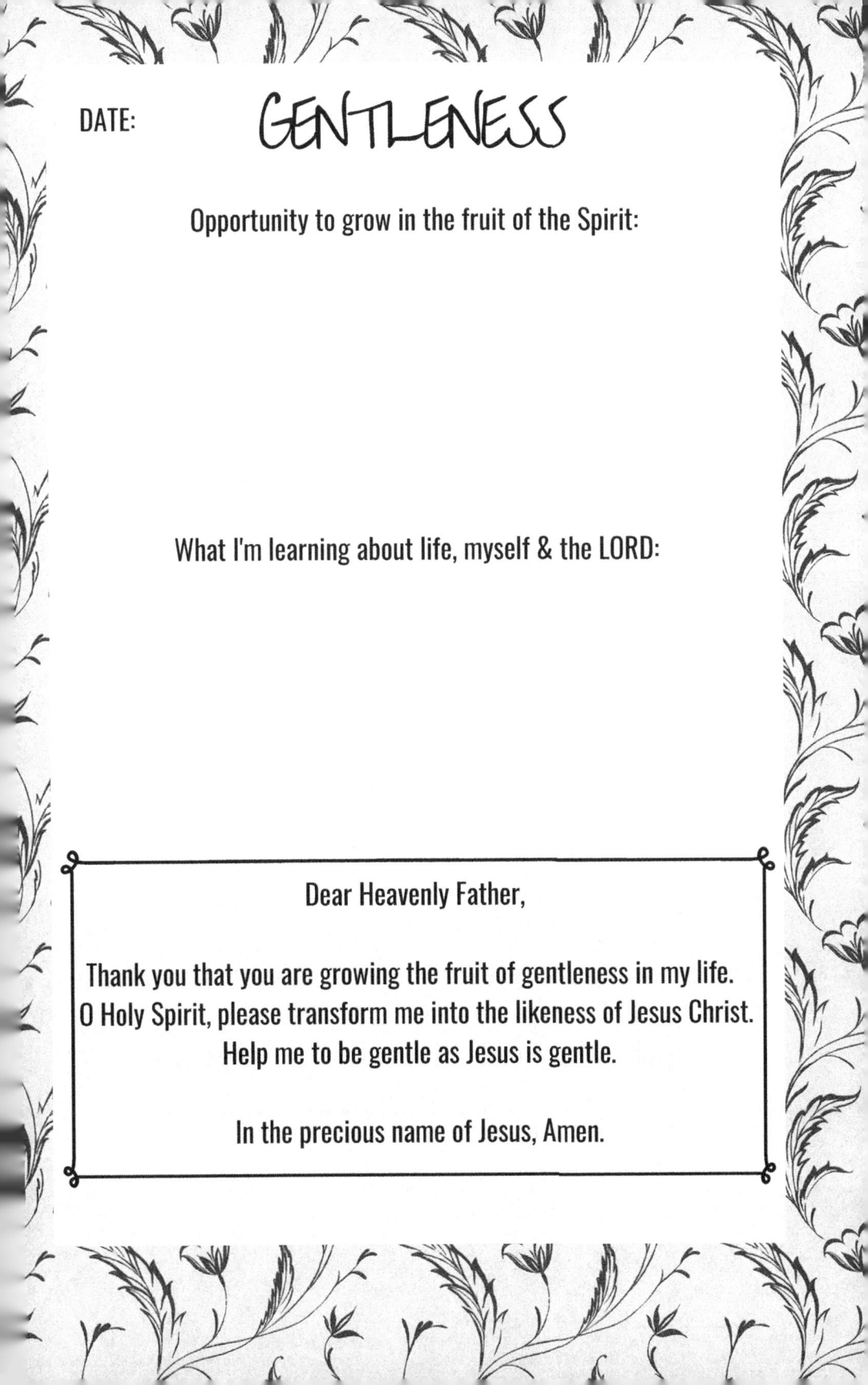

GENTLENESS

Opportunity to grow in the fruit of the Spirit:

What I'm learning about life, myself & the LORD:

Dear Heavenly Father,

Thank you that you are growing the fruit of gentleness in my life. O Holy Spirit, please transform me into the likeness of Jesus Christ. Help me to be gentle as Jesus is gentle.

In the precious name of Jesus, Amen.

DATE: # SELF-CONTROL

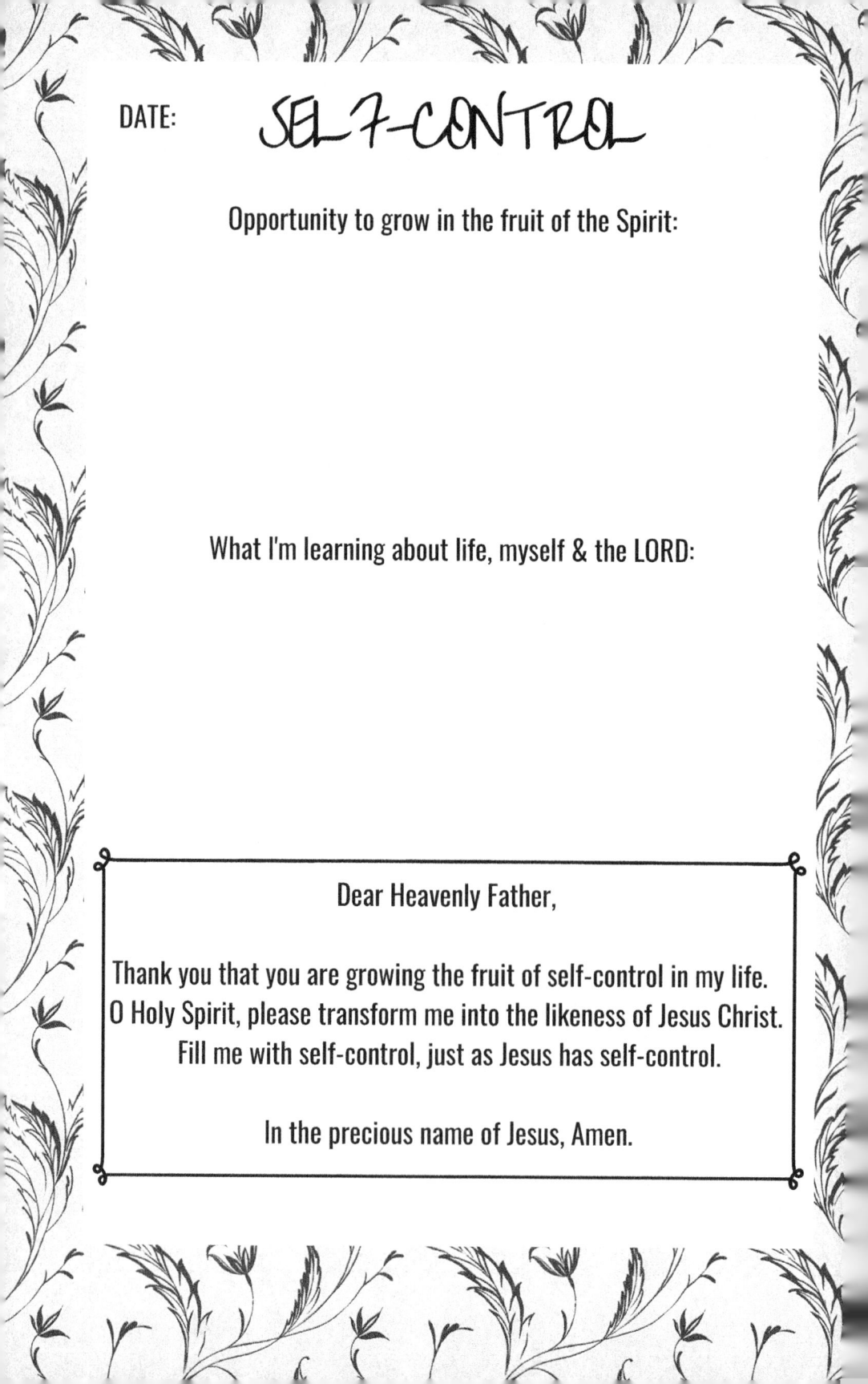

Opportunity to grow in the fruit of the Spirit:

What I'm learning about life, myself & the LORD:

Dear Heavenly Father,

Thank you that you are growing the fruit of self-control in my life. O Holy Spirit, please transform me into the likeness of Jesus Christ. Fill me with self-control, just as Jesus has self-control.

In the precious name of Jesus, Amen.

love,
joy,
peace,
patience,
kindness,
goodness,
faithfulness,
gentleness,
self-control

DATE:

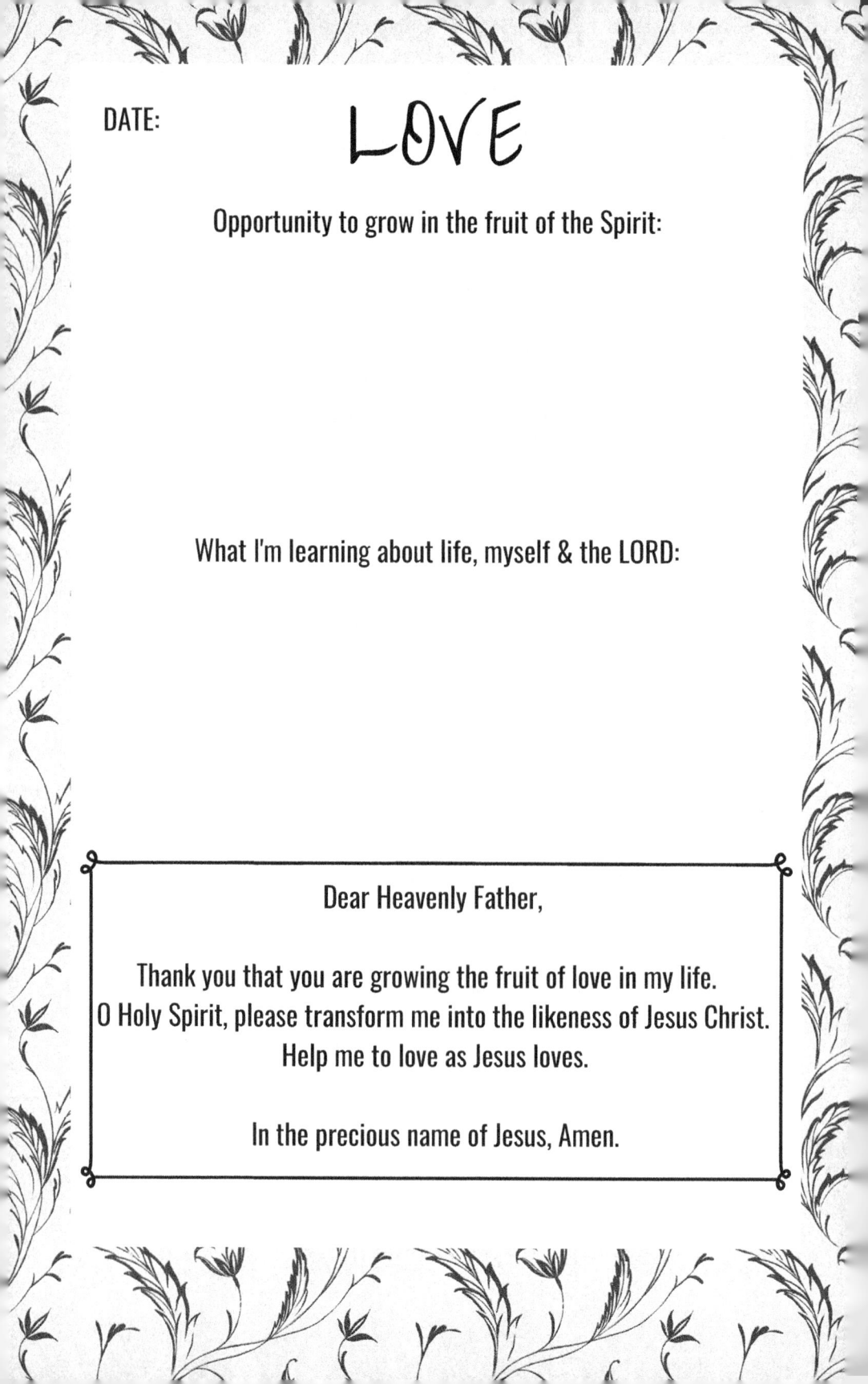

LOVE

Opportunity to grow in the fruit of the Spirit:

What I'm learning about life, myself & the LORD:

Dear Heavenly Father,

Thank you that you are growing the fruit of love in my life.
O Holy Spirit, please transform me into the likeness of Jesus Christ.
Help me to love as Jesus loves.

In the precious name of Jesus, Amen.

DATE:

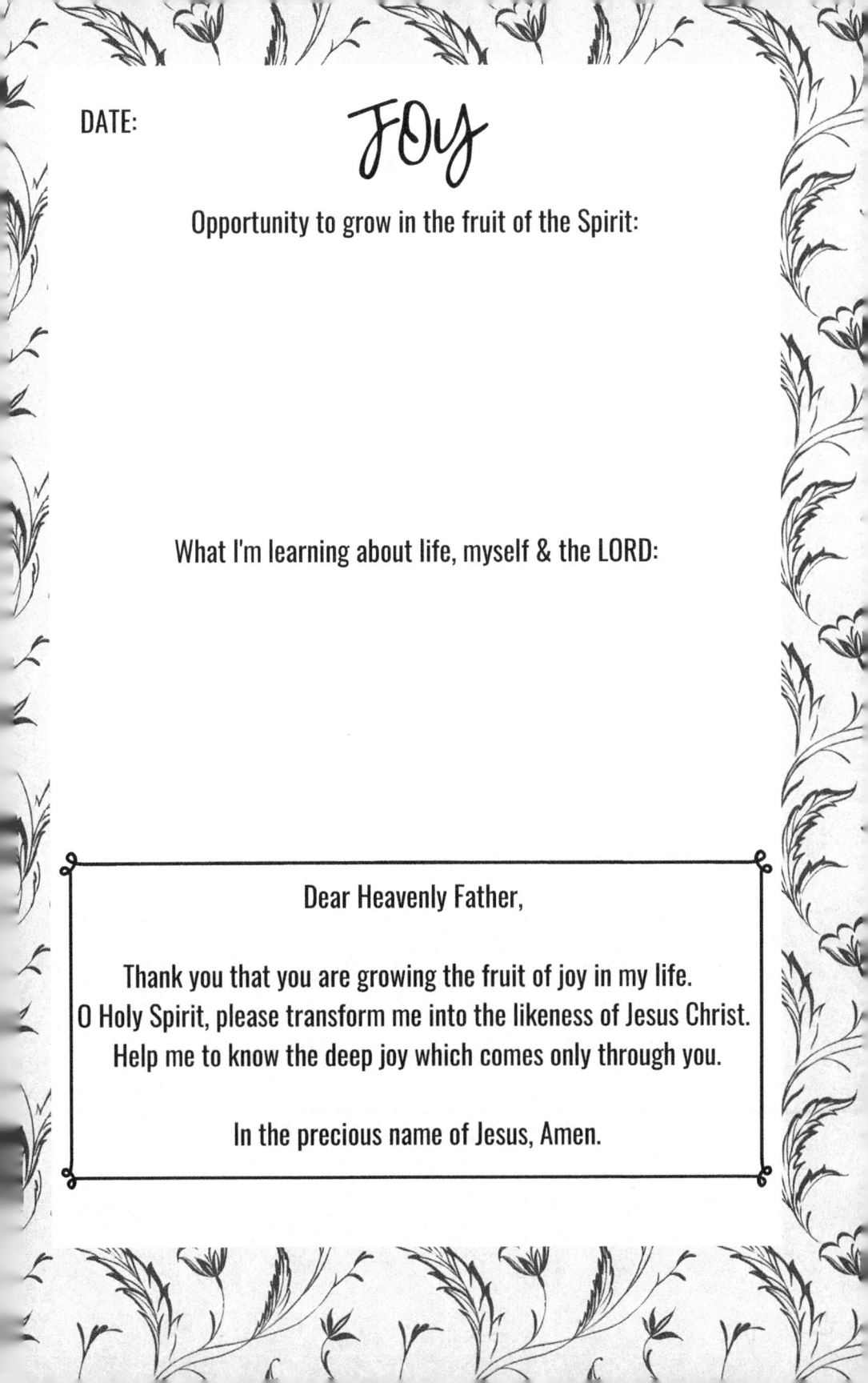

JOY

Opportunity to grow in the fruit of the Spirit:

What I'm learning about life, myself & the LORD:

Dear Heavenly Father,

Thank you that you are growing the fruit of joy in my life.
O Holy Spirit, please transform me into the likeness of Jesus Christ.
Help me to know the deep joy which comes only through you.

In the precious name of Jesus, Amen.

DATE:

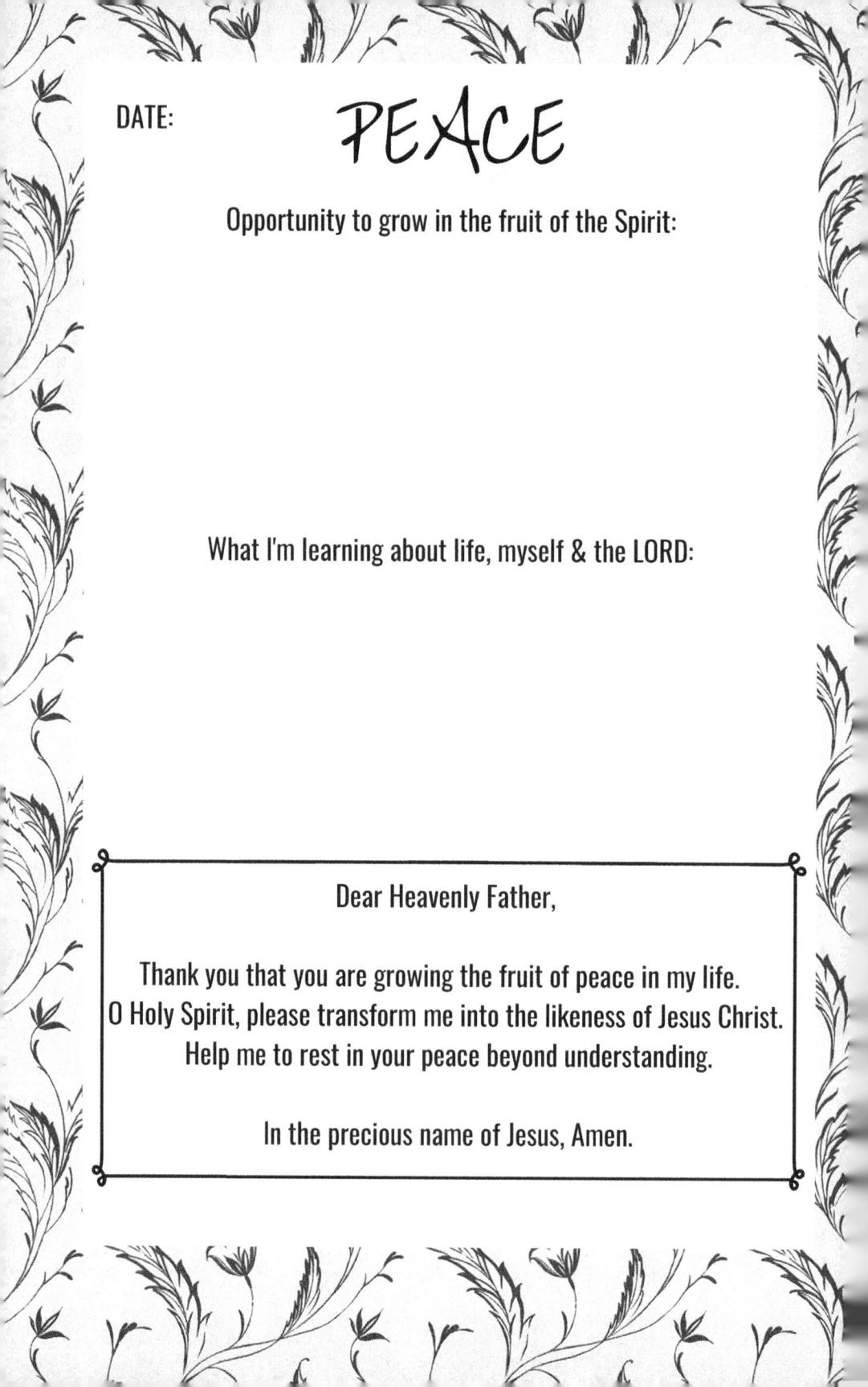

PEACE

Opportunity to grow in the fruit of the Spirit:

What I'm learning about life, myself & the LORD:

Dear Heavenly Father,

Thank you that you are growing the fruit of peace in my life.
O Holy Spirit, please transform me into the likeness of Jesus Christ.
Help me to rest in your peace beyond understanding.

In the precious name of Jesus, Amen.

DATE:

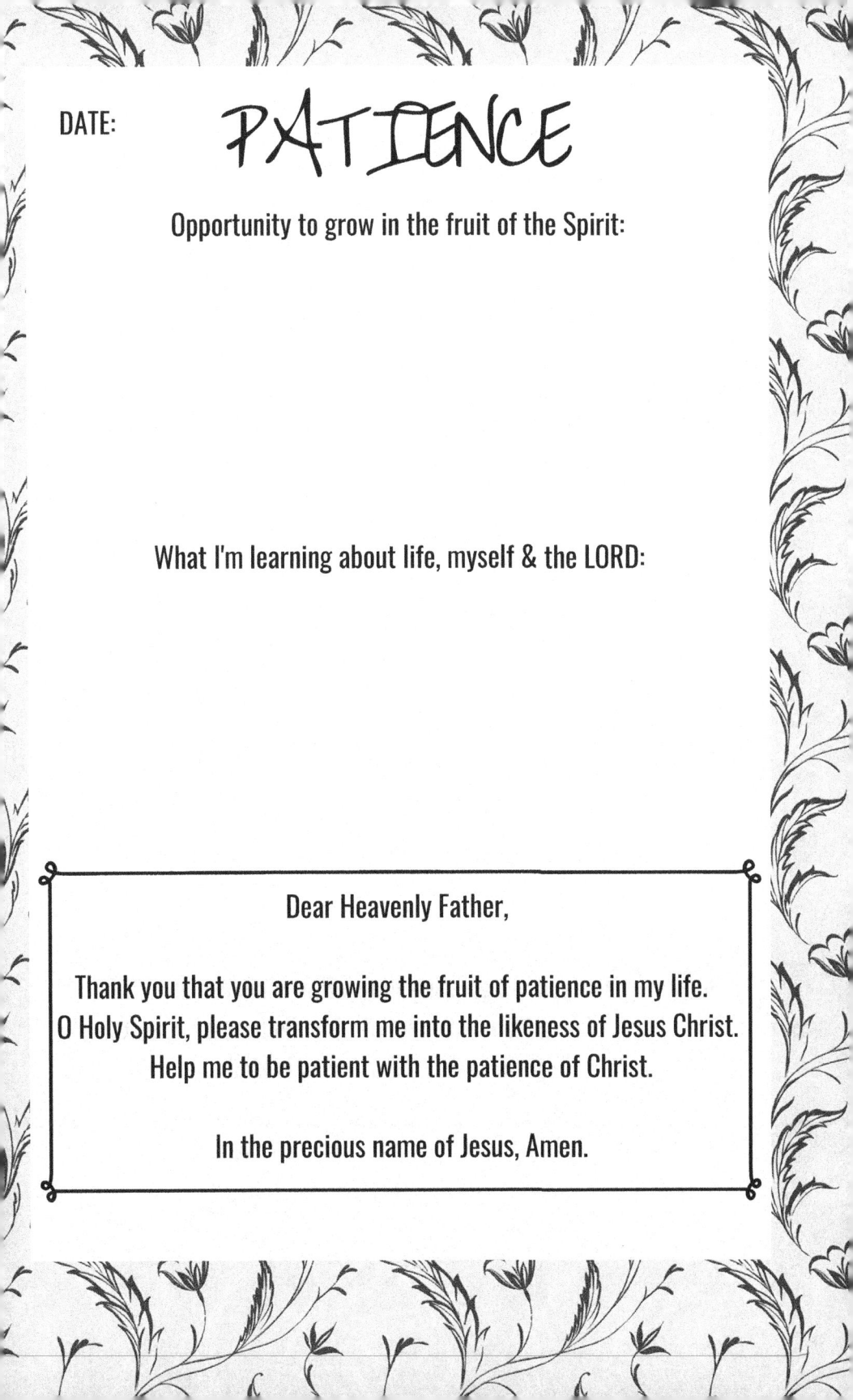

PATIENCE

Opportunity to grow in the fruit of the Spirit:

What I'm learning about life, myself & the LORD:

Dear Heavenly Father,

Thank you that you are growing the fruit of patience in my life.
O Holy Spirit, please transform me into the likeness of Jesus Christ.
Help me to be patient with the patience of Christ.

In the precious name of Jesus, Amen.

DATE:

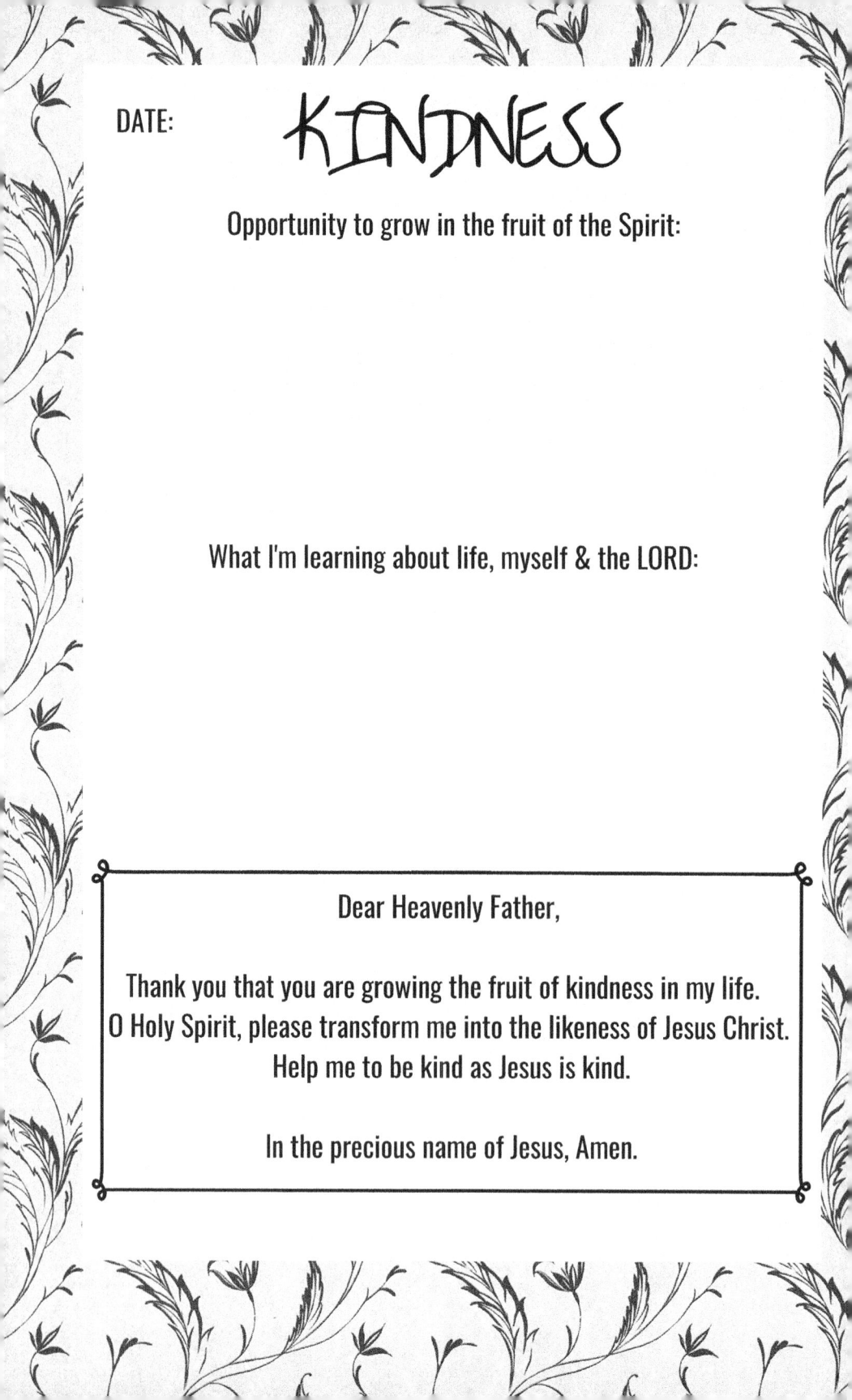

KINDNESS

Opportunity to grow in the fruit of the Spirit:

What I'm learning about life, myself & the LORD:

Dear Heavenly Father,

Thank you that you are growing the fruit of kindness in my life.
O Holy Spirit, please transform me into the likeness of Jesus Christ.
Help me to be kind as Jesus is kind.

In the precious name of Jesus, Amen.

DATE:

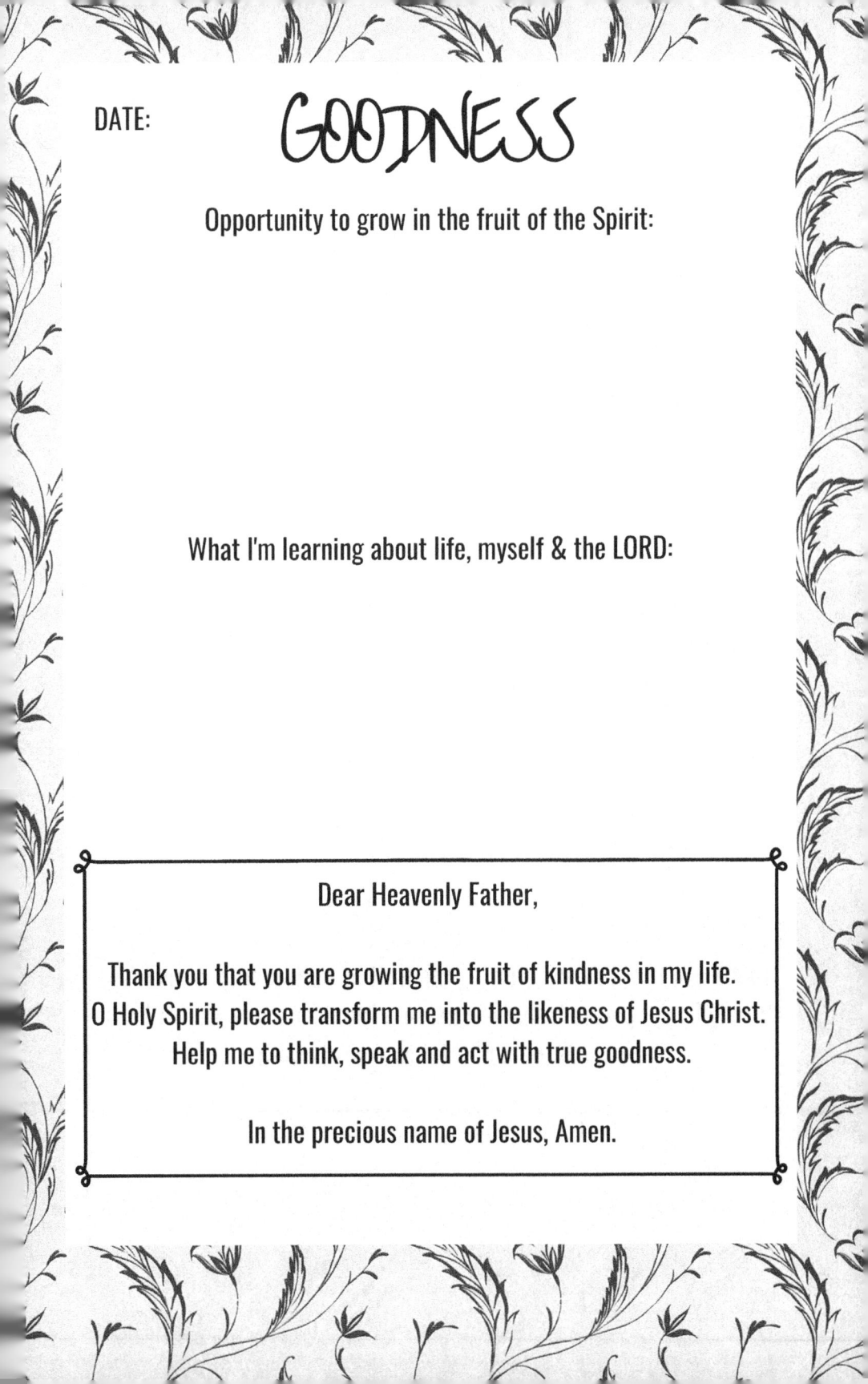

GOODNESS

Opportunity to grow in the fruit of the Spirit:

What I'm learning about life, myself & the LORD:

Dear Heavenly Father,

Thank you that you are growing the fruit of kindness in my life.
O Holy Spirit, please transform me into the likeness of Jesus Christ.
Help me to think, speak and act with true goodness.

In the precious name of Jesus, Amen.

DATE: # FAITHFULNESS

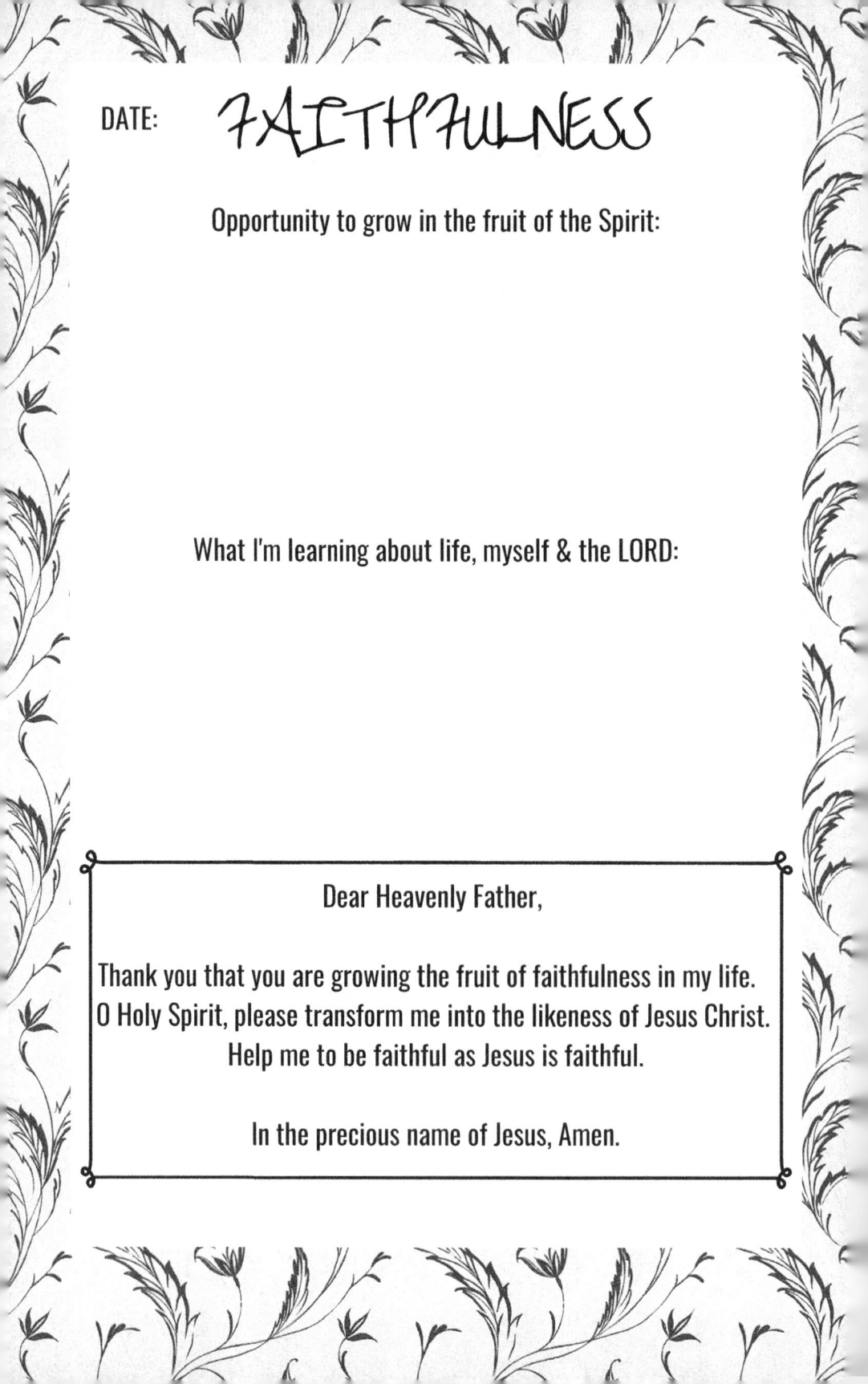

Opportunity to grow in the fruit of the Spirit:

What I'm learning about life, myself & the LORD:

Dear Heavenly Father,

Thank you that you are growing the fruit of faithfulness in my life. O Holy Spirit, please transform me into the likeness of Jesus Christ. Help me to be faithful as Jesus is faithful.

In the precious name of Jesus, Amen.

DATE:

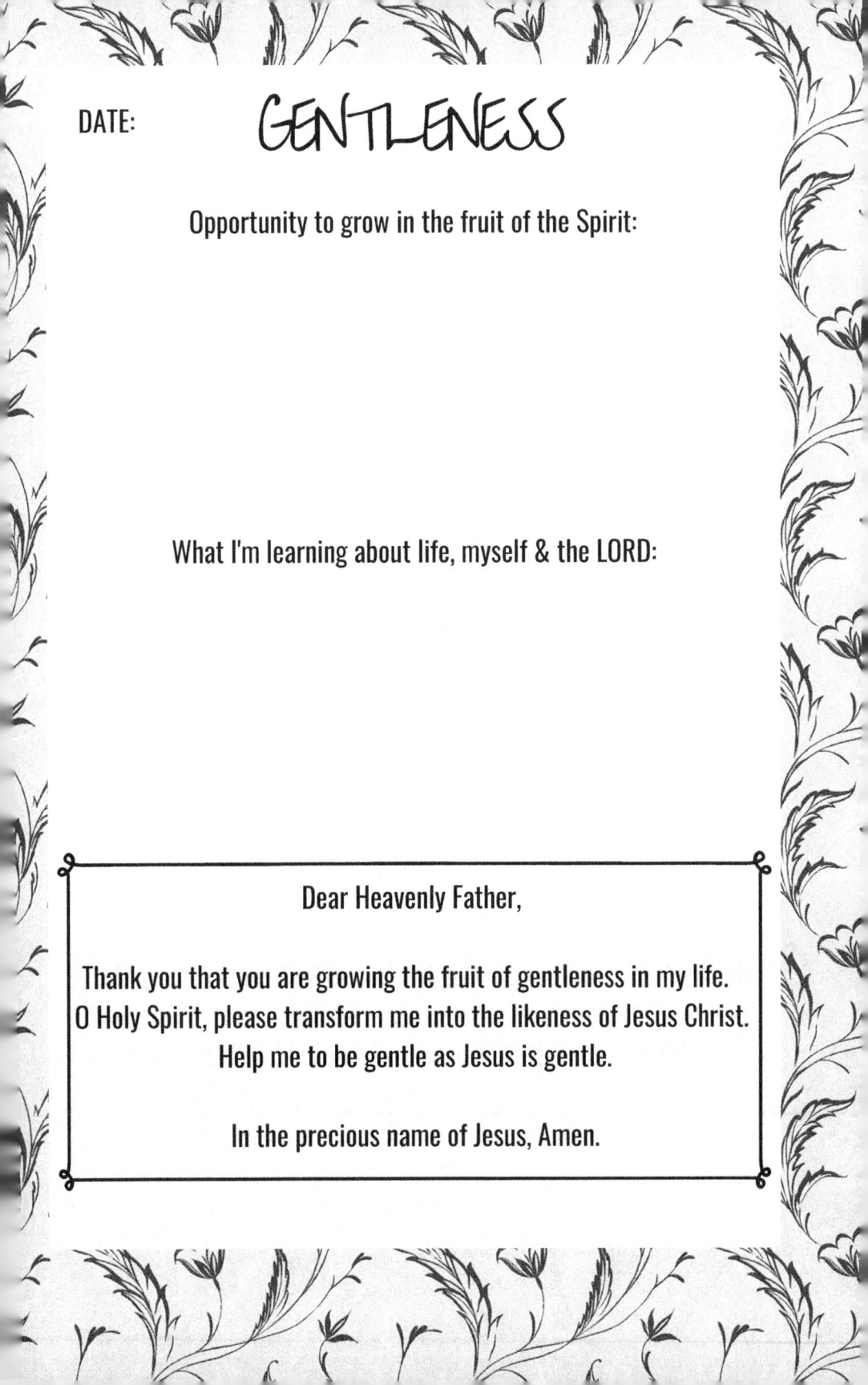

GENTLENESS

Opportunity to grow in the fruit of the Spirit:

What I'm learning about life, myself & the LORD:

Dear Heavenly Father,

Thank you that you are growing the fruit of gentleness in my life. O Holy Spirit, please transform me into the likeness of Jesus Christ. Help me to be gentle as Jesus is gentle.

In the precious name of Jesus, Amen.

DATE:

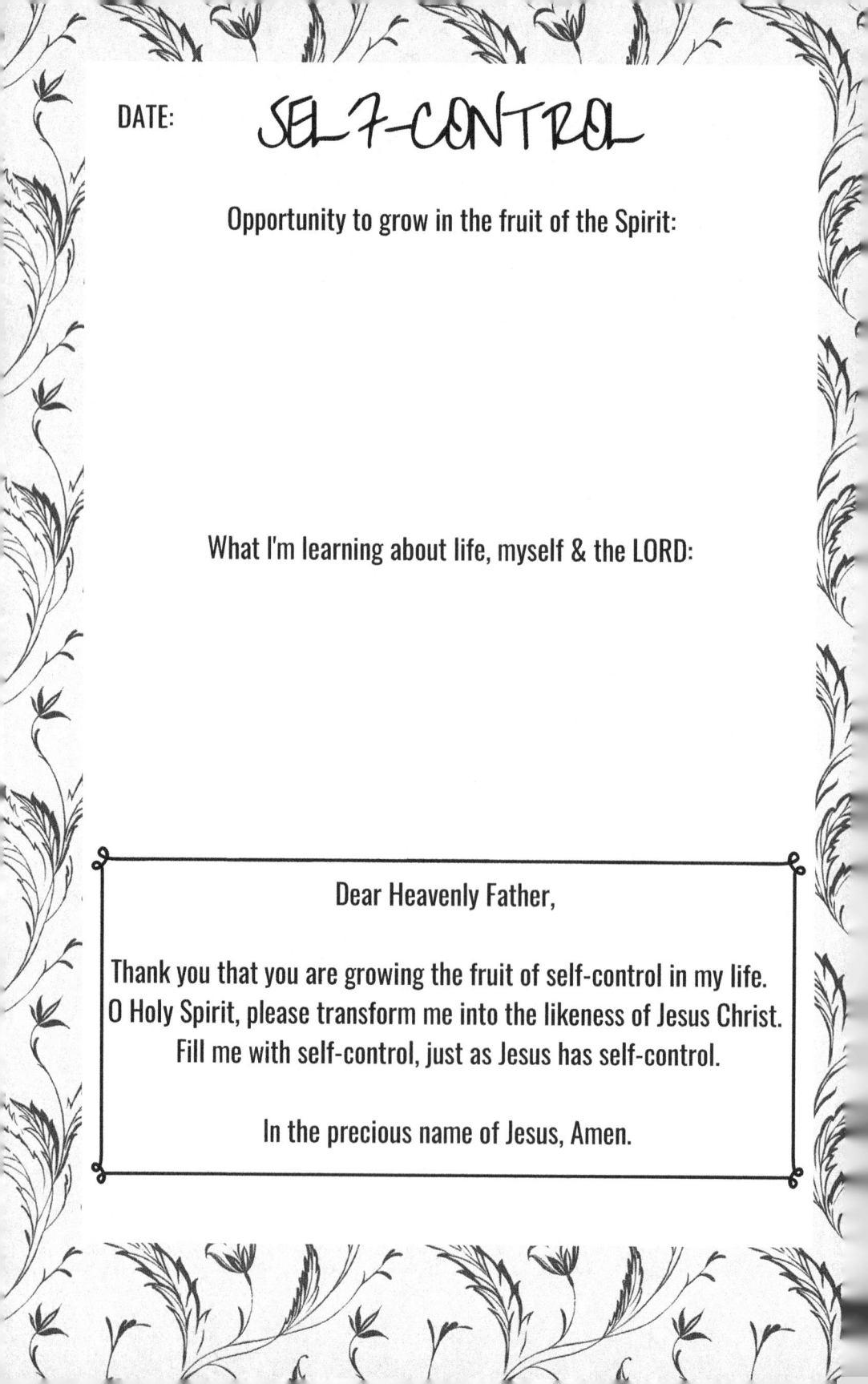

SELF-CONTROL

Opportunity to grow in the fruit of the Spirit:

What I'm learning about life, myself & the LORD:

Dear Heavenly Father,

Thank you that you are growing the fruit of self-control in my life.
O Holy Spirit, please transform me into the likeness of Jesus Christ.
Fill me with self-control, just as Jesus has self-control.

In the precious name of Jesus, Amen.

Against these things there is no law.

DATE:

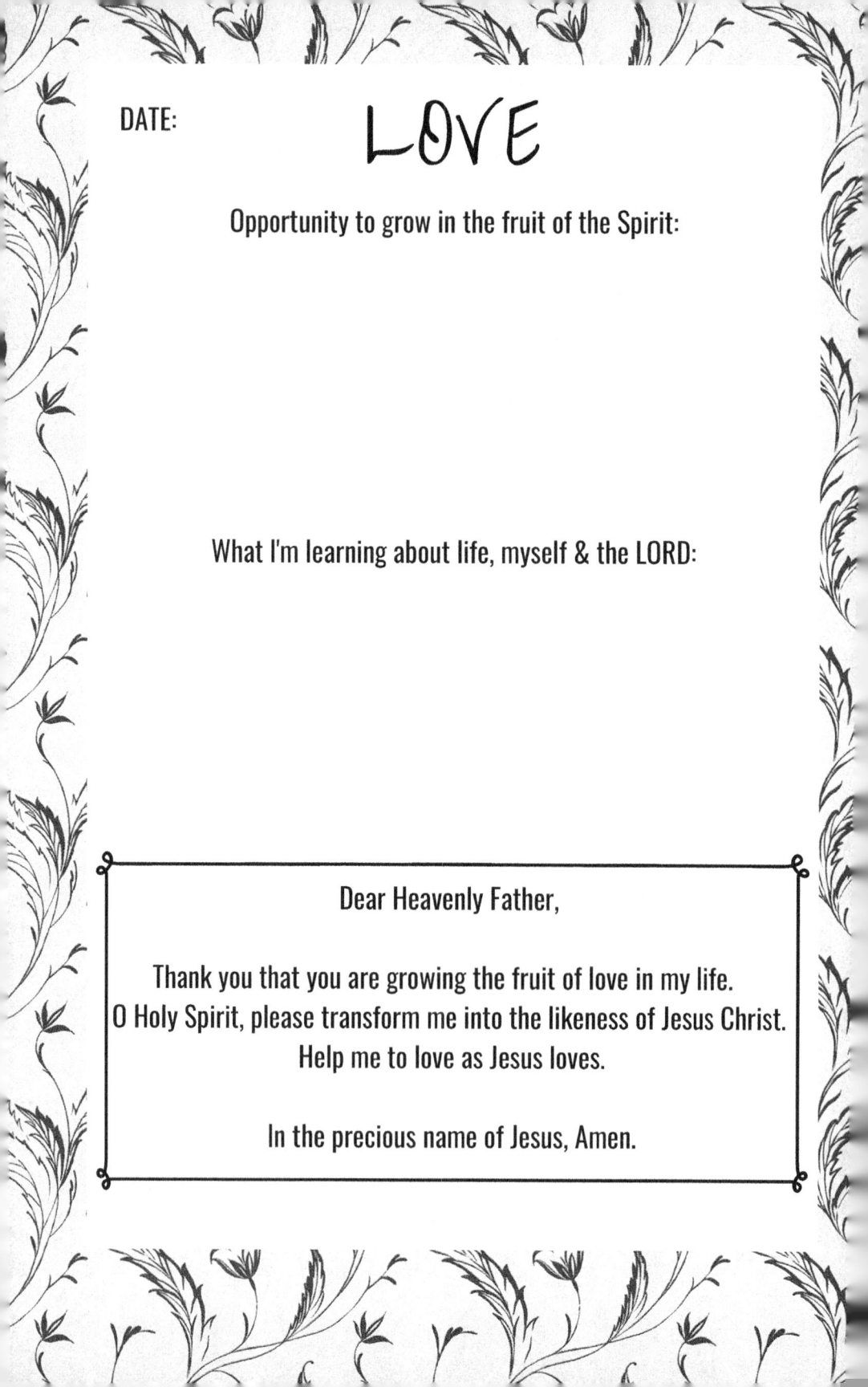

LOVE

Opportunity to grow in the fruit of the Spirit:

What I'm learning about life, myself & the LORD:

Dear Heavenly Father,

Thank you that you are growing the fruit of love in my life.
O Holy Spirit, please transform me into the likeness of Jesus Christ.
Help me to love as Jesus loves.

In the precious name of Jesus, Amen.

DATE:

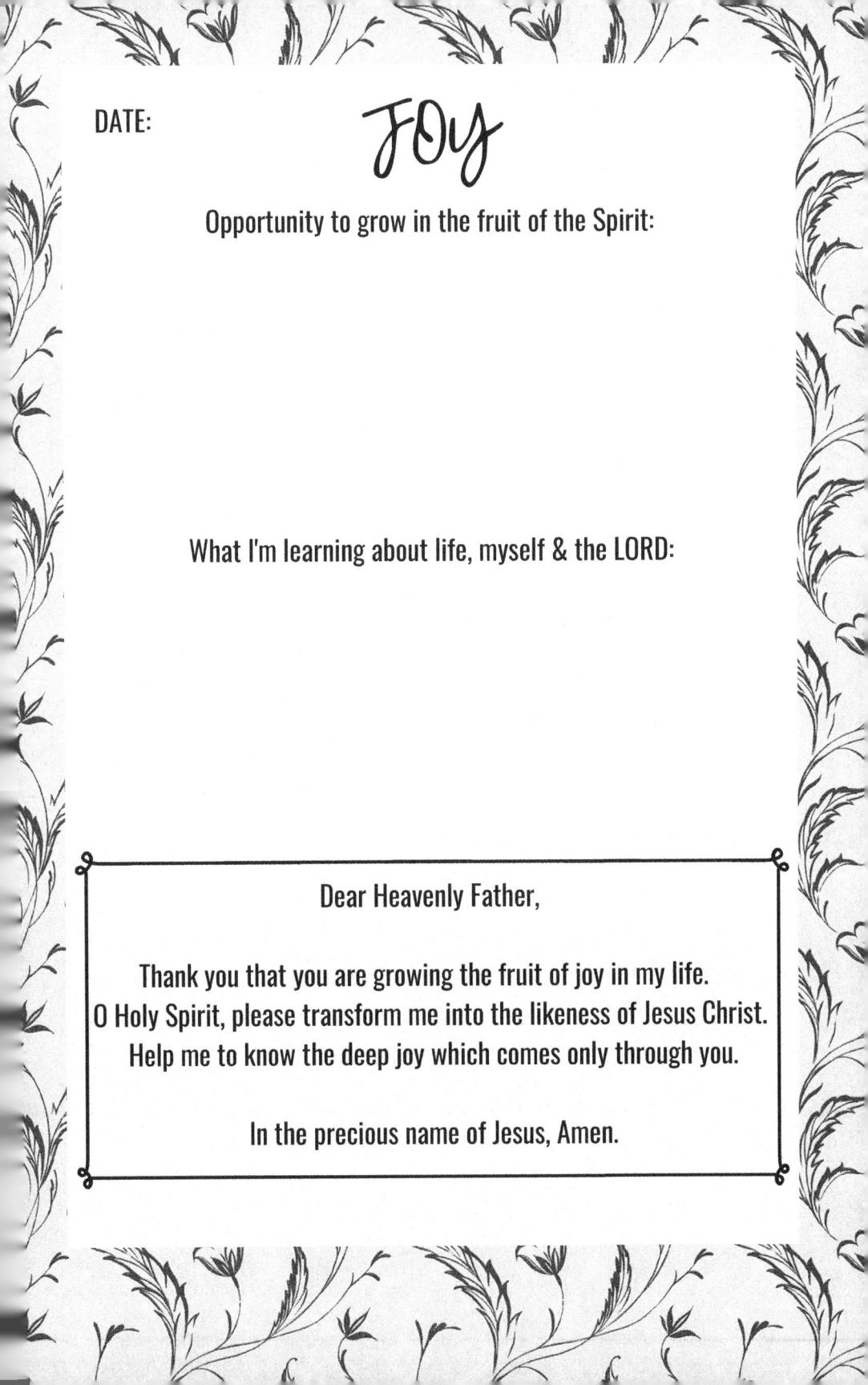

JOY

Opportunity to grow in the fruit of the Spirit:

What I'm learning about life, myself & the LORD:

Dear Heavenly Father,

Thank you that you are growing the fruit of joy in my life.
O Holy Spirit, please transform me into the likeness of Jesus Christ.
Help me to know the deep joy which comes only through you.

In the precious name of Jesus, Amen.

DATE:

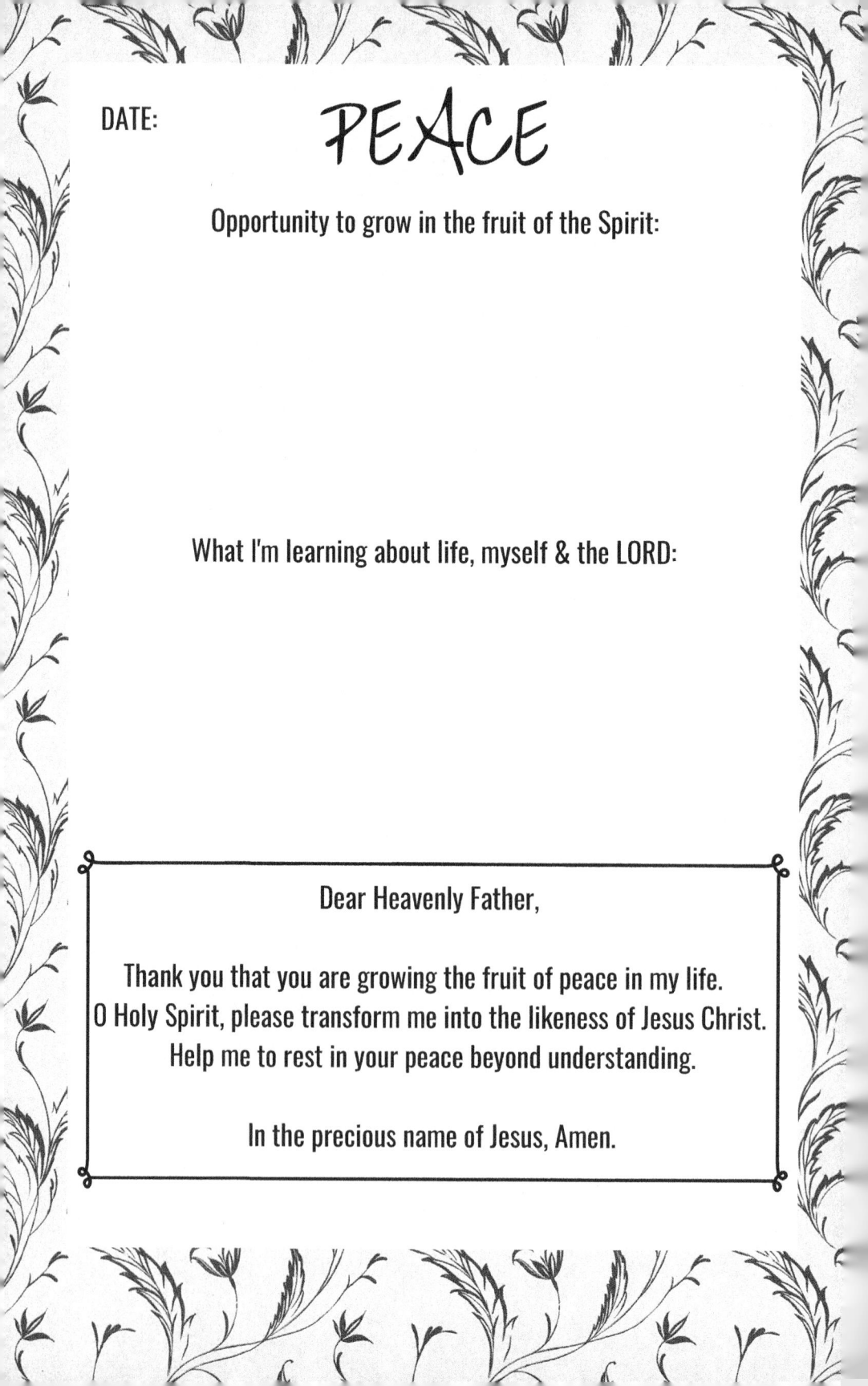

PEACE

Opportunity to grow in the fruit of the Spirit:

What I'm learning about life, myself & the LORD:

Dear Heavenly Father,

Thank you that you are growing the fruit of peace in my life.
O Holy Spirit, please transform me into the likeness of Jesus Christ.
Help me to rest in your peace beyond understanding.

In the precious name of Jesus, Amen.

DATE:

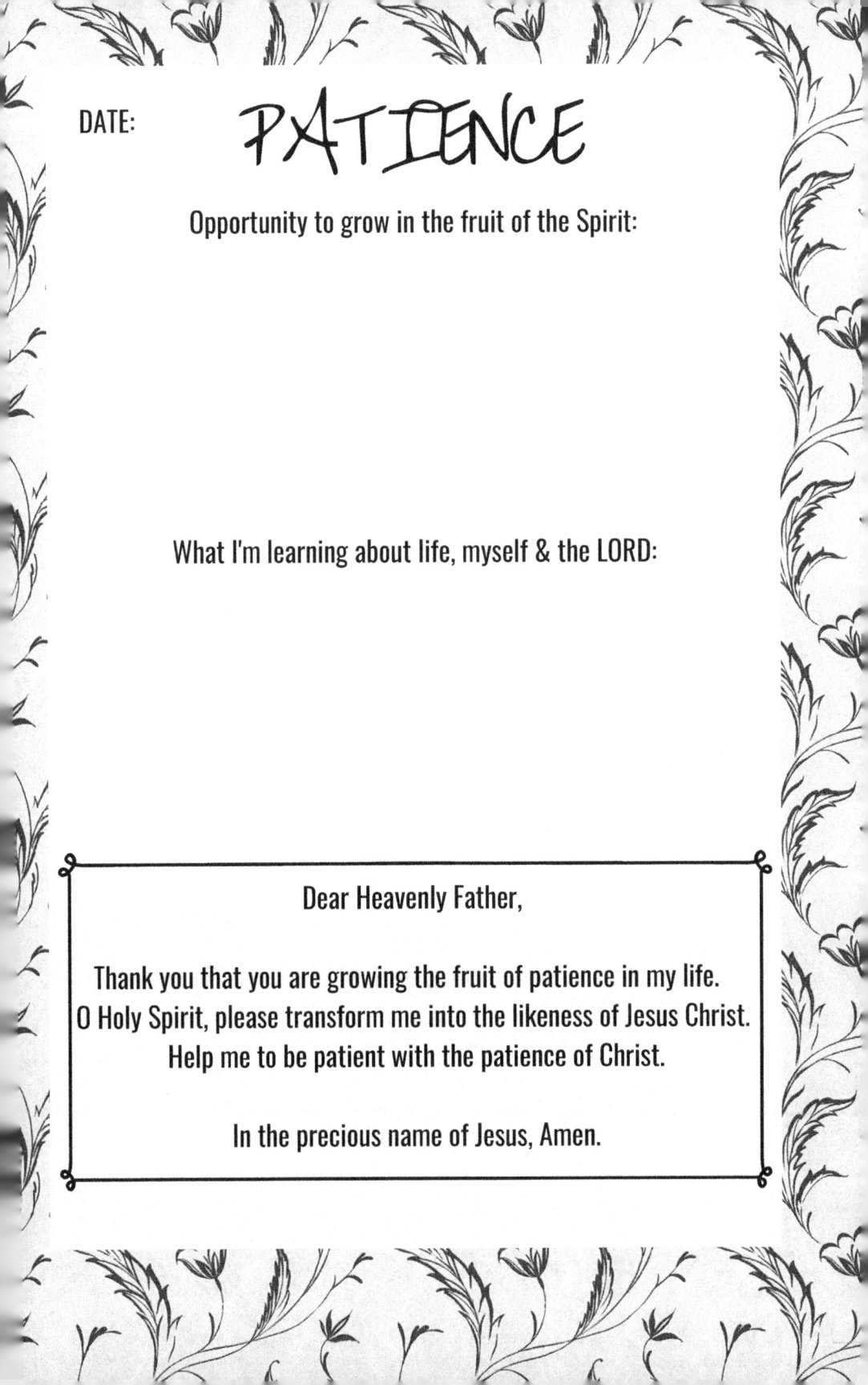

PATIENCE

Opportunity to grow in the fruit of the Spirit:

What I'm learning about life, myself & the LORD:

Dear Heavenly Father,

Thank you that you are growing the fruit of patience in my life.
O Holy Spirit, please transform me into the likeness of Jesus Christ.
Help me to be patient with the patience of Christ.

In the precious name of Jesus, Amen.

DATE:

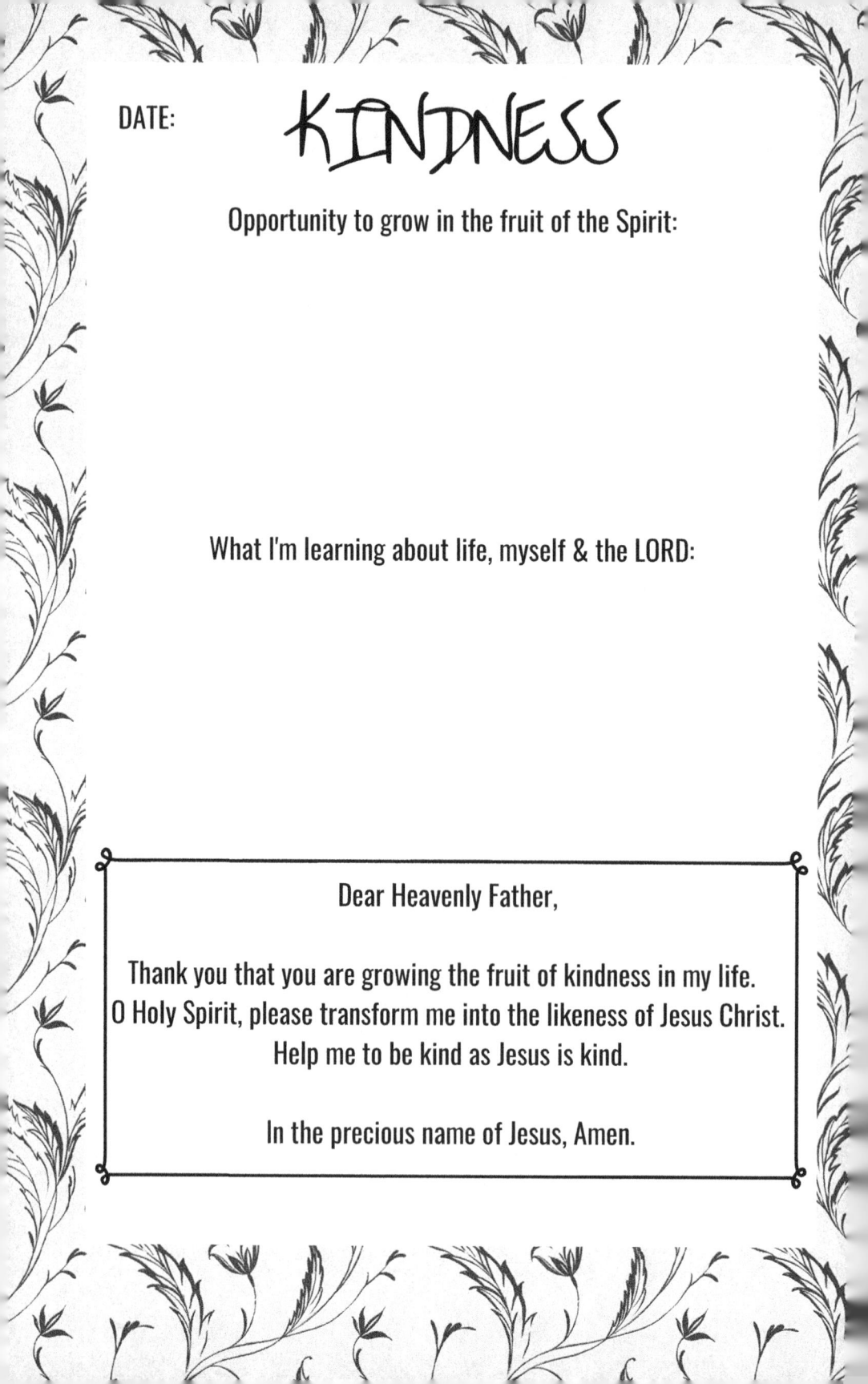

KINDNESS

Opportunity to grow in the fruit of the Spirit:

What I'm learning about life, myself & the LORD:

Dear Heavenly Father,

Thank you that you are growing the fruit of kindness in my life.
O Holy Spirit, please transform me into the likeness of Jesus Christ.
Help me to be kind as Jesus is kind.

In the precious name of Jesus, Amen.

DATE:

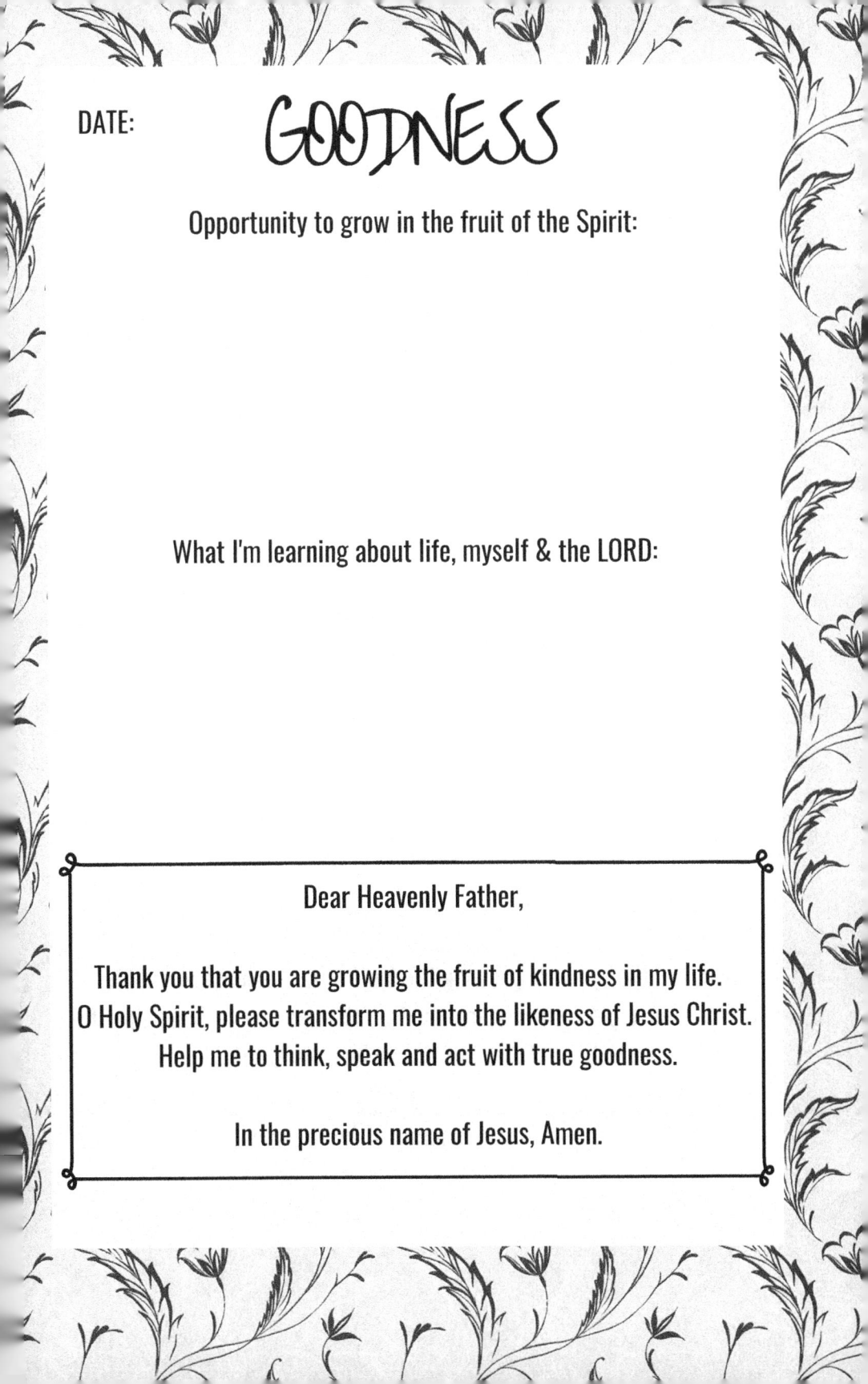

GOODNESS

Opportunity to grow in the fruit of the Spirit:

What I'm learning about life, myself & the LORD:

Dear Heavenly Father,

Thank you that you are growing the fruit of kindness in my life.
O Holy Spirit, please transform me into the likeness of Jesus Christ.
Help me to think, speak and act with true goodness.

In the precious name of Jesus, Amen.

DATE:

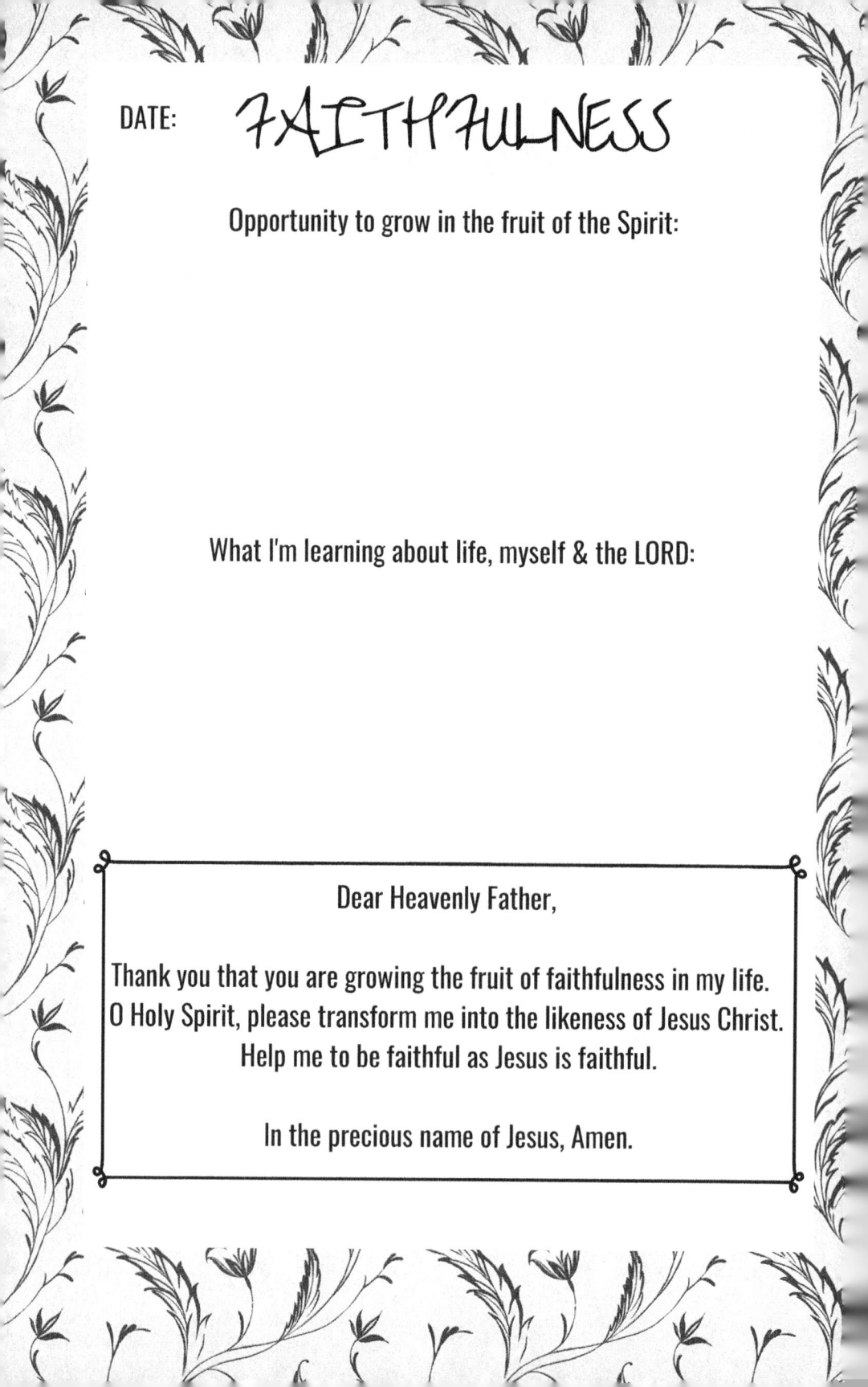

FAITHFULNESS

Opportunity to grow in the fruit of the Spirit:

What I'm learning about life, myself & the LORD:

Dear Heavenly Father,

Thank you that you are growing the fruit of faithfulness in my life. O Holy Spirit, please transform me into the likeness of Jesus Christ. Help me to be faithful as Jesus is faithful.

In the precious name of Jesus, Amen.

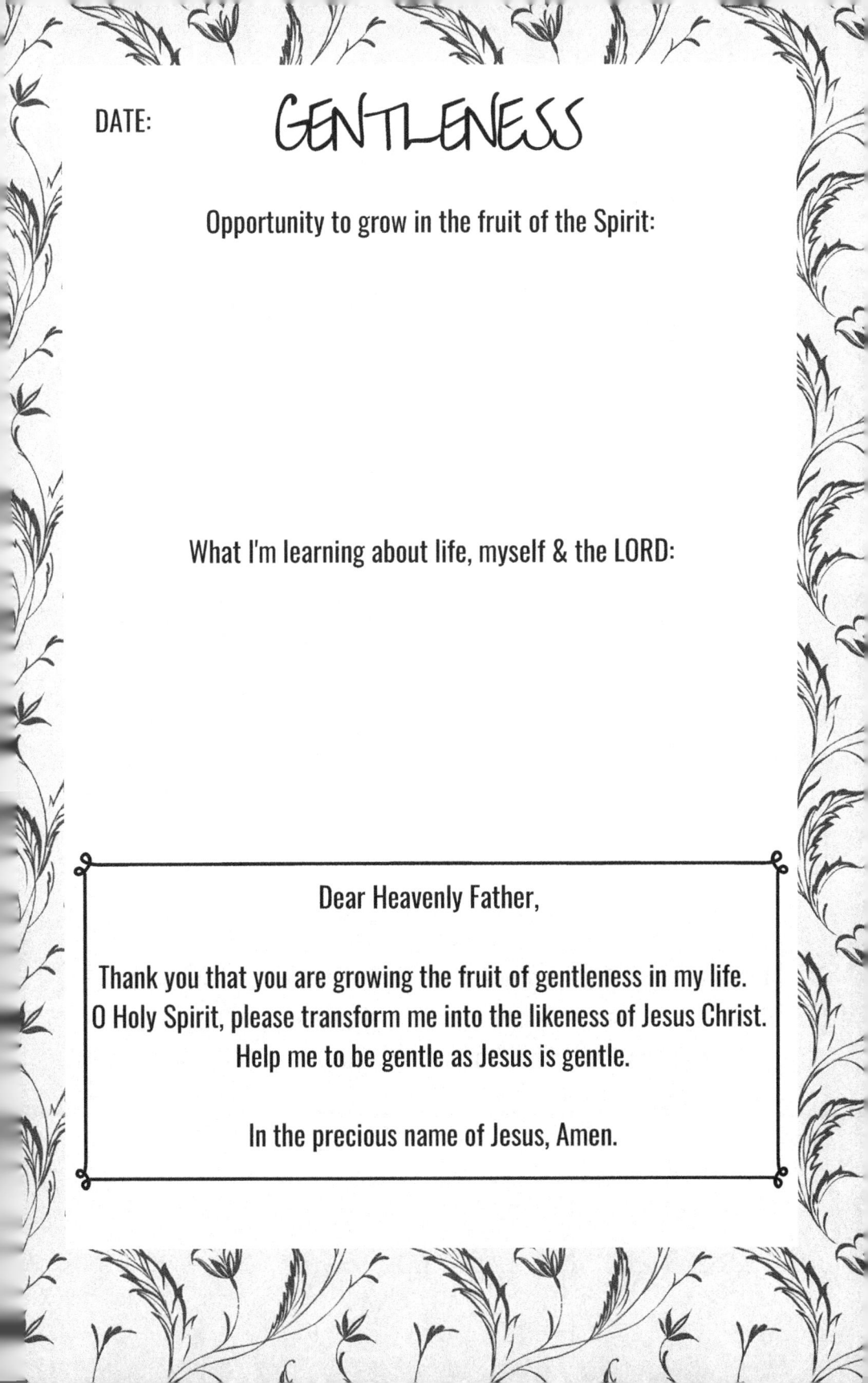

DATE:

GENTLENESS

Opportunity to grow in the fruit of the Spirit:

What I'm learning about life, myself & the LORD:

Dear Heavenly Father,

Thank you that you are growing the fruit of gentleness in my life.
O Holy Spirit, please transform me into the likeness of Jesus Christ.
Help me to be gentle as Jesus is gentle.

In the precious name of Jesus, Amen.

DATE:

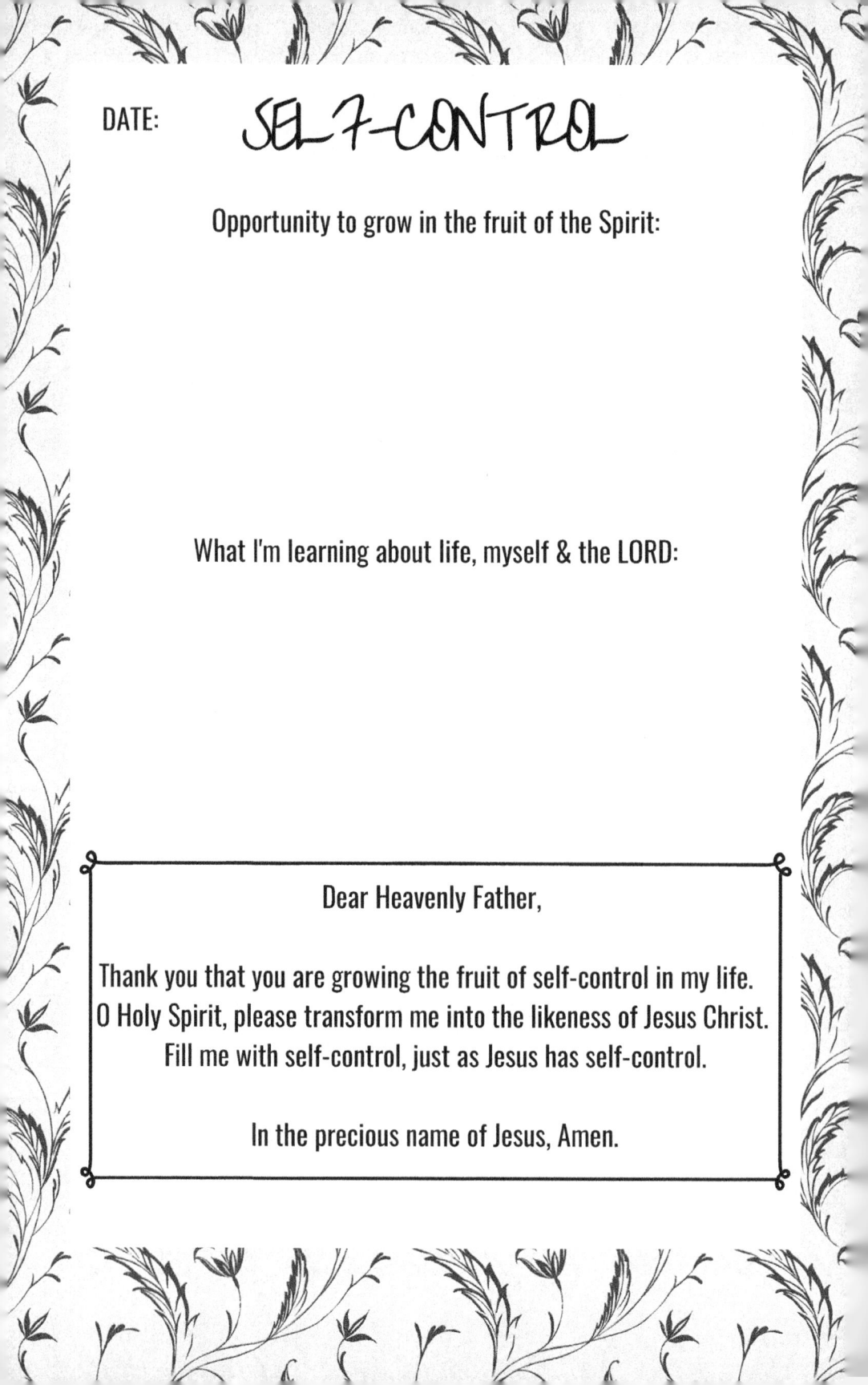

SELF-CONTROL

Opportunity to grow in the fruit of the Spirit:

What I'm learning about life, myself & the LORD:

Dear Heavenly Father,

Thank you that you are growing the fruit of self-control in my life. O Holy Spirit, please transform me into the likeness of Jesus Christ. Fill me with self-control, just as Jesus has self-control.

In the precious name of Jesus, Amen.

DATE:

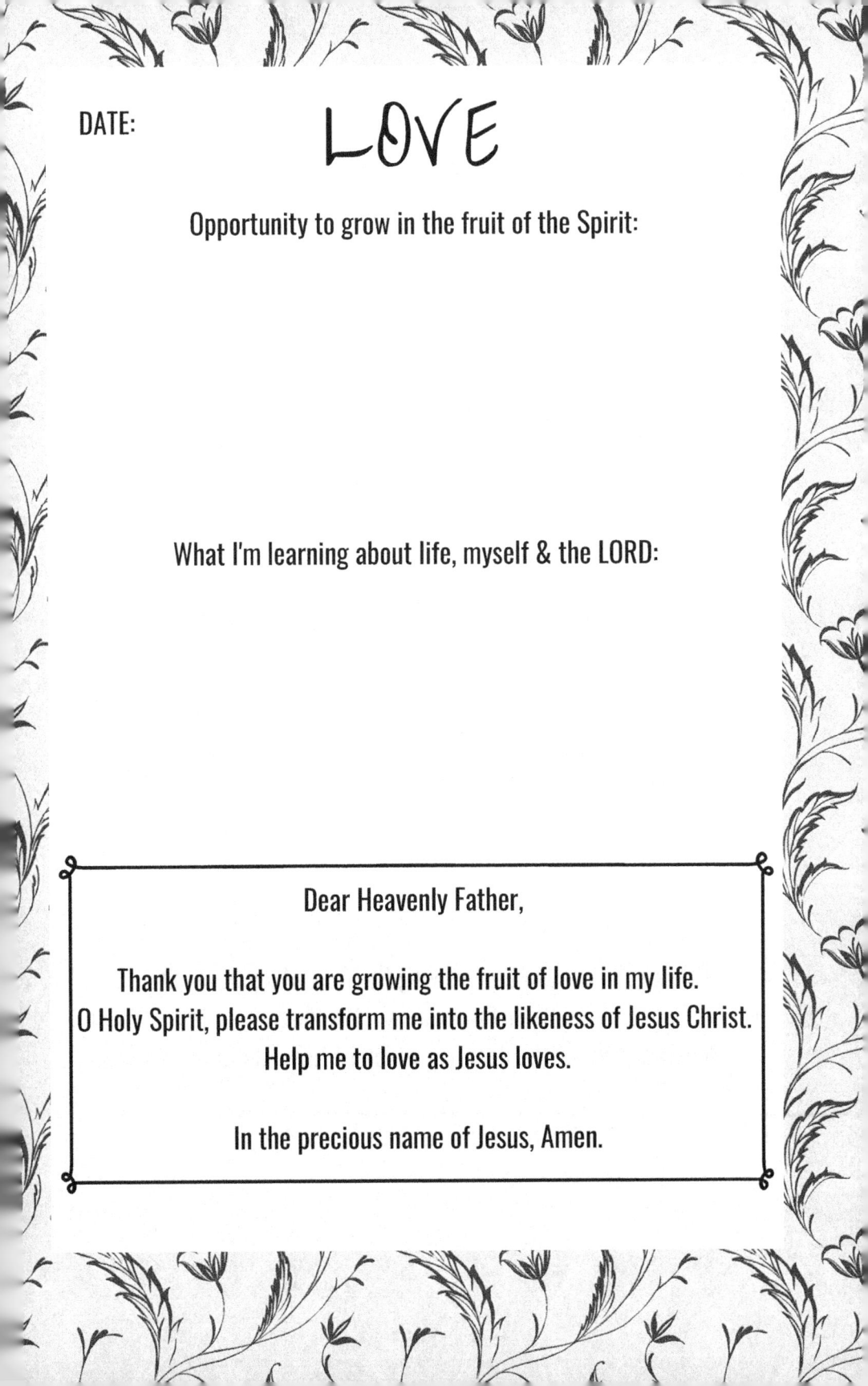

LOVE

Opportunity to grow in the fruit of the Spirit:

What I'm learning about life, myself & the LORD:

Dear Heavenly Father,

Thank you that you are growing the fruit of love in my life.
O Holy Spirit, please transform me into the likeness of Jesus Christ.
Help me to love as Jesus loves.

In the precious name of Jesus, Amen.

DATE:

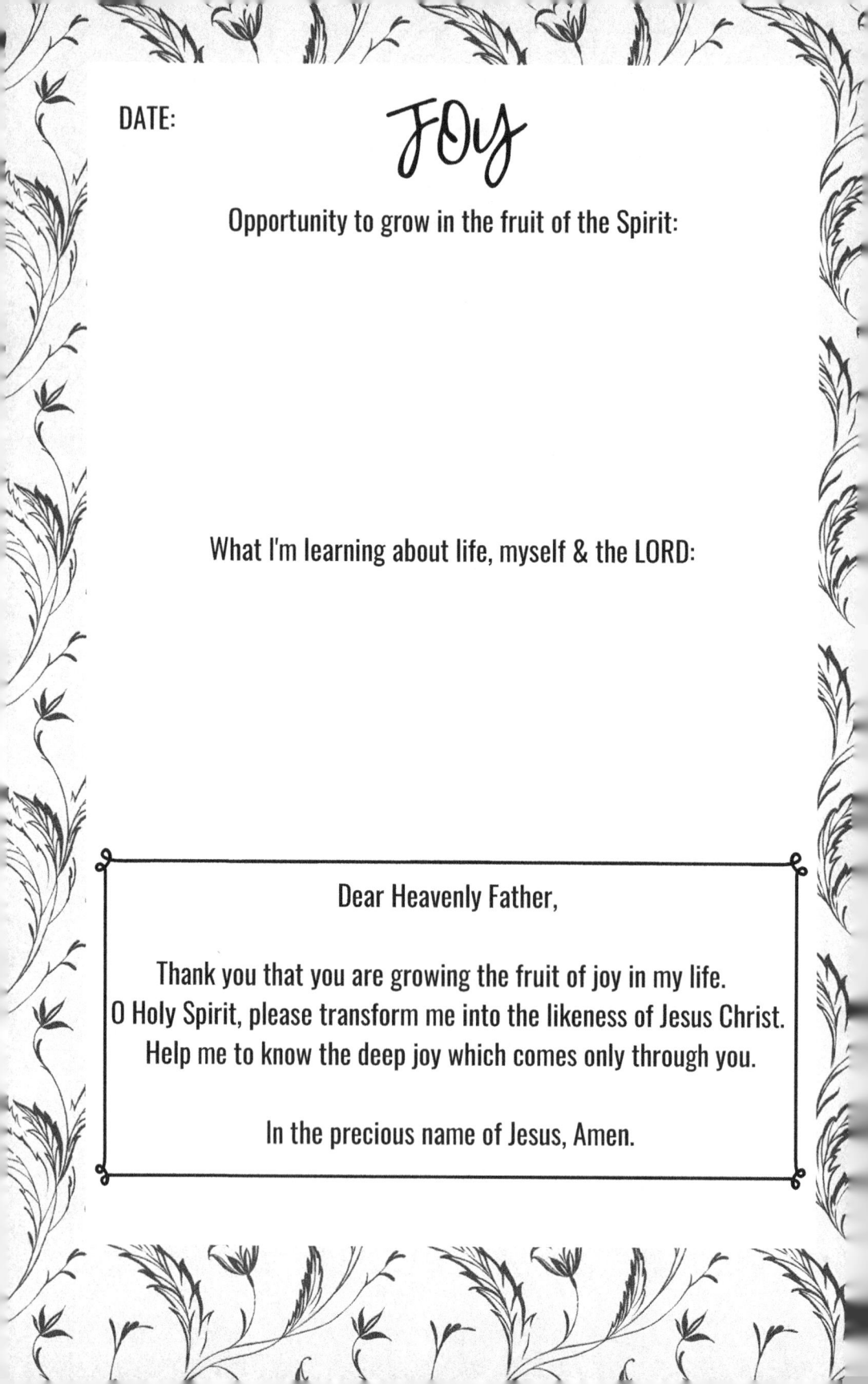

JOY

Opportunity to grow in the fruit of the Spirit:

What I'm learning about life, myself & the LORD:

Dear Heavenly Father,

Thank you that you are growing the fruit of joy in my life.
O Holy Spirit, please transform me into the likeness of Jesus Christ.
Help me to know the deep joy which comes only through you.

In the precious name of Jesus, Amen.

DATE:

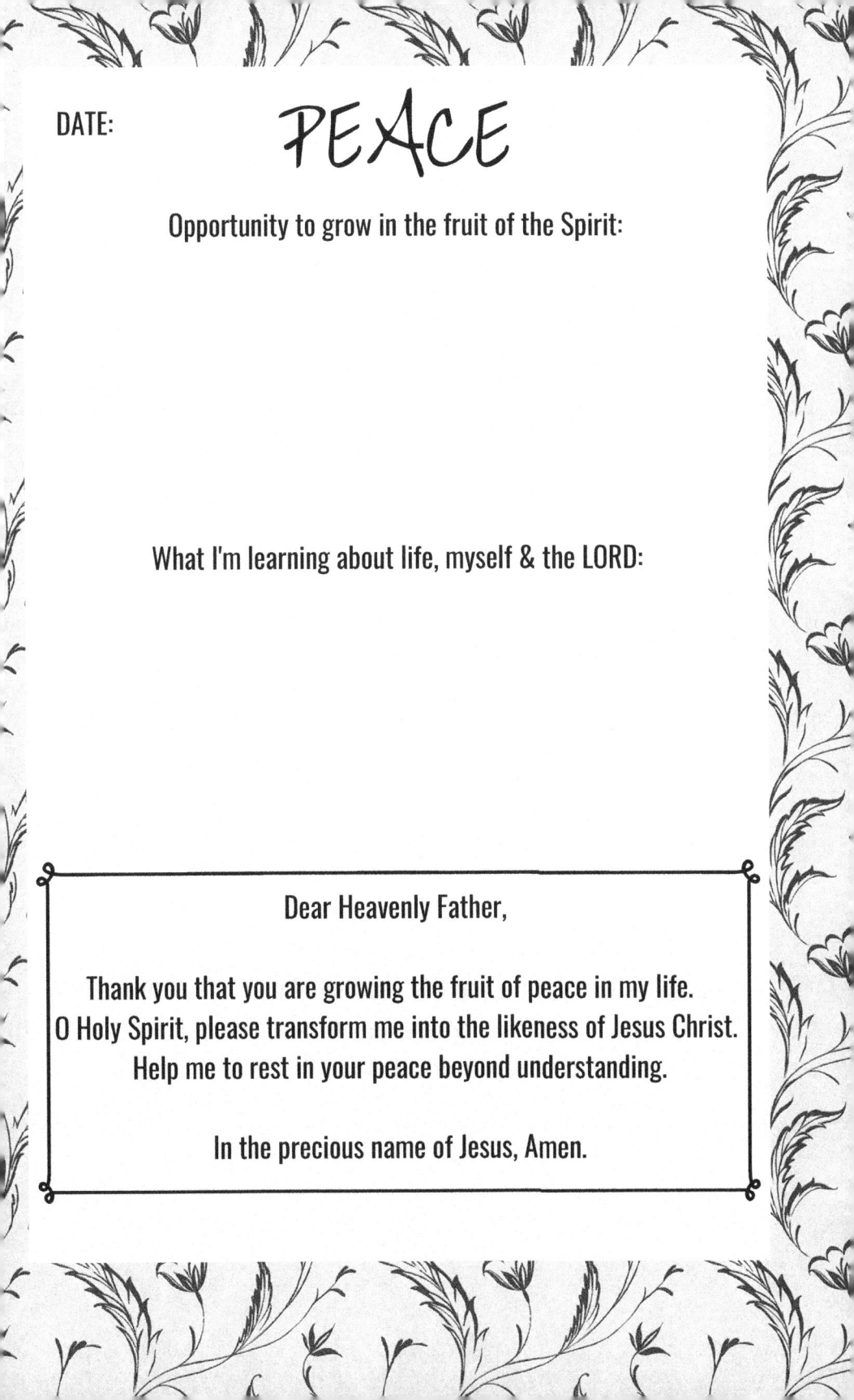

PEACE

Opportunity to grow in the fruit of the Spirit:

What I'm learning about life, myself & the LORD:

Dear Heavenly Father,

Thank you that you are growing the fruit of peace in my life.
O Holy Spirit, please transform me into the likeness of Jesus Christ.
Help me to rest in your peace beyond understanding.

In the precious name of Jesus, Amen.

DATE:

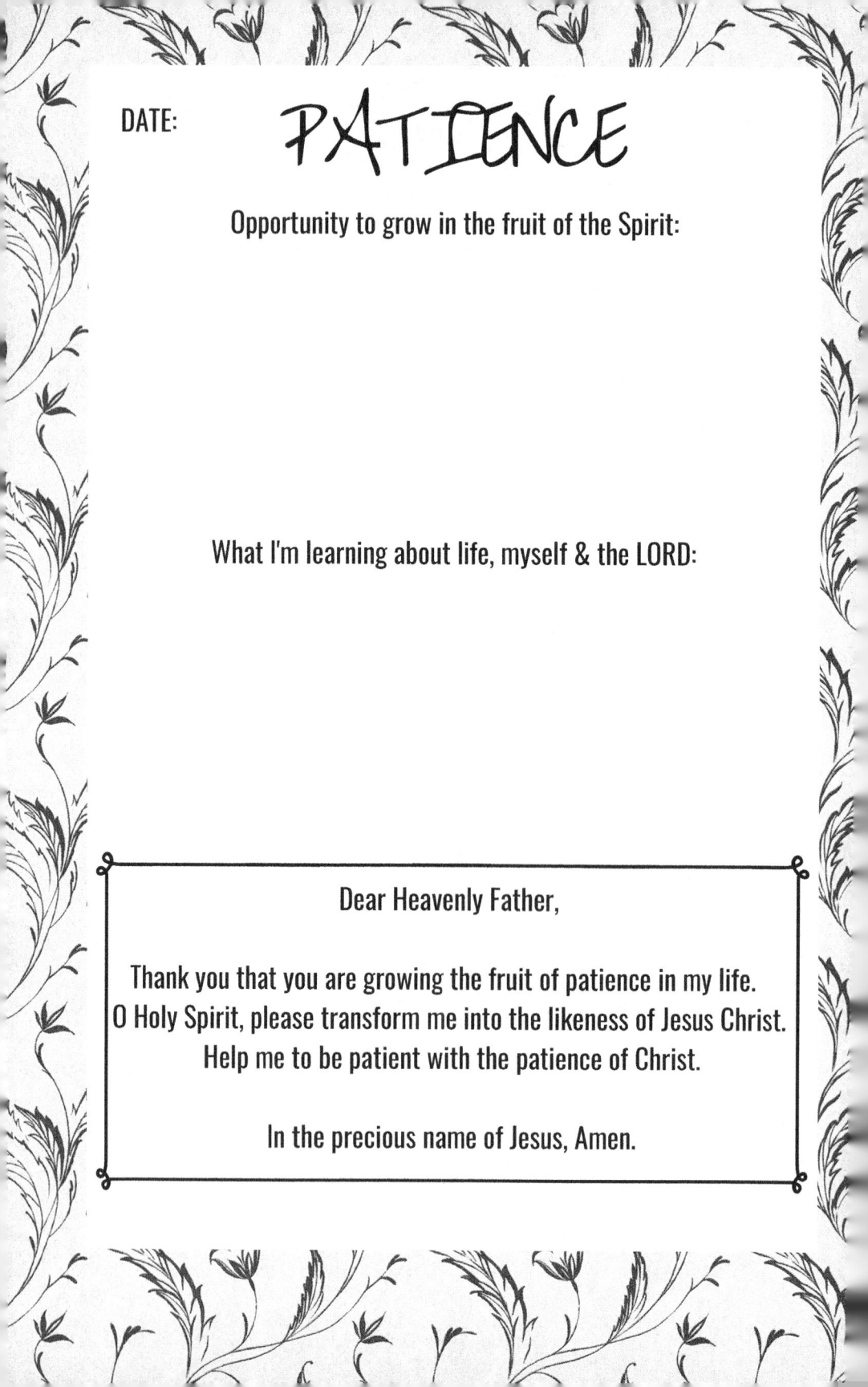

PATIENCE

Opportunity to grow in the fruit of the Spirit:

What I'm learning about life, myself & the LORD:

Dear Heavenly Father,

Thank you that you are growing the fruit of patience in my life.
O Holy Spirit, please transform me into the likeness of Jesus Christ.
Help me to be patient with the patience of Christ.

In the precious name of Jesus, Amen.

DATE:

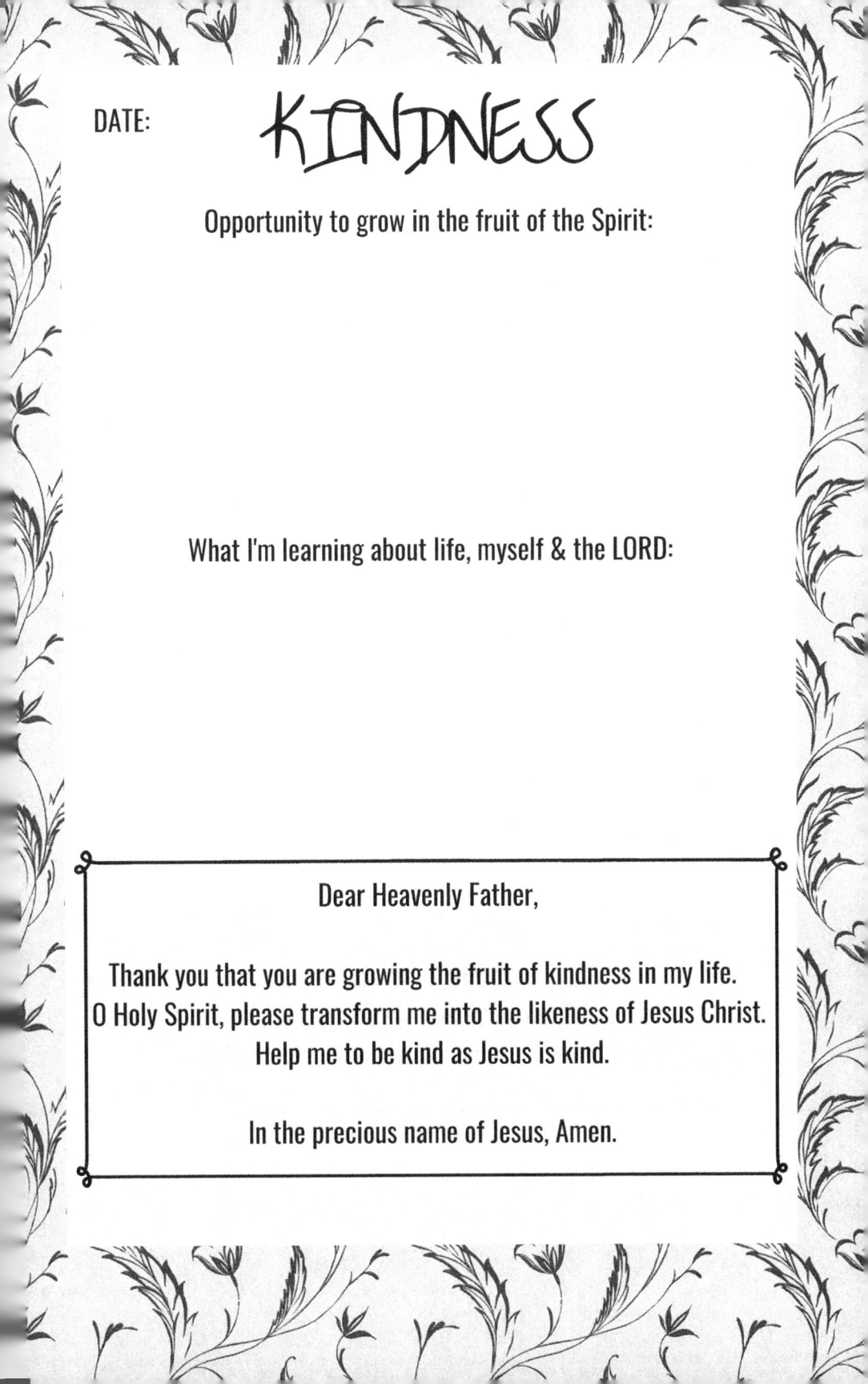

KINDNESS

Opportunity to grow in the fruit of the Spirit:

What I'm learning about life, myself & the LORD:

Dear Heavenly Father,

Thank you that you are growing the fruit of kindness in my life.
O Holy Spirit, please transform me into the likeness of Jesus Christ.
Help me to be kind as Jesus is kind.

In the precious name of Jesus, Amen.

DATE: # GOODNESS

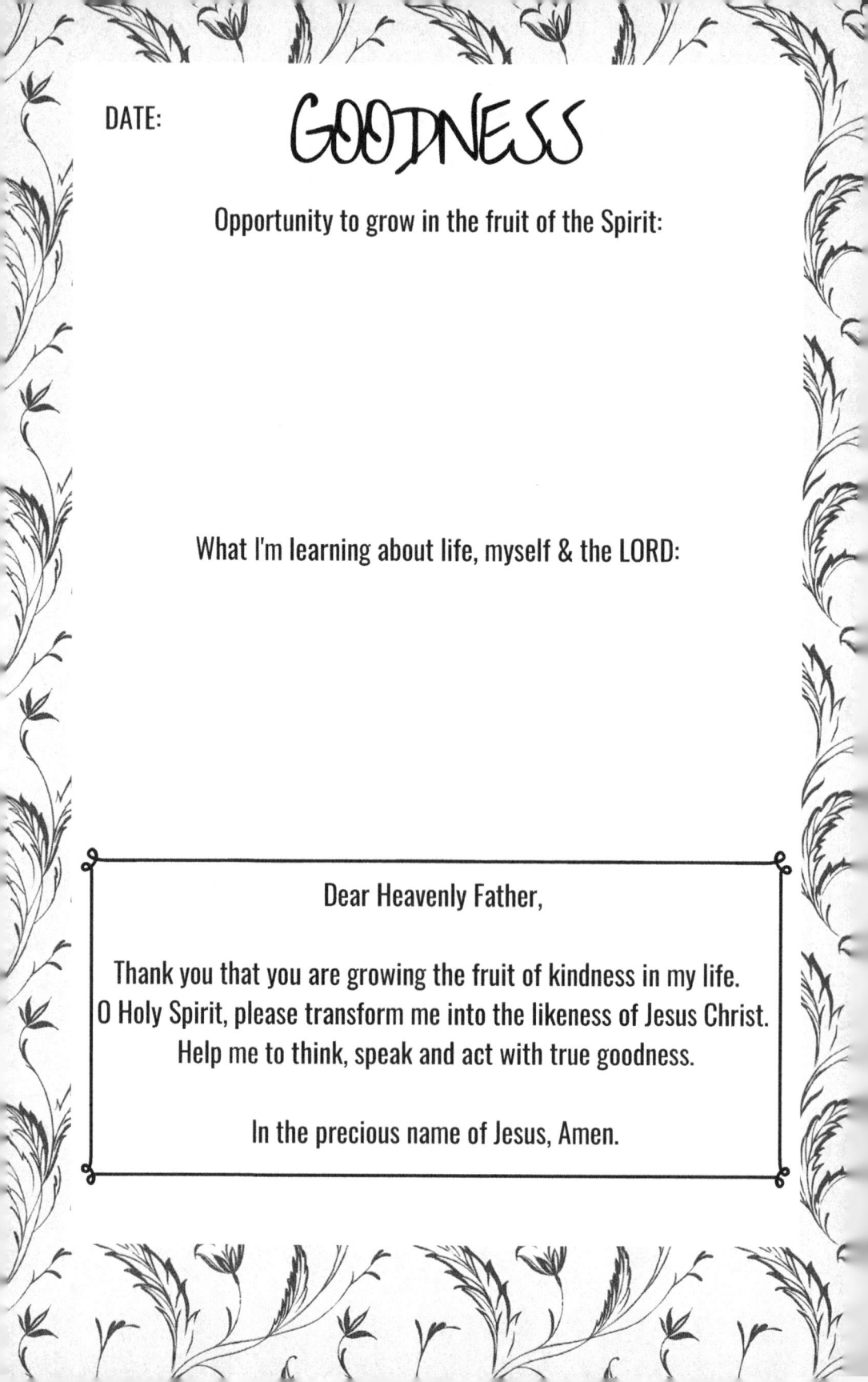

Opportunity to grow in the fruit of the Spirit:

What I'm learning about life, myself & the LORD:

Dear Heavenly Father,

Thank you that you are growing the fruit of kindness in my life.
O Holy Spirit, please transform me into the likeness of Jesus Christ.
Help me to think, speak and act with true goodness.

In the precious name of Jesus, Amen.

DATE: **FAITHFULNESS**

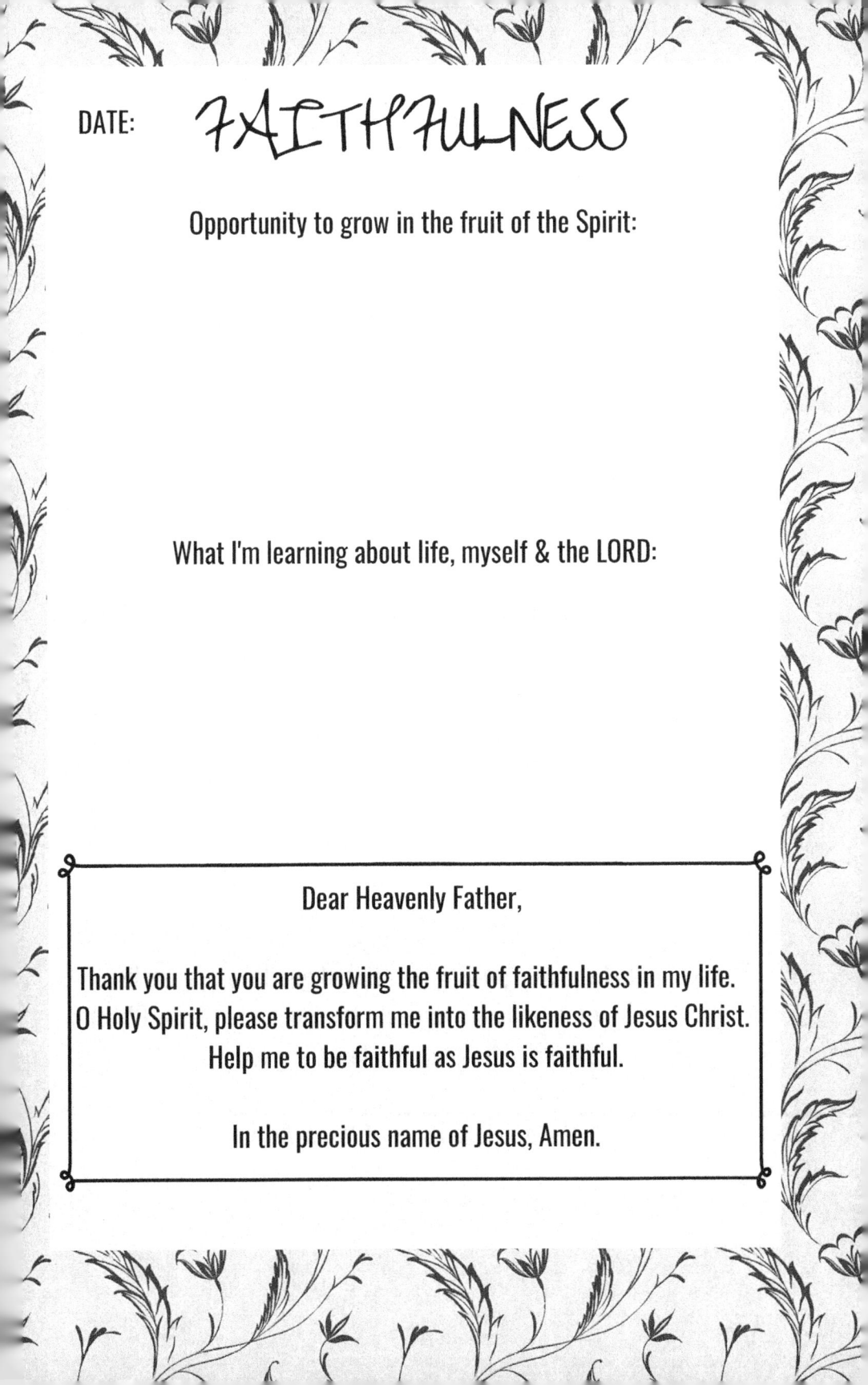

Opportunity to grow in the fruit of the Spirit:

What I'm learning about life, myself & the LORD:

Dear Heavenly Father,

Thank you that you are growing the fruit of faithfulness in my life.
O Holy Spirit, please transform me into the likeness of Jesus Christ.
Help me to be faithful as Jesus is faithful.

In the precious name of Jesus, Amen.

DATE:

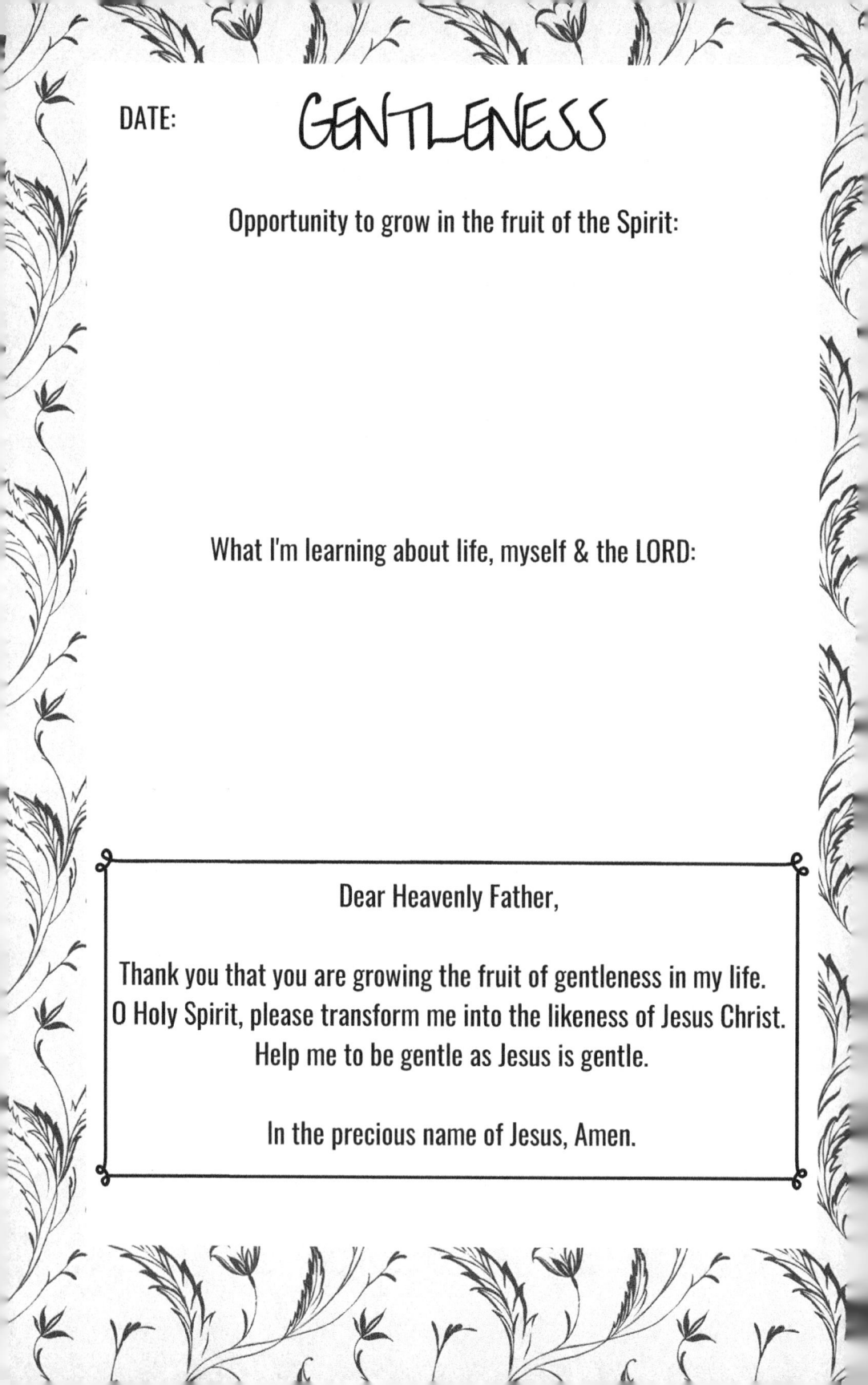

GENTLENESS

Opportunity to grow in the fruit of the Spirit:

What I'm learning about life, myself & the LORD:

Dear Heavenly Father,

Thank you that you are growing the fruit of gentleness in my life.
O Holy Spirit, please transform me into the likeness of Jesus Christ.
Help me to be gentle as Jesus is gentle.

In the precious name of Jesus, Amen.

DATE:

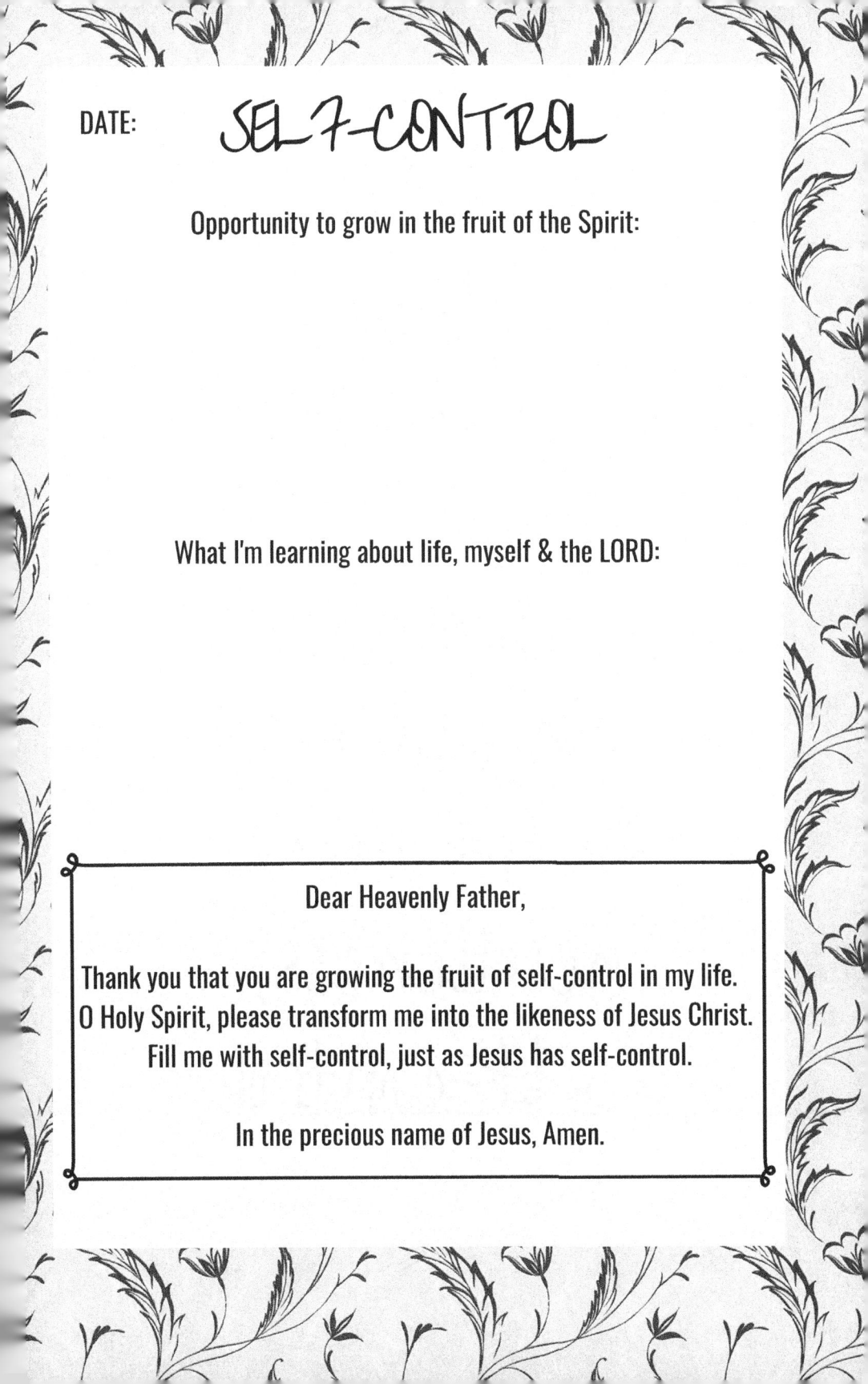

SELF-CONTROL

Opportunity to grow in the fruit of the Spirit:

What I'm learning about life, myself & the LORD:

Dear Heavenly Father,

Thank you that you are growing the fruit of self-control in my life. O Holy Spirit, please transform me into the likeness of Jesus Christ. Fill me with self-control, just as Jesus has self-control.

In the precious name of Jesus, Amen.

love,
joy,
peace,
patience,
kindness,
goodness,
faithfulness,
gentleness,
self-control

DATE:

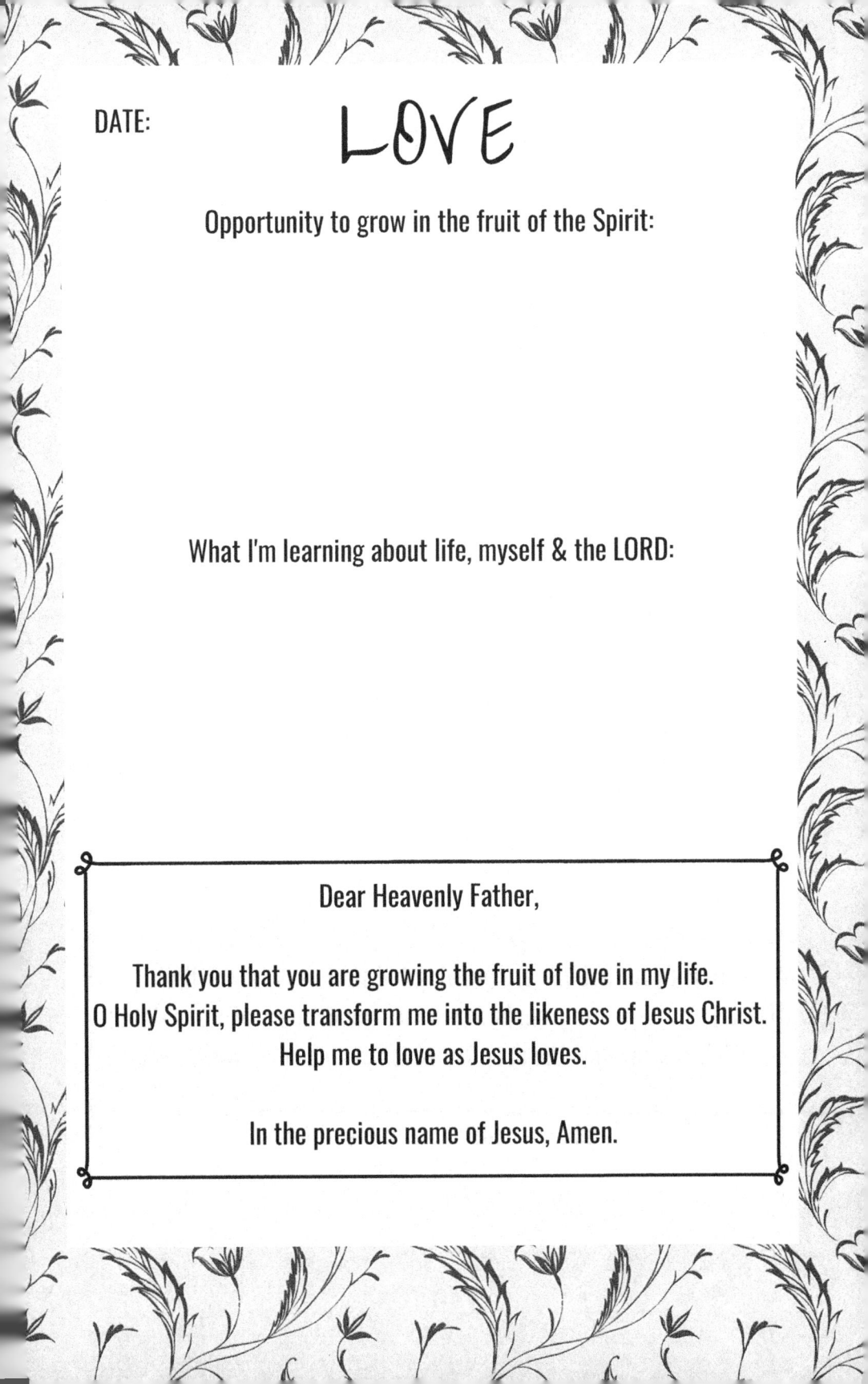

LOVE

Opportunity to grow in the fruit of the Spirit:

What I'm learning about life, myself & the LORD:

Dear Heavenly Father,

Thank you that you are growing the fruit of love in my life.
O Holy Spirit, please transform me into the likeness of Jesus Christ.
Help me to love as Jesus loves.

In the precious name of Jesus, Amen.

DATE:

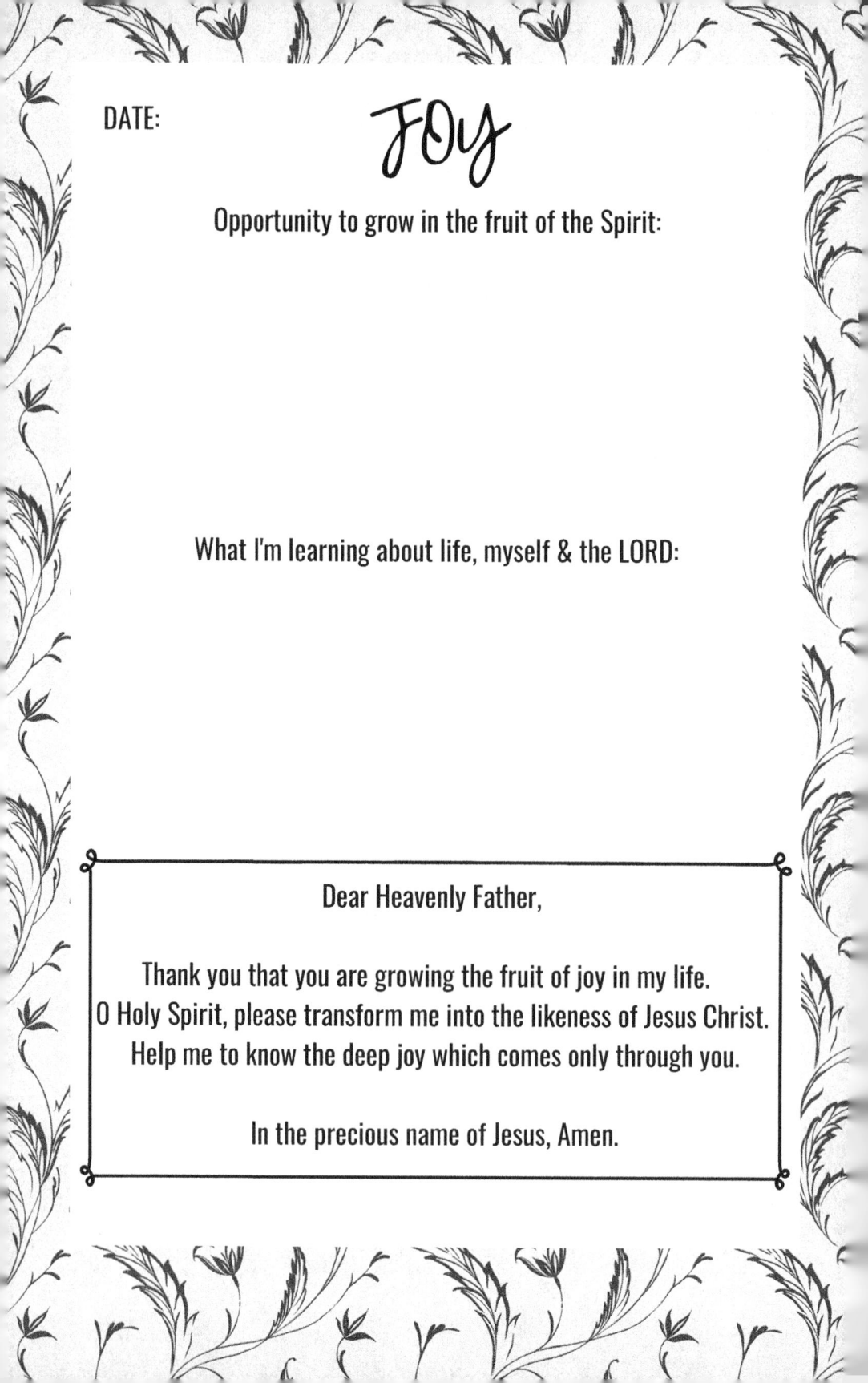

JOY

Opportunity to grow in the fruit of the Spirit:

What I'm learning about life, myself & the LORD:

Dear Heavenly Father,

Thank you that you are growing the fruit of joy in my life.
O Holy Spirit, please transform me into the likeness of Jesus Christ.
Help me to know the deep joy which comes only through you.

In the precious name of Jesus, Amen.

DATE:

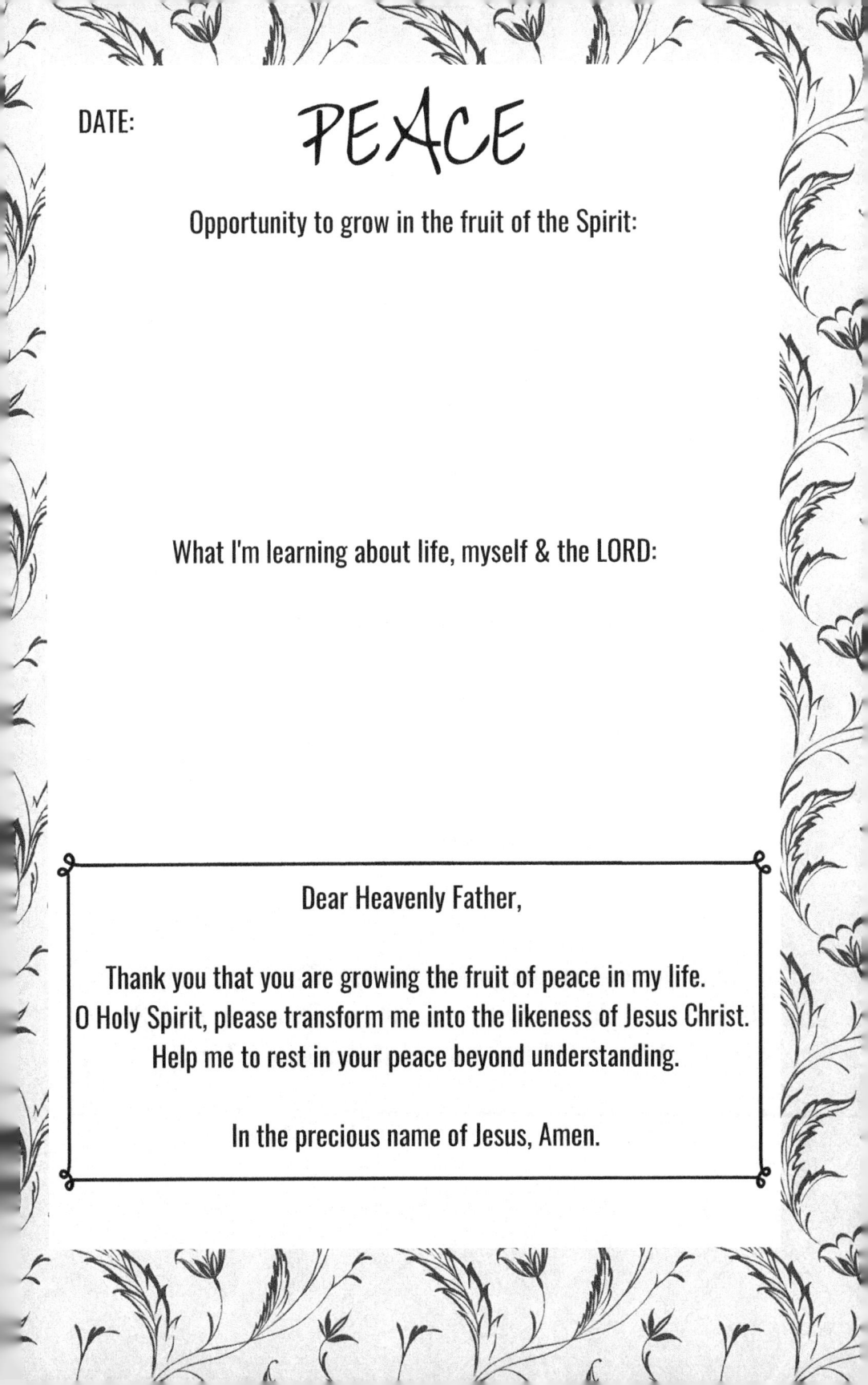

PEACE

Opportunity to grow in the fruit of the Spirit:

What I'm learning about life, myself & the LORD:

Dear Heavenly Father,

Thank you that you are growing the fruit of peace in my life.
O Holy Spirit, please transform me into the likeness of Jesus Christ.
Help me to rest in your peace beyond understanding.

In the precious name of Jesus, Amen.

DATE:

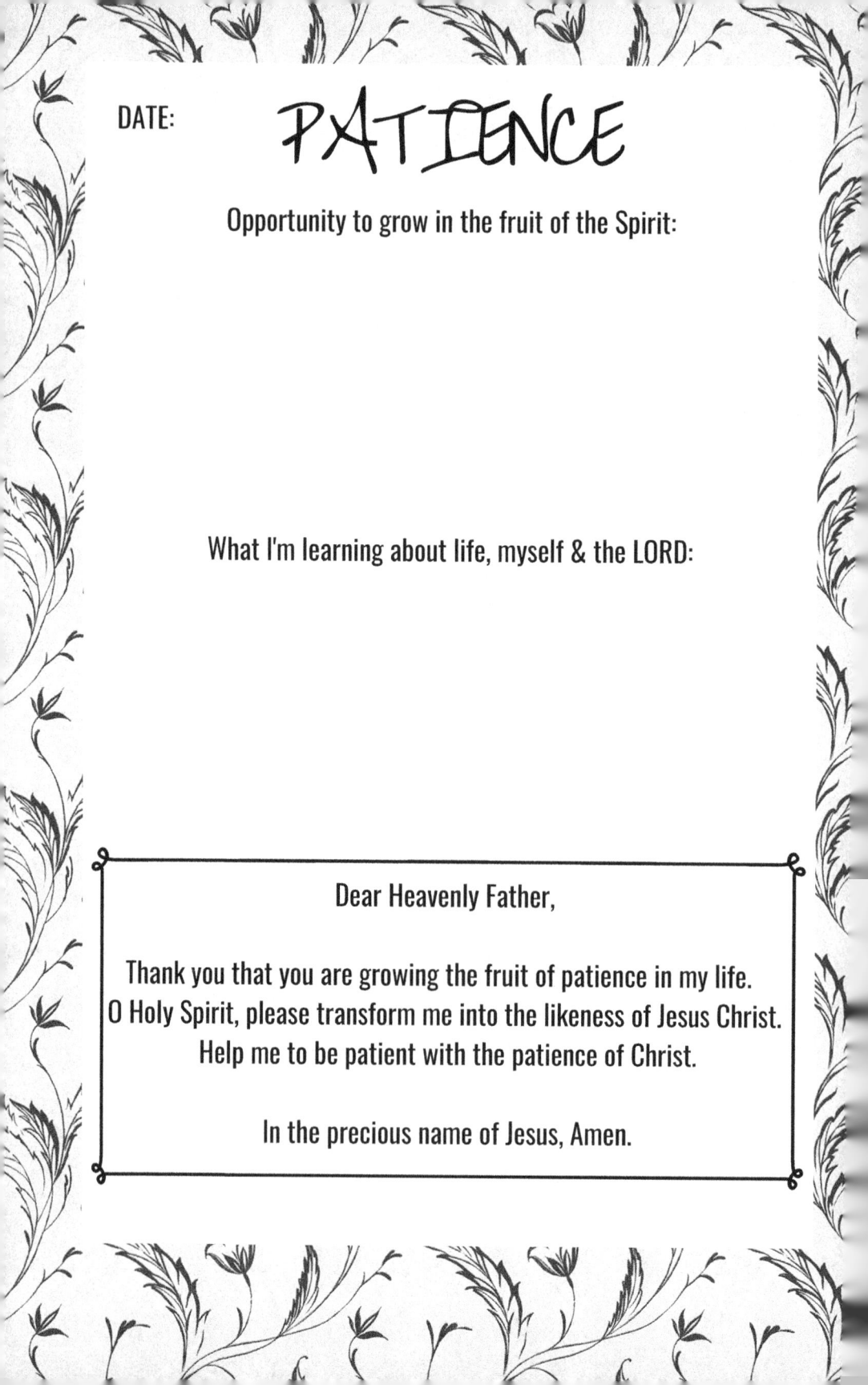

PATIENCE

Opportunity to grow in the fruit of the Spirit:

What I'm learning about life, myself & the LORD:

Dear Heavenly Father,

Thank you that you are growing the fruit of patience in my life.
O Holy Spirit, please transform me into the likeness of Jesus Christ.
Help me to be patient with the patience of Christ.

In the precious name of Jesus, Amen.

DATE:

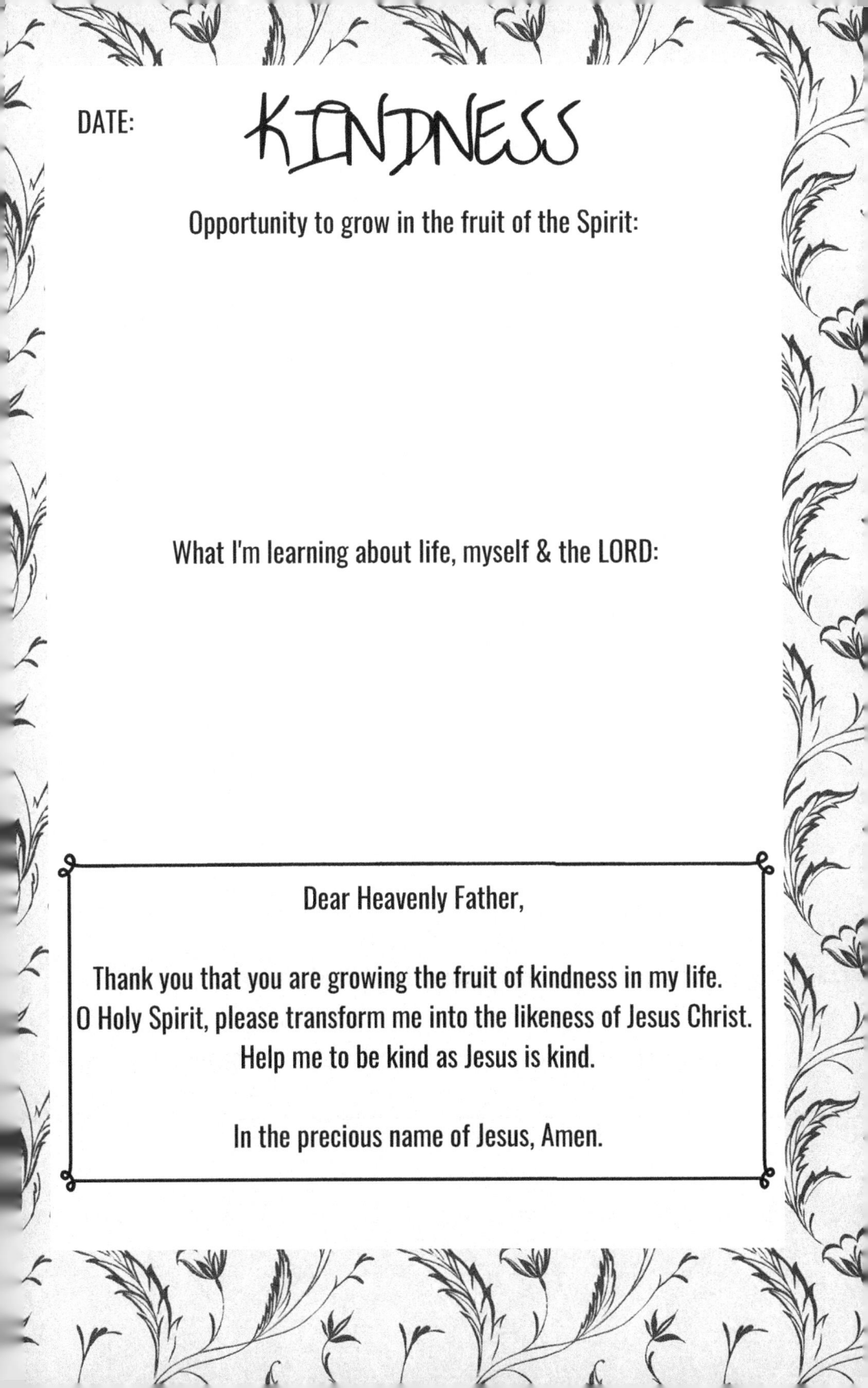

KINDNESS

Opportunity to grow in the fruit of the Spirit:

What I'm learning about life, myself & the LORD:

Dear Heavenly Father,

Thank you that you are growing the fruit of kindness in my life.
O Holy Spirit, please transform me into the likeness of Jesus Christ.
Help me to be kind as Jesus is kind.

In the precious name of Jesus, Amen.

DATE: # GOODNESS

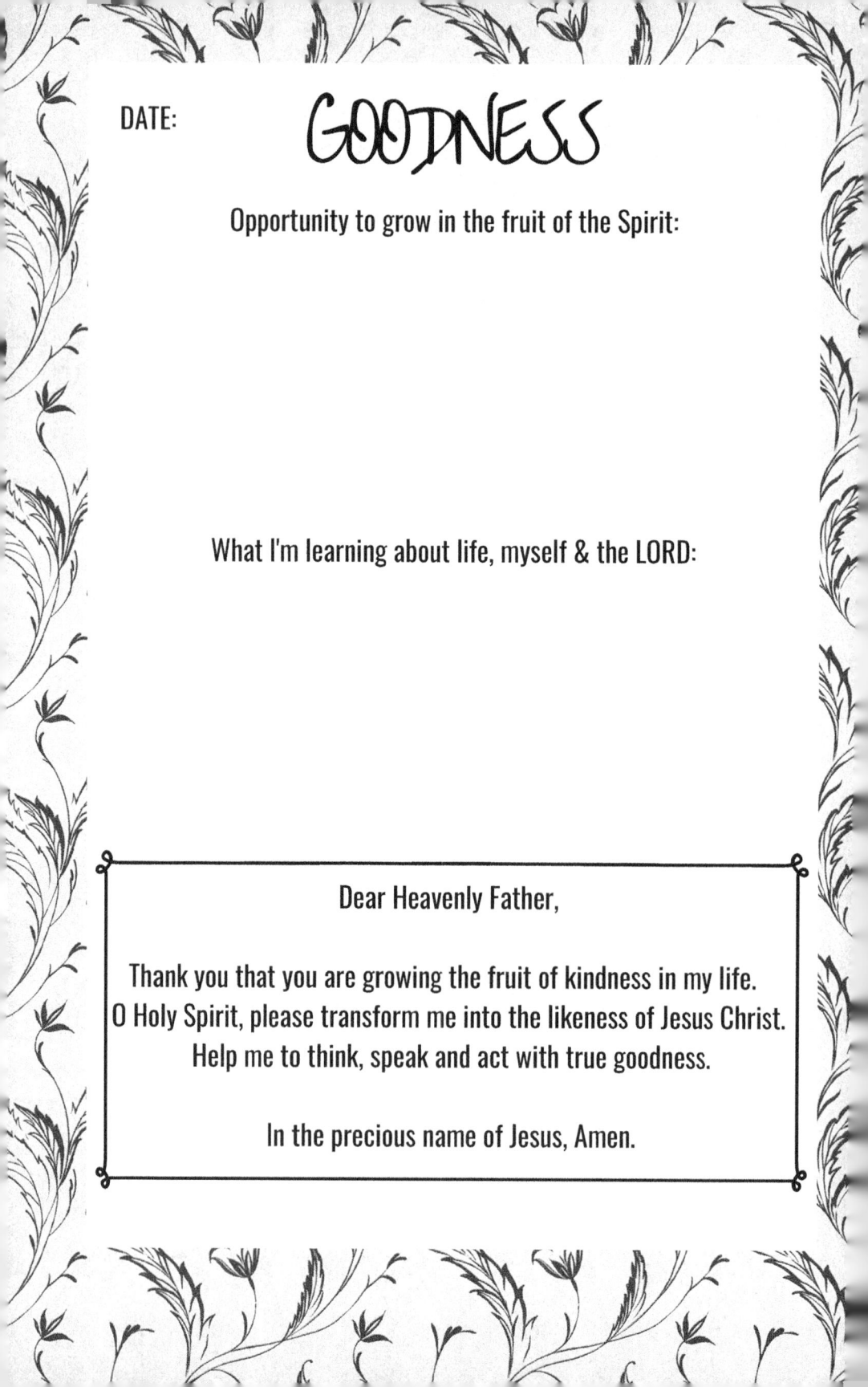

Opportunity to grow in the fruit of the Spirit:

What I'm learning about life, myself & the LORD:

Dear Heavenly Father,

Thank you that you are growing the fruit of kindness in my life.
O Holy Spirit, please transform me into the likeness of Jesus Christ.
Help me to think, speak and act with true goodness.

In the precious name of Jesus, Amen.

DATE: **FAITHFULNESS**

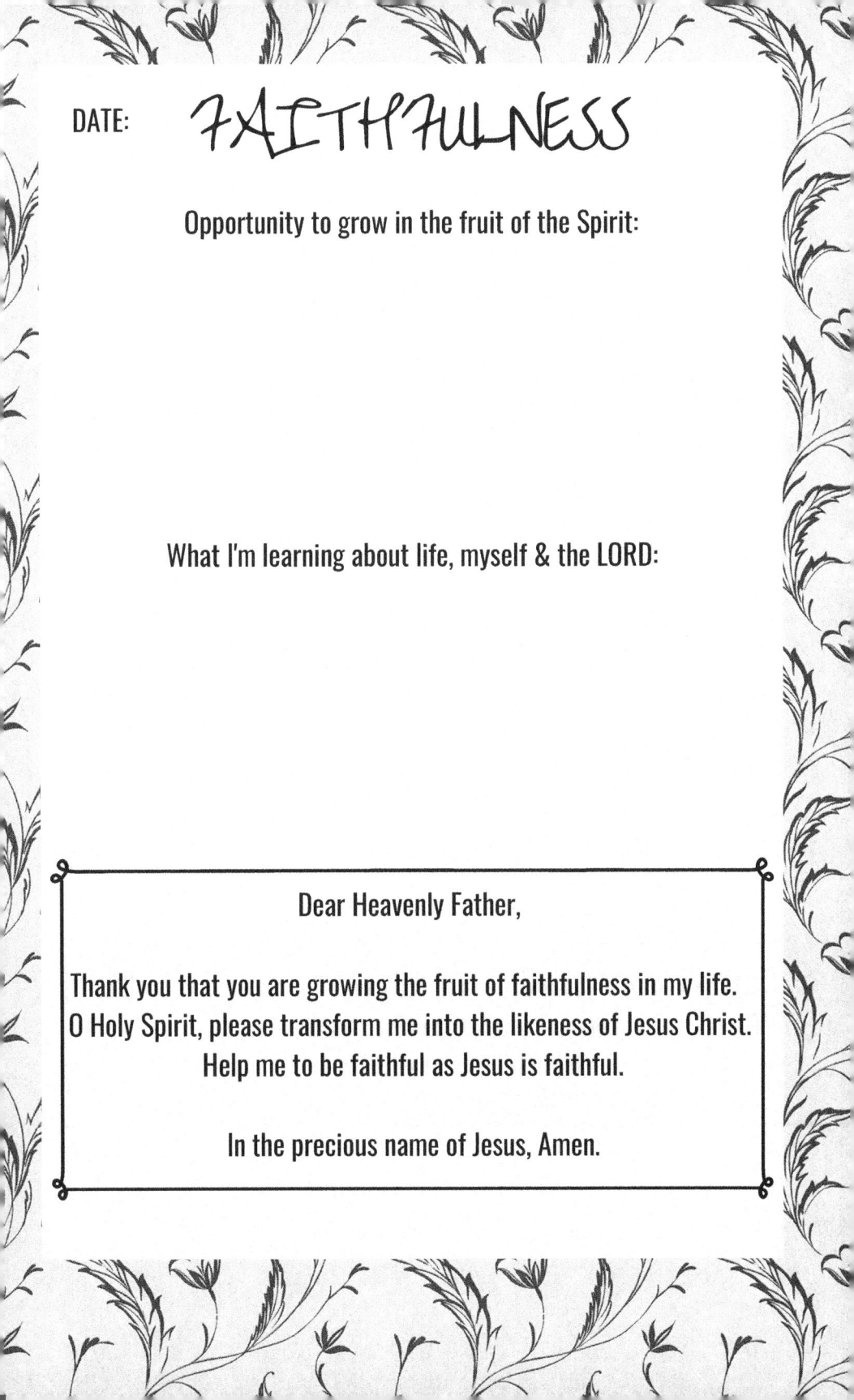

Opportunity to grow in the fruit of the Spirit:

What I'm learning about life, myself & the LORD:

Dear Heavenly Father,

Thank you that you are growing the fruit of faithfulness in my life. O Holy Spirit, please transform me into the likeness of Jesus Christ. Help me to be faithful as Jesus is faithful.

In the precious name of Jesus, Amen.

DATE:

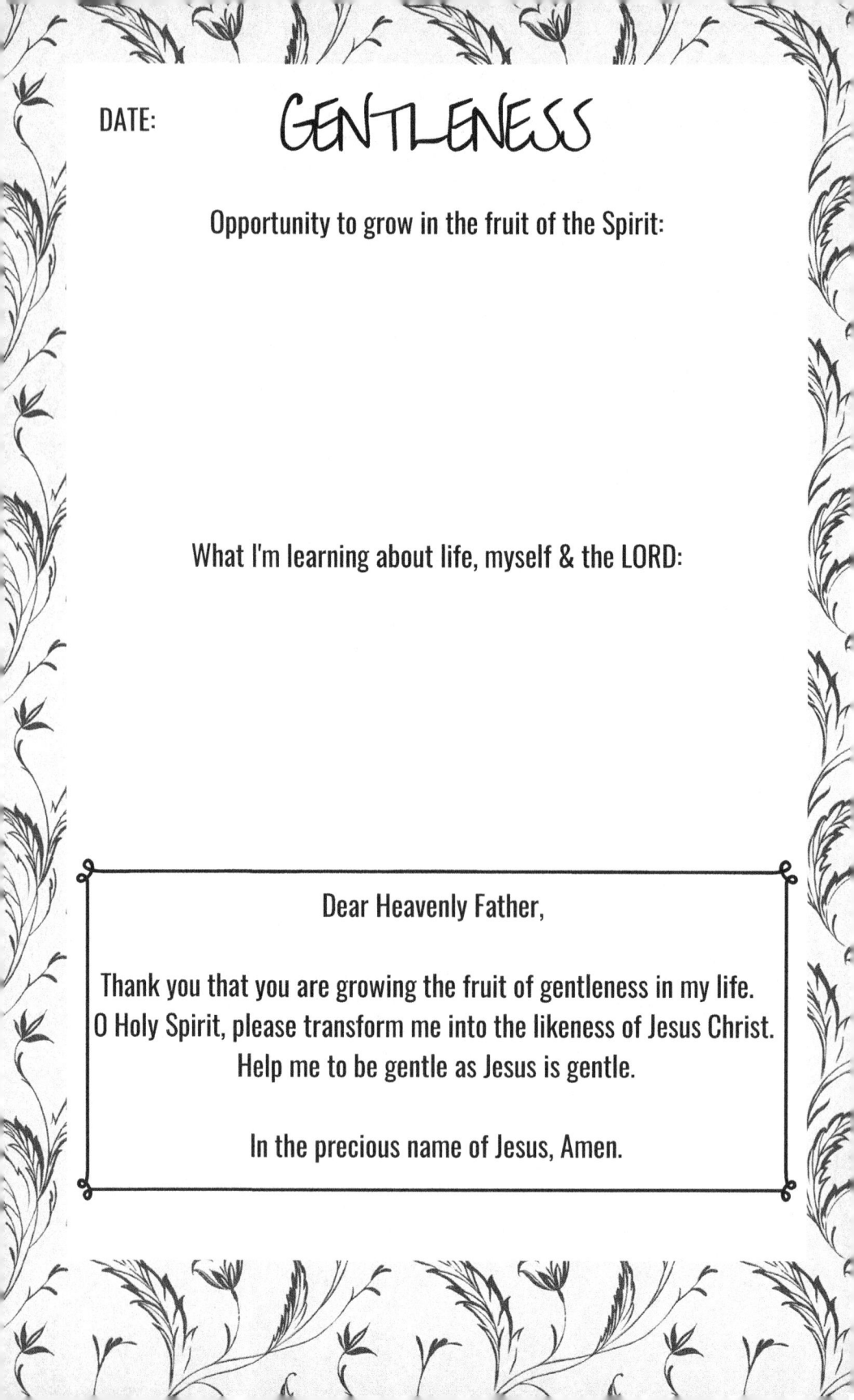

GENTLENESS

Opportunity to grow in the fruit of the Spirit:

What I'm learning about life, myself & the LORD:

Dear Heavenly Father,

Thank you that you are growing the fruit of gentleness in my life.
O Holy Spirit, please transform me into the likeness of Jesus Christ.
Help me to be gentle as Jesus is gentle.

In the precious name of Jesus, Amen.

DATE:

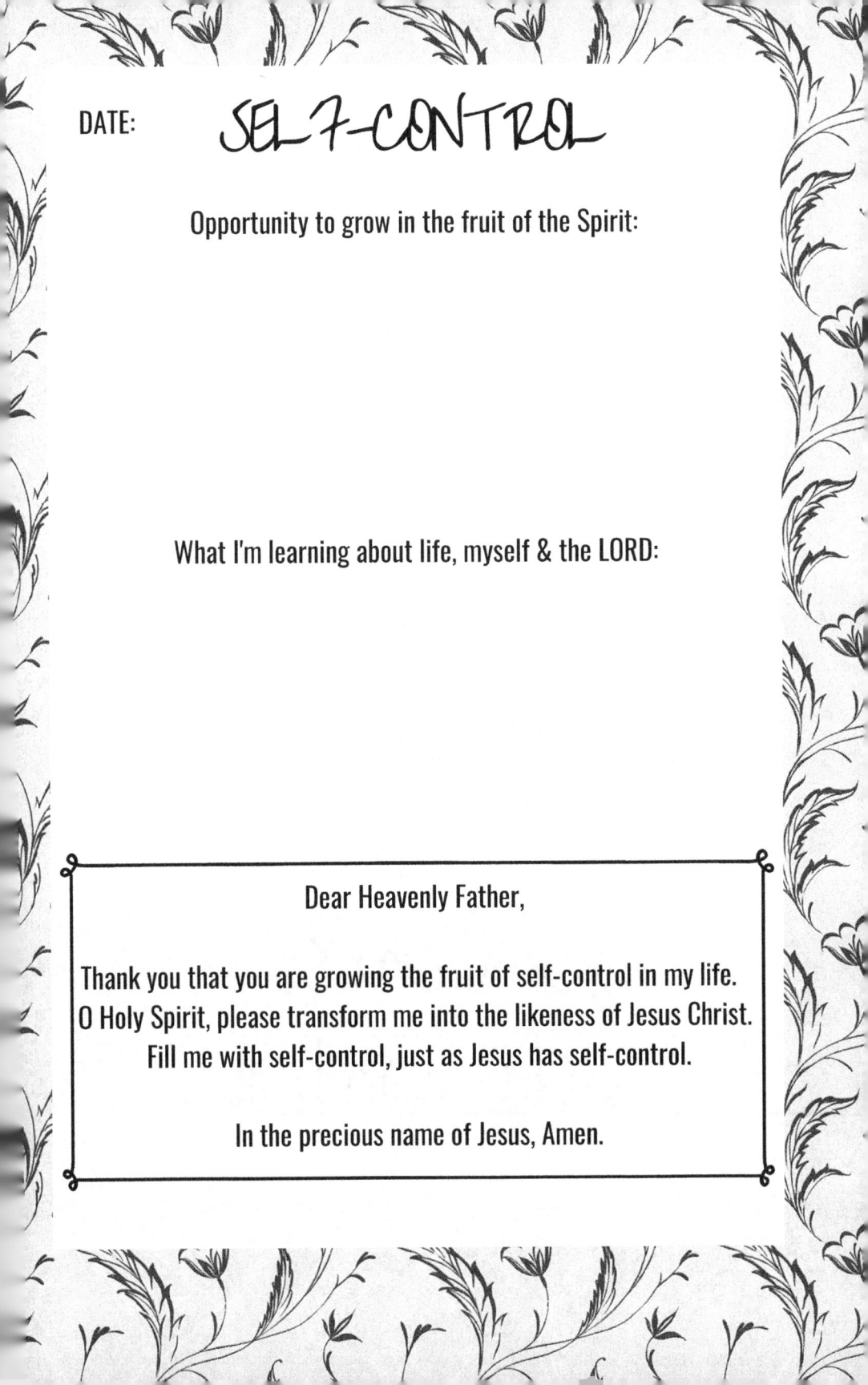

SELF-CONTROL

Opportunity to grow in the fruit of the Spirit:

What I'm learning about life, myself & the LORD:

Dear Heavenly Father,

Thank you that you are growing the fruit of self-control in my life. O Holy Spirit, please transform me into the likeness of Jesus Christ. Fill me with self-control, just as Jesus has self-control.

In the precious name of Jesus, Amen.

love,
joy,
peace,
patience,
kindness,
goodness,
faithfulness,
gentleness,
self-control

DATE:

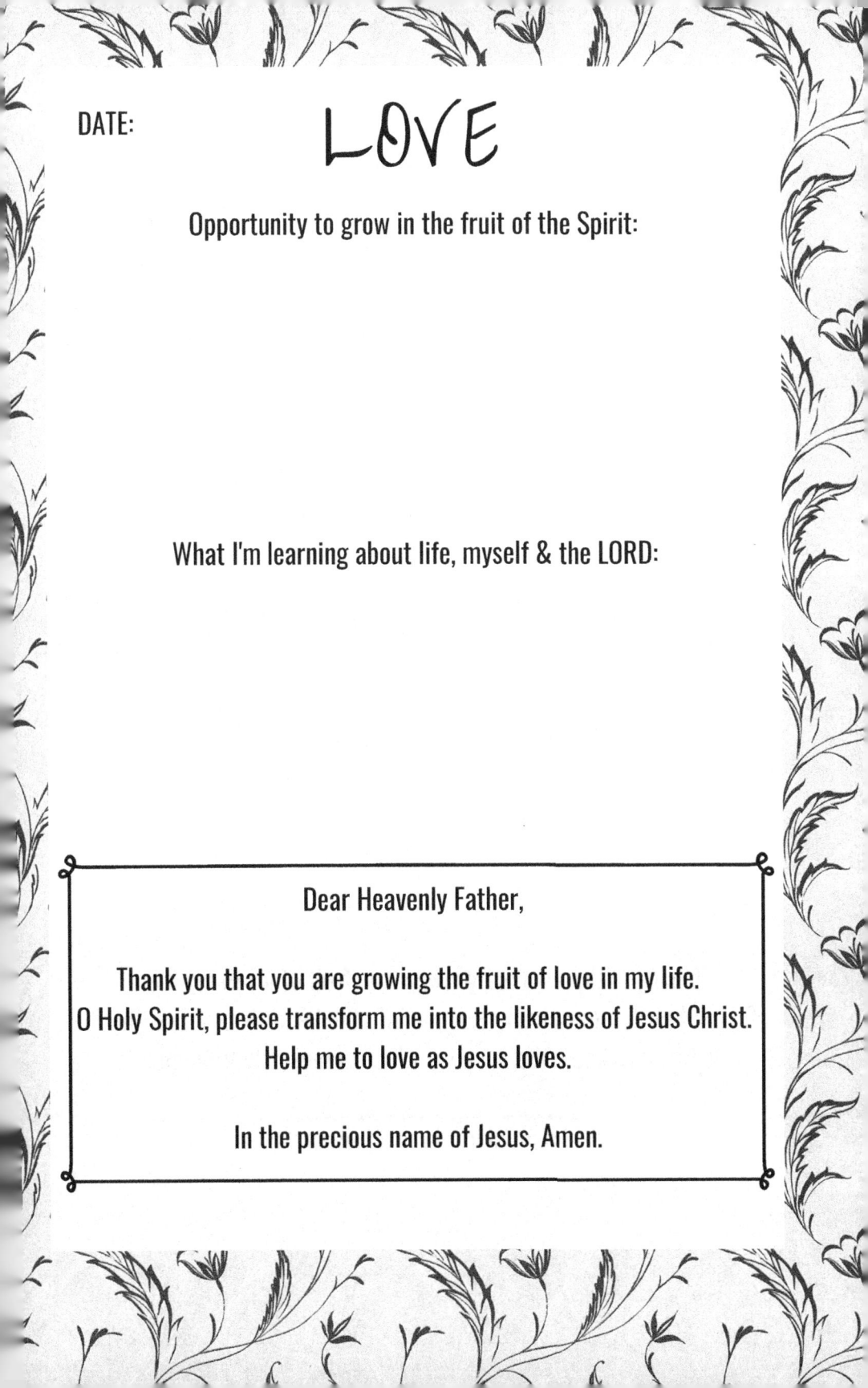

LOVE

Opportunity to grow in the fruit of the Spirit:

What I'm learning about life, myself & the LORD:

Dear Heavenly Father,

Thank you that you are growing the fruit of love in my life.
O Holy Spirit, please transform me into the likeness of Jesus Christ.
Help me to love as Jesus loves.

In the precious name of Jesus, Amen.

DATE:

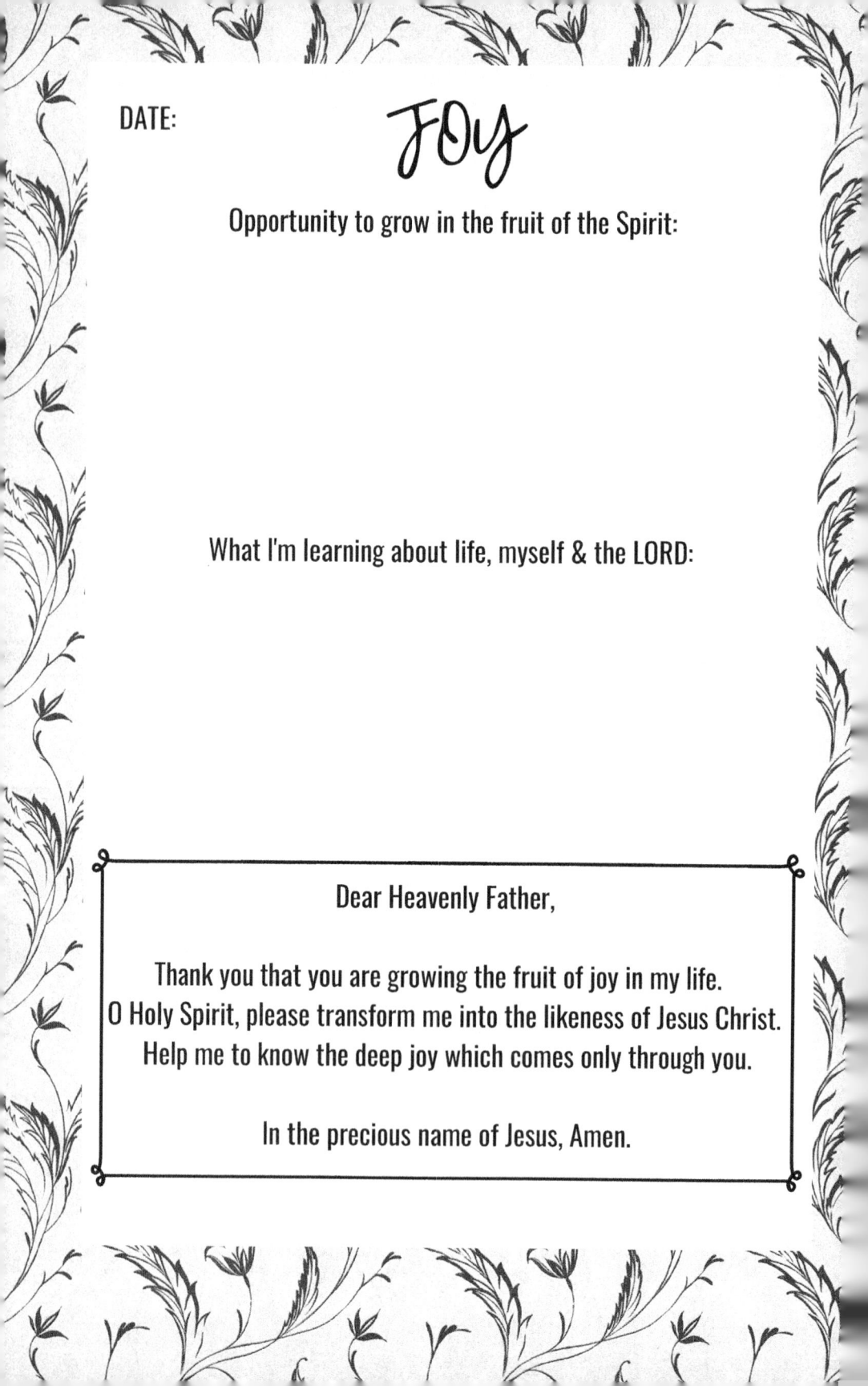

JOY

Opportunity to grow in the fruit of the Spirit:

What I'm learning about life, myself & the LORD:

Dear Heavenly Father,

Thank you that you are growing the fruit of joy in my life.
O Holy Spirit, please transform me into the likeness of Jesus Christ.
Help me to know the deep joy which comes only through you.

In the precious name of Jesus, Amen.

DATE:

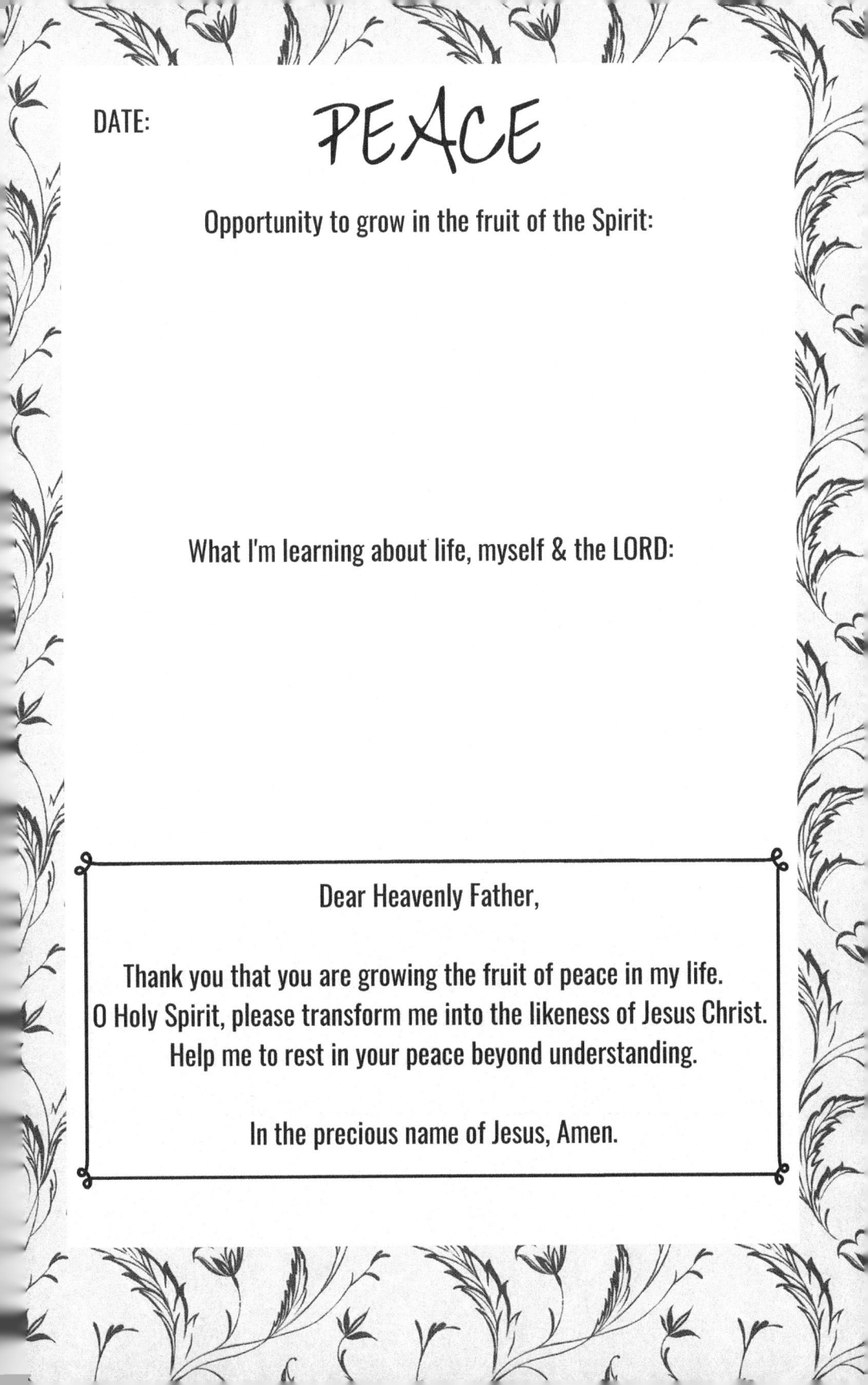

PEACE

Opportunity to grow in the fruit of the Spirit:

What I'm learning about life, myself & the LORD:

Dear Heavenly Father,

Thank you that you are growing the fruit of peace in my life.
O Holy Spirit, please transform me into the likeness of Jesus Christ.
Help me to rest in your peace beyond understanding.

In the precious name of Jesus, Amen.

DATE:

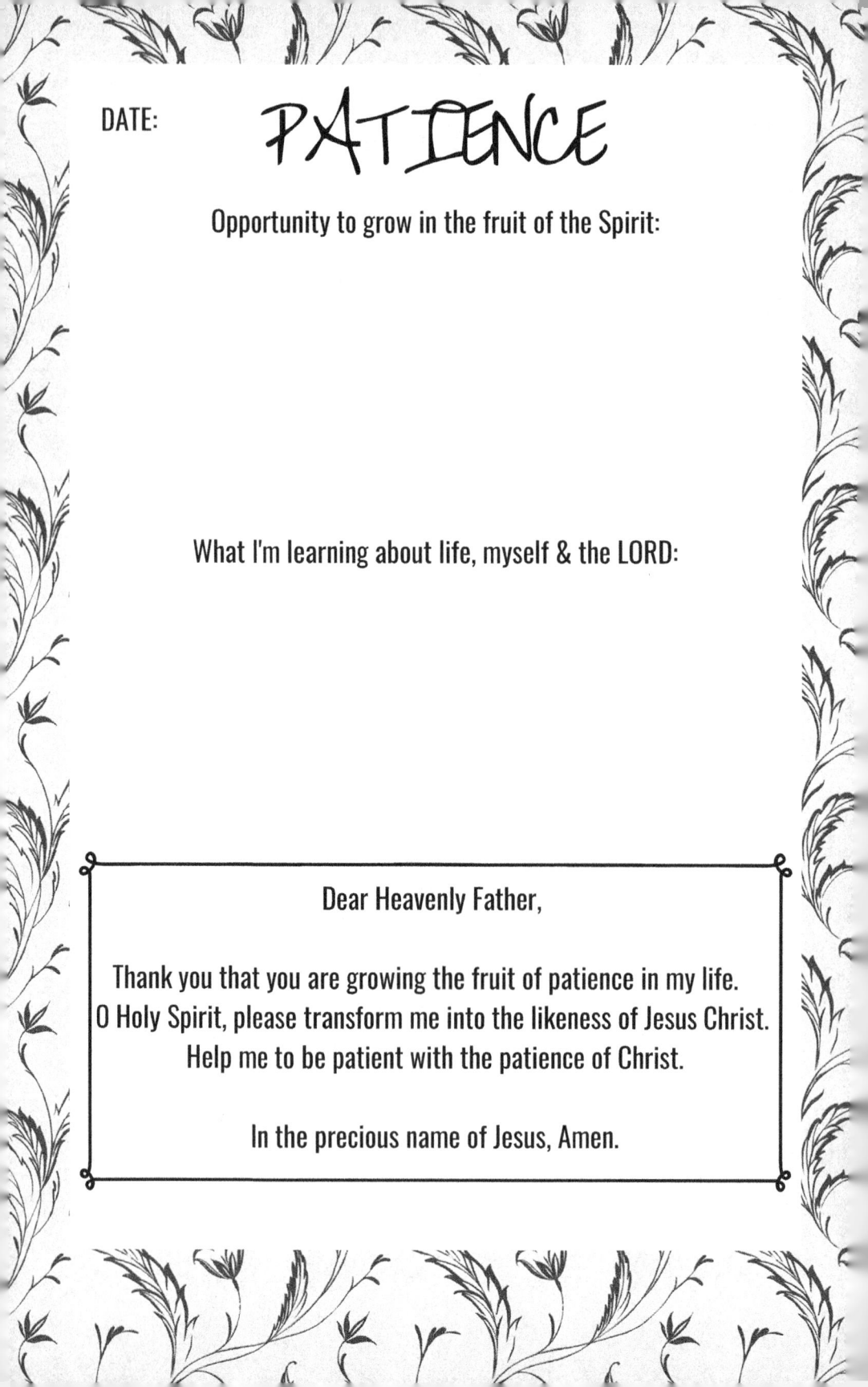

PATIENCE

Opportunity to grow in the fruit of the Spirit:

What I'm learning about life, myself & the LORD:

Dear Heavenly Father,

Thank you that you are growing the fruit of patience in my life.
O Holy Spirit, please transform me into the likeness of Jesus Christ.
Help me to be patient with the patience of Christ.

In the precious name of Jesus, Amen.

DATE:

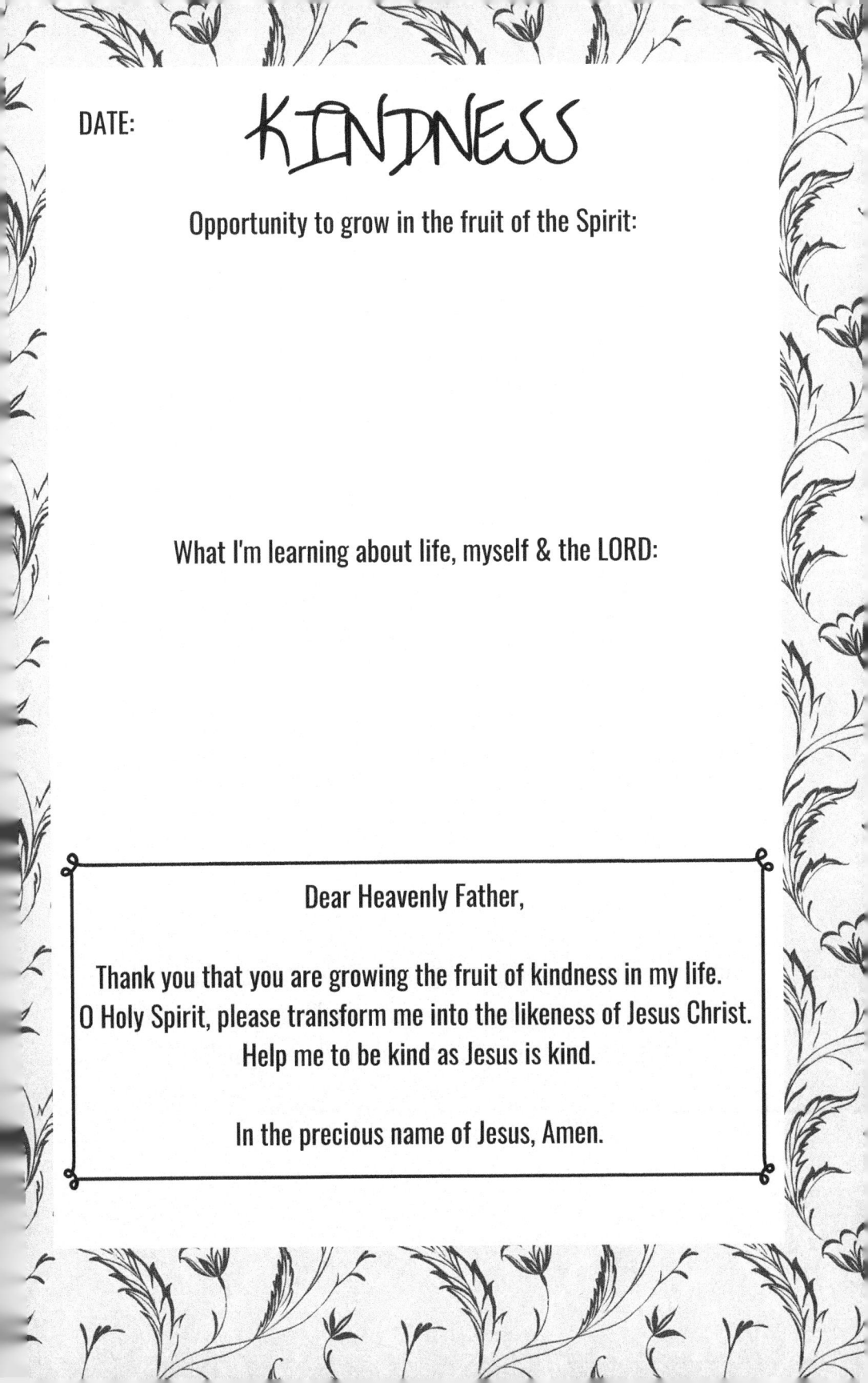

KINDNESS

Opportunity to grow in the fruit of the Spirit:

What I'm learning about life, myself & the LORD:

Dear Heavenly Father,

Thank you that you are growing the fruit of kindness in my life.
O Holy Spirit, please transform me into the likeness of Jesus Christ.
Help me to be kind as Jesus is kind.

In the precious name of Jesus, Amen.

DATE:

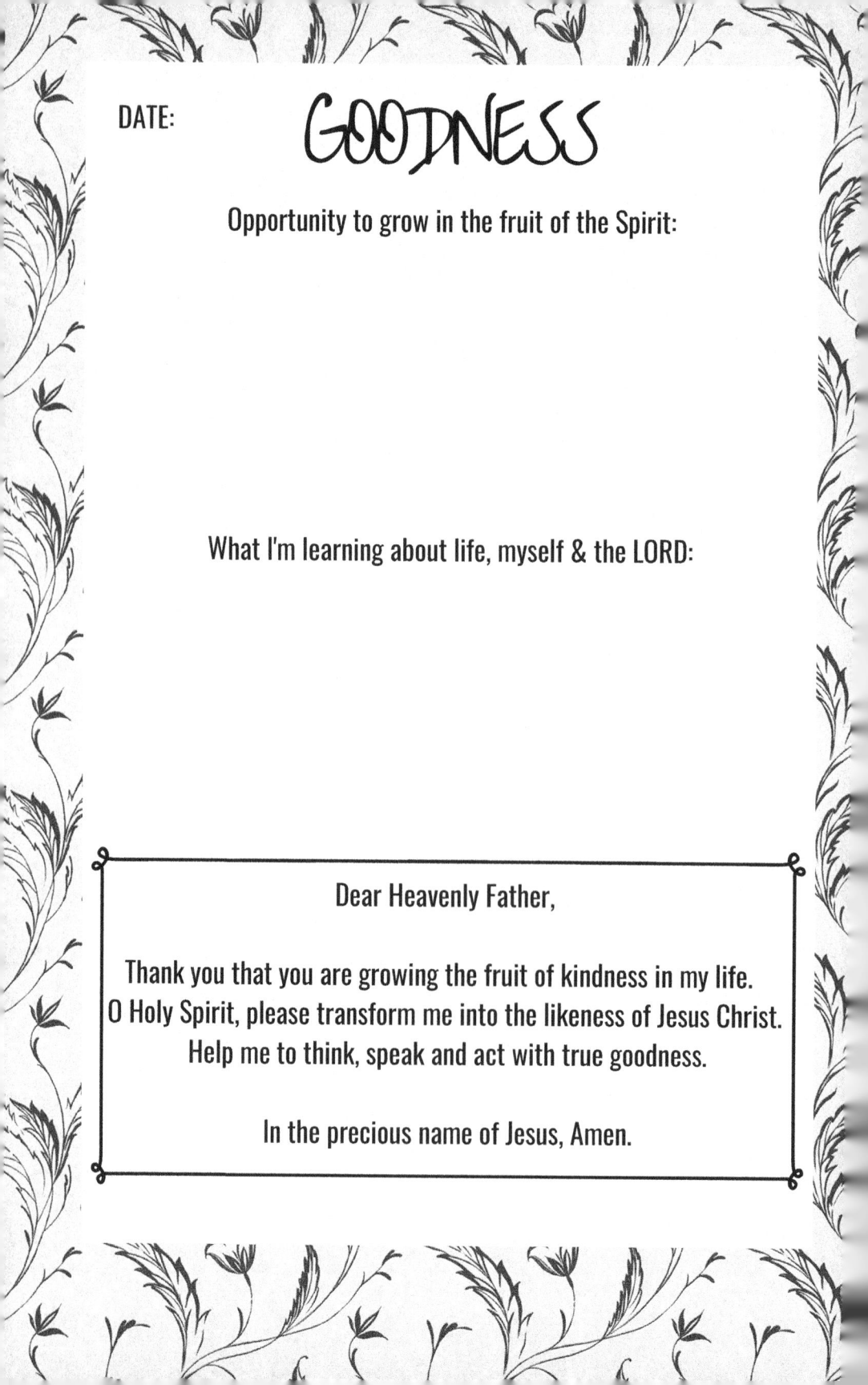

GOODNESS

Opportunity to grow in the fruit of the Spirit:

What I'm learning about life, myself & the LORD:

Dear Heavenly Father,

Thank you that you are growing the fruit of kindness in my life.
O Holy Spirit, please transform me into the likeness of Jesus Christ.
Help me to think, speak and act with true goodness.

In the precious name of Jesus, Amen.

DATE: # FAITHFULNESS

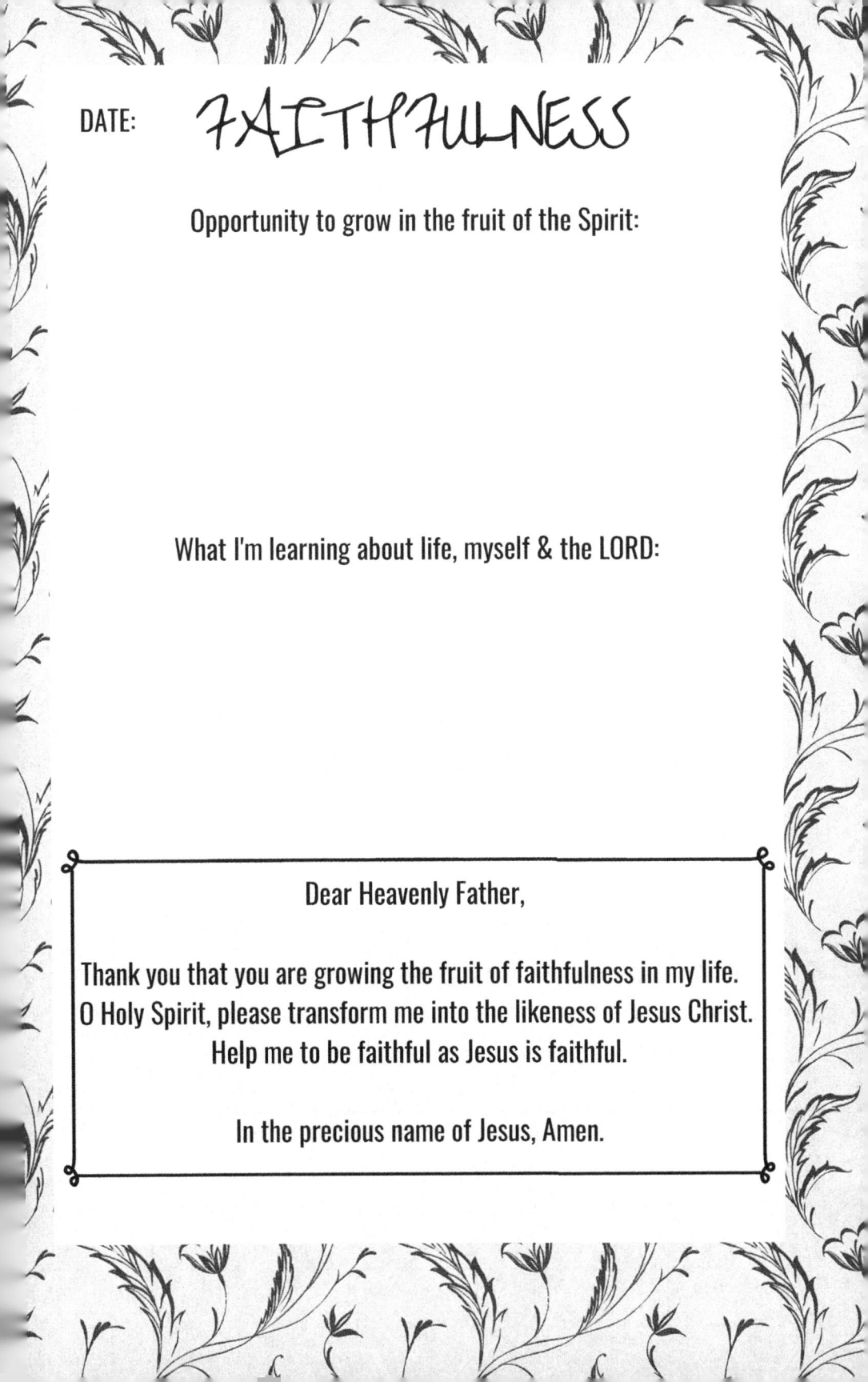

Opportunity to grow in the fruit of the Spirit:

What I'm learning about life, myself & the LORD:

Dear Heavenly Father,

Thank you that you are growing the fruit of faithfulness in my life.
O Holy Spirit, please transform me into the likeness of Jesus Christ.
Help me to be faithful as Jesus is faithful.

In the precious name of Jesus, Amen.

DATE:

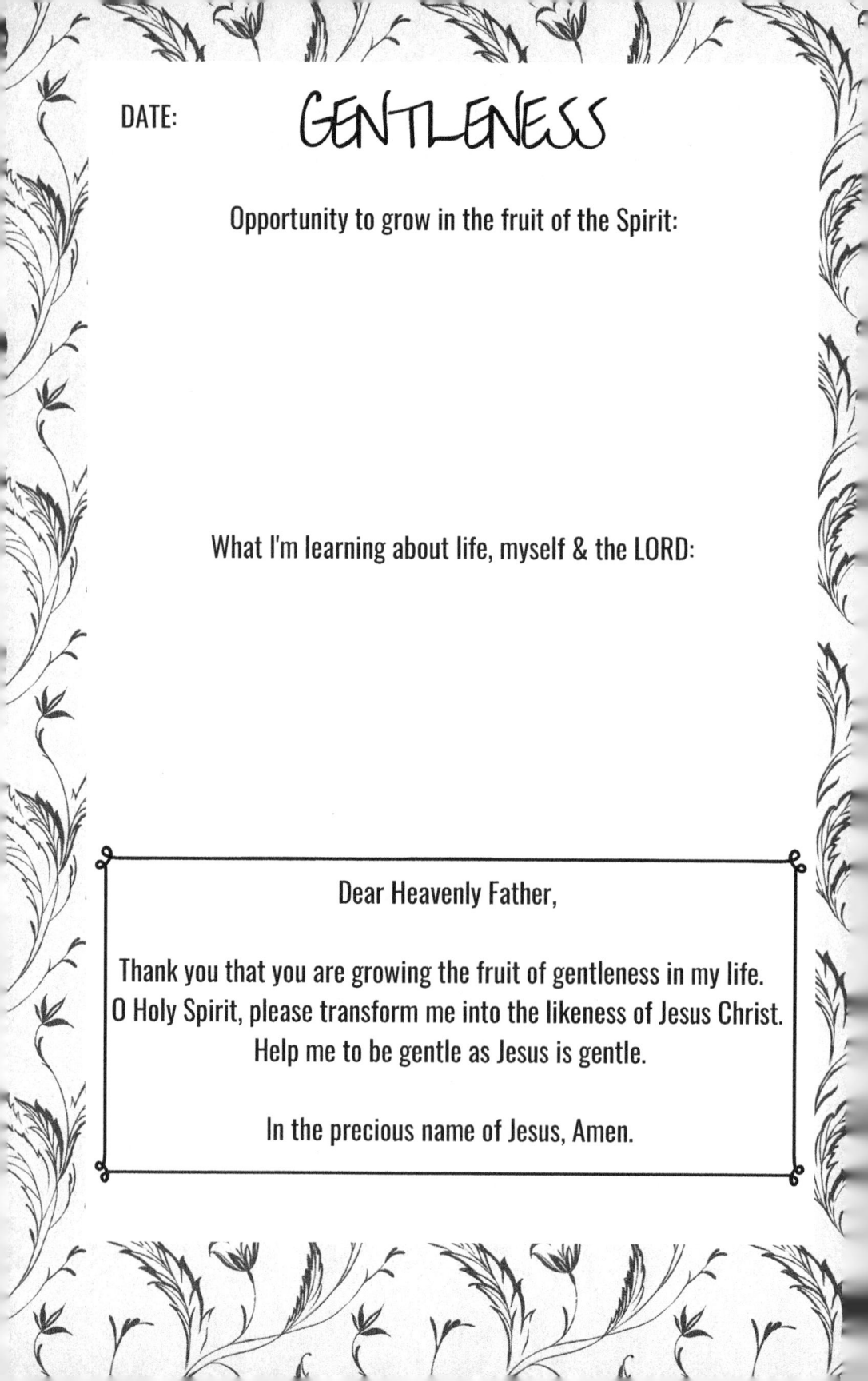

GENTLENESS

Opportunity to grow in the fruit of the Spirit:

What I'm learning about life, myself & the LORD:

Dear Heavenly Father,

Thank you that you are growing the fruit of gentleness in my life.
O Holy Spirit, please transform me into the likeness of Jesus Christ.
Help me to be gentle as Jesus is gentle.

In the precious name of Jesus, Amen.

DATE:

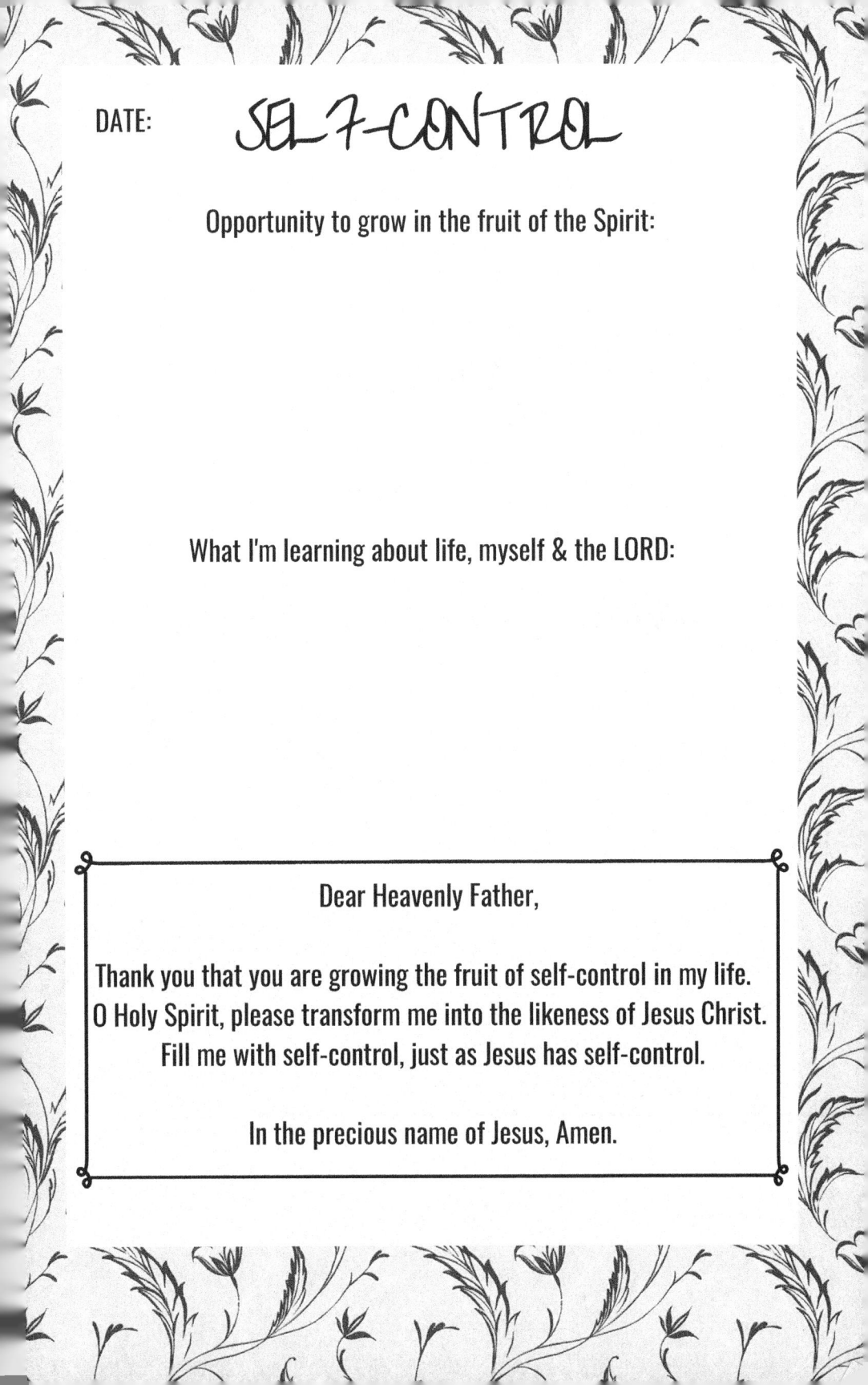

SELF-CONTROL

Opportunity to grow in the fruit of the Spirit:

What I'm learning about life, myself & the LORD:

Dear Heavenly Father,

Thank you that you are growing the fruit of self-control in my life. O Holy Spirit, please transform me into the likeness of Jesus Christ. Fill me with self-control, just as Jesus has self-control.

In the precious name of Jesus, Amen.

Against these things there is no law.

DATE:

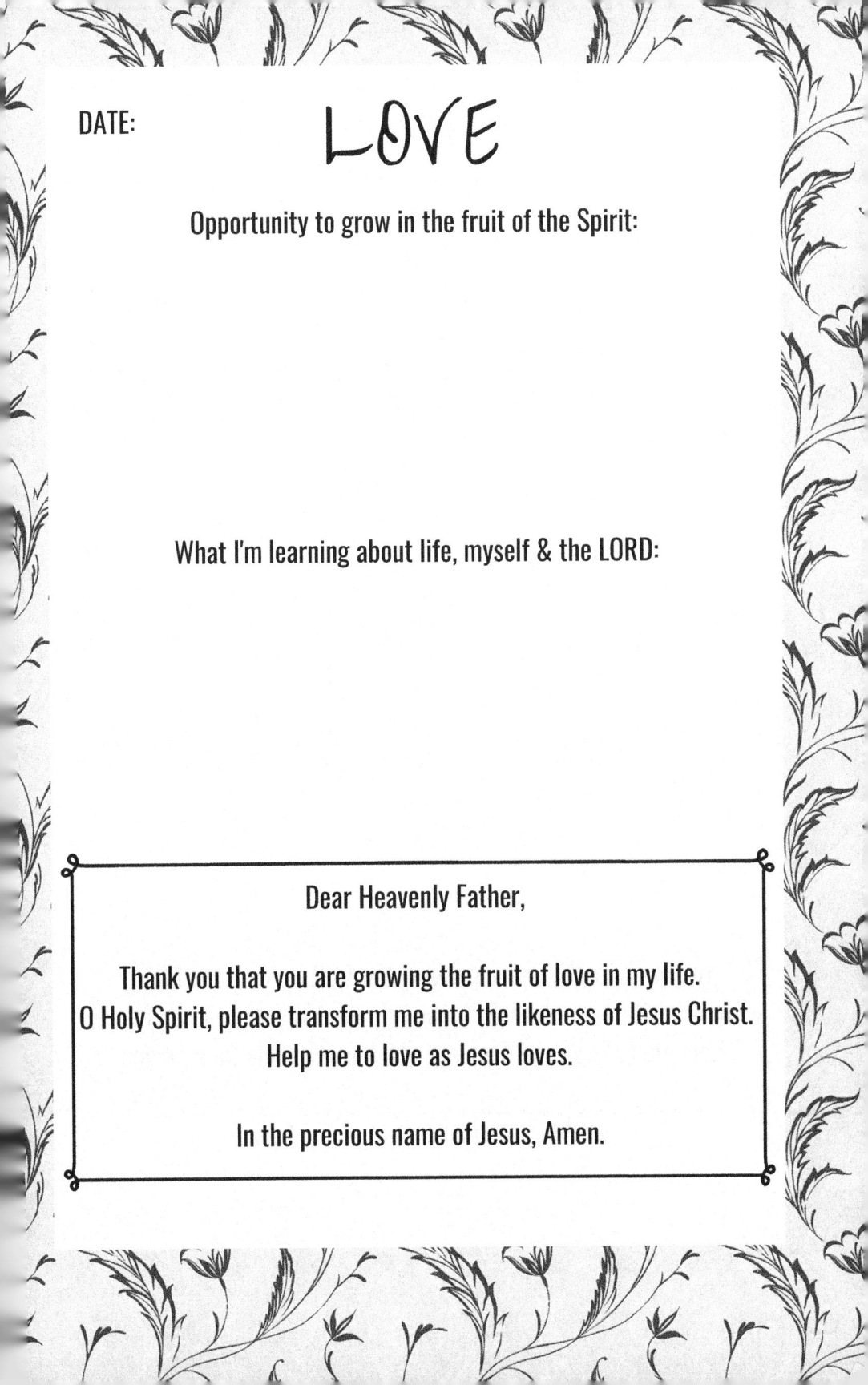

LOVE

Opportunity to grow in the fruit of the Spirit:

What I'm learning about life, myself & the LORD:

Dear Heavenly Father,

Thank you that you are growing the fruit of love in my life.
O Holy Spirit, please transform me into the likeness of Jesus Christ.
Help me to love as Jesus loves.

In the precious name of Jesus, Amen.

DATE:

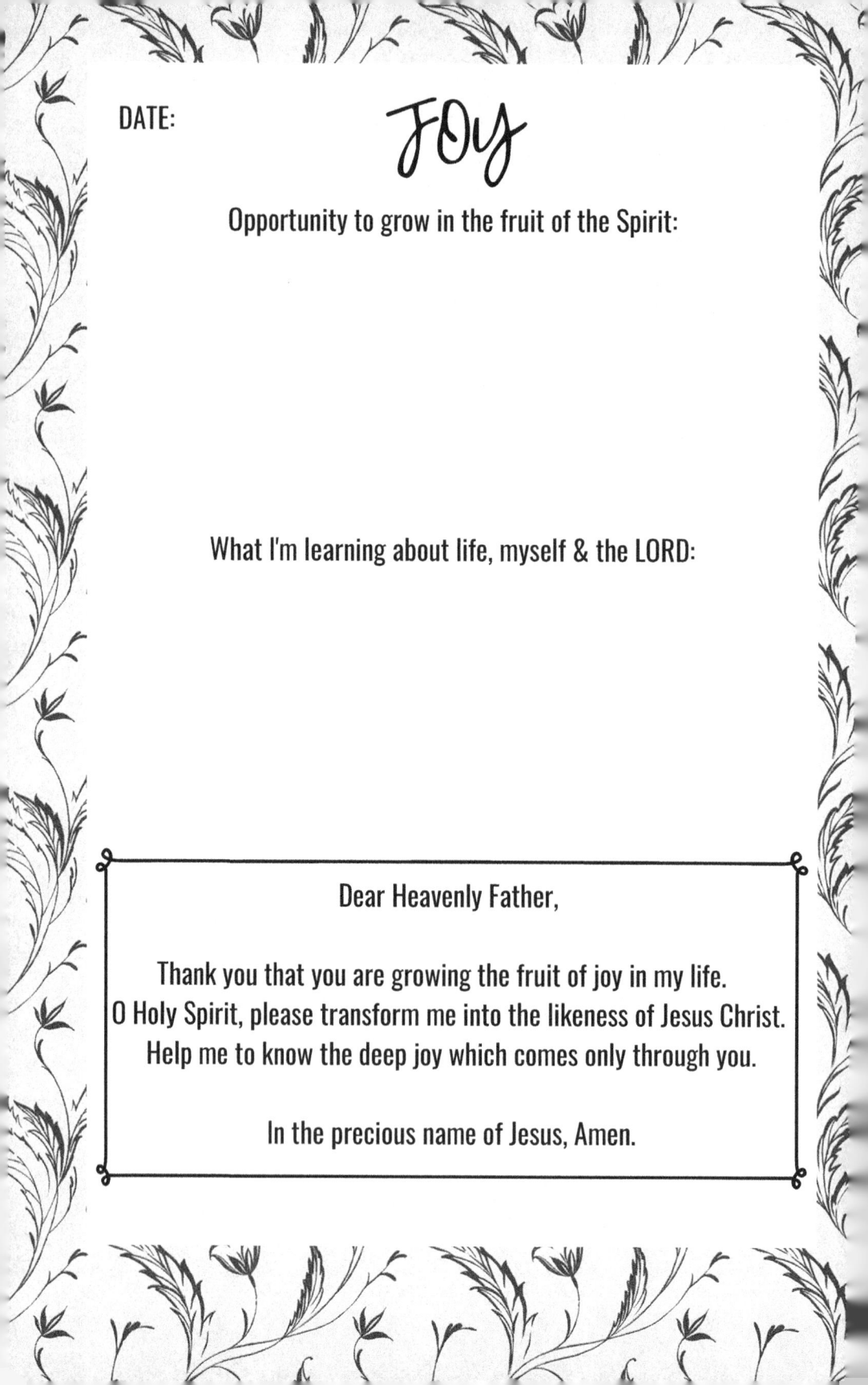

JOY

Opportunity to grow in the fruit of the Spirit:

What I'm learning about life, myself & the LORD:

Dear Heavenly Father,

Thank you that you are growing the fruit of joy in my life.
O Holy Spirit, please transform me into the likeness of Jesus Christ.
Help me to know the deep joy which comes only through you.

In the precious name of Jesus, Amen.

DATE:

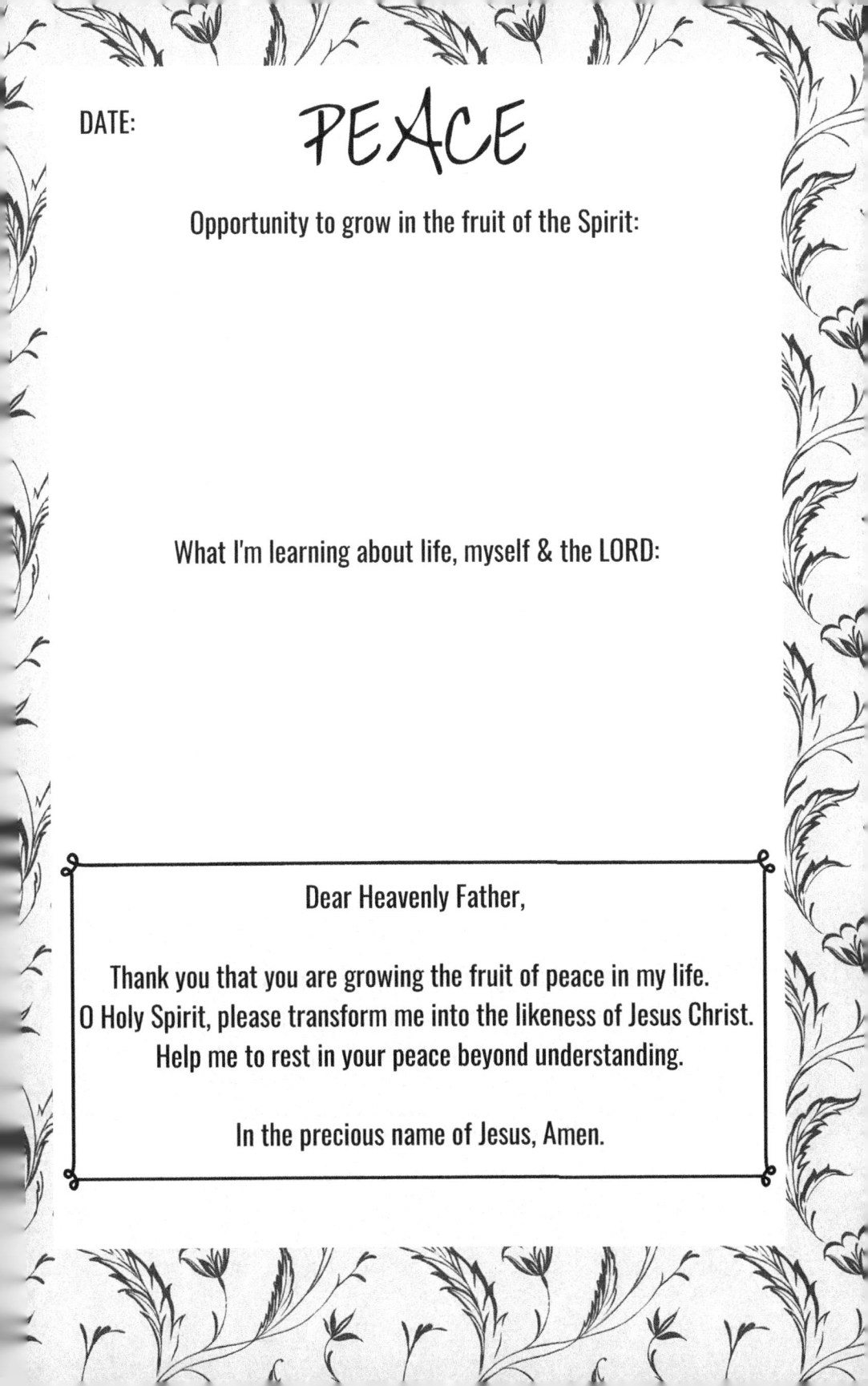

PEACE

Opportunity to grow in the fruit of the Spirit:

What I'm learning about life, myself & the LORD:

Dear Heavenly Father,

Thank you that you are growing the fruit of peace in my life.
O Holy Spirit, please transform me into the likeness of Jesus Christ.
Help me to rest in your peace beyond understanding.

In the precious name of Jesus, Amen.

DATE:

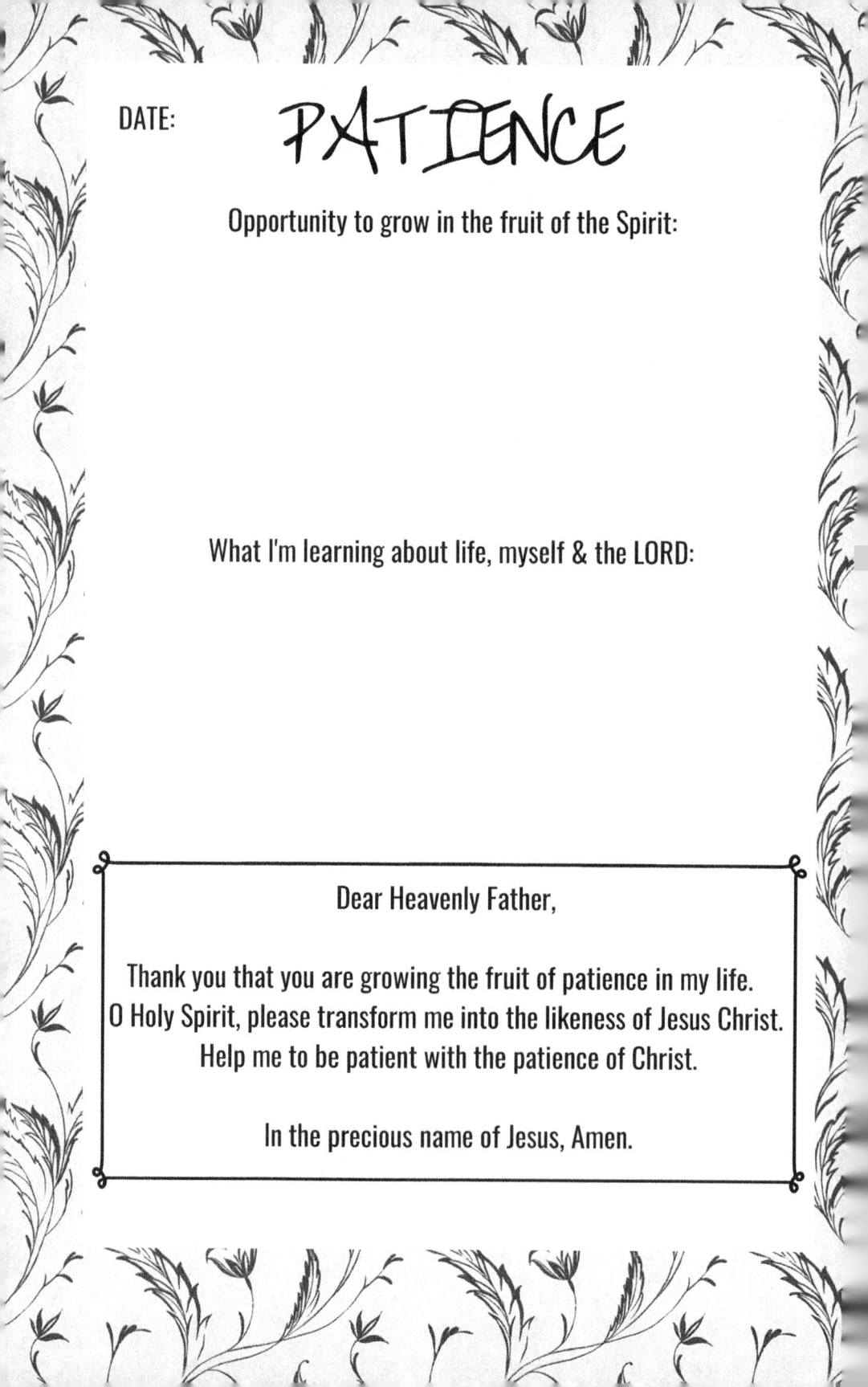

PATIENCE

Opportunity to grow in the fruit of the Spirit:

What I'm learning about life, myself & the LORD:

Dear Heavenly Father,

Thank you that you are growing the fruit of patience in my life.
O Holy Spirit, please transform me into the likeness of Jesus Christ.
Help me to be patient with the patience of Christ.

In the precious name of Jesus, Amen.

DATE:

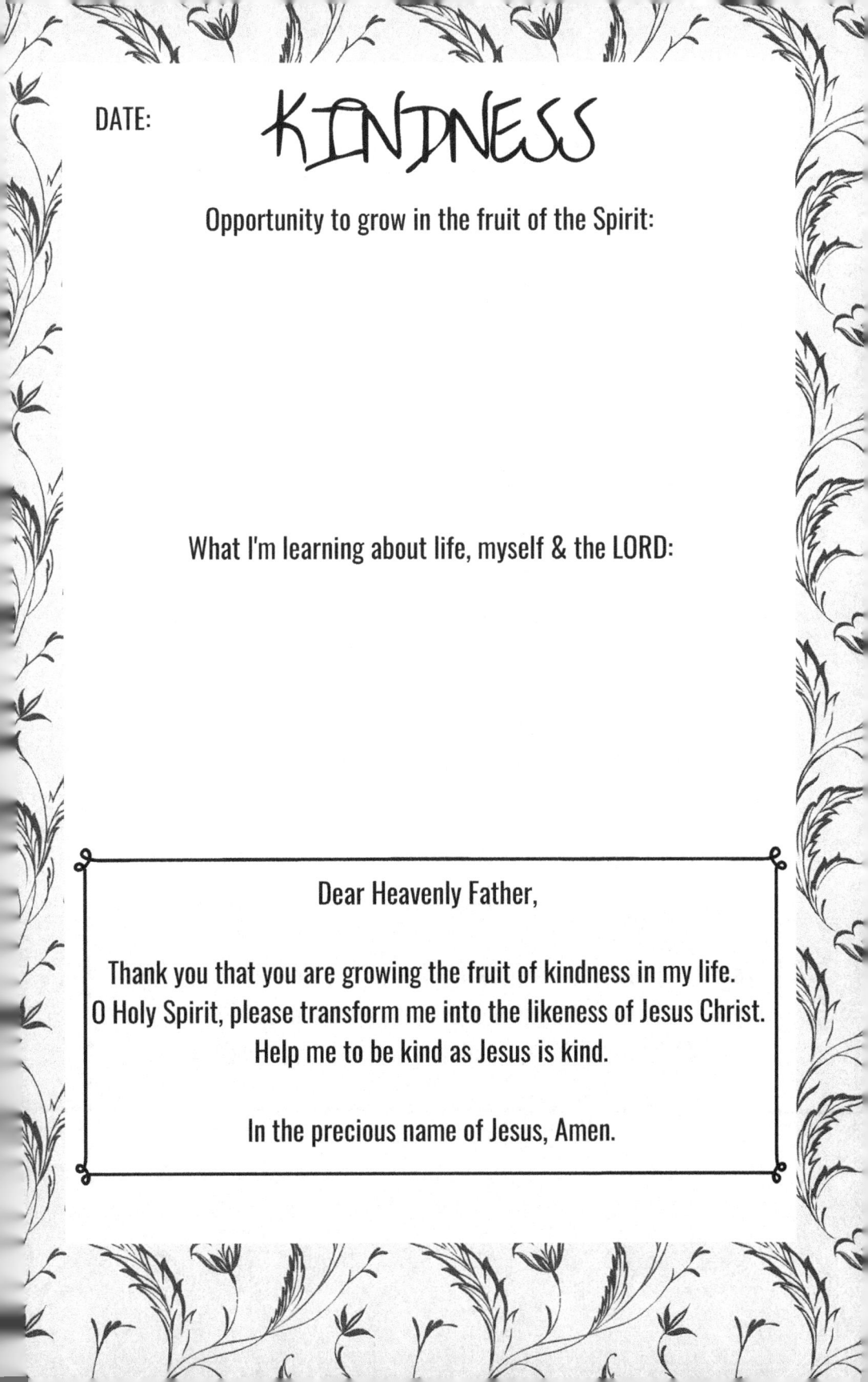

KINDNESS

Opportunity to grow in the fruit of the Spirit:

What I'm learning about life, myself & the LORD:

Dear Heavenly Father,

Thank you that you are growing the fruit of kindness in my life.
O Holy Spirit, please transform me into the likeness of Jesus Christ.
Help me to be kind as Jesus is kind.

In the precious name of Jesus, Amen.

DATE:

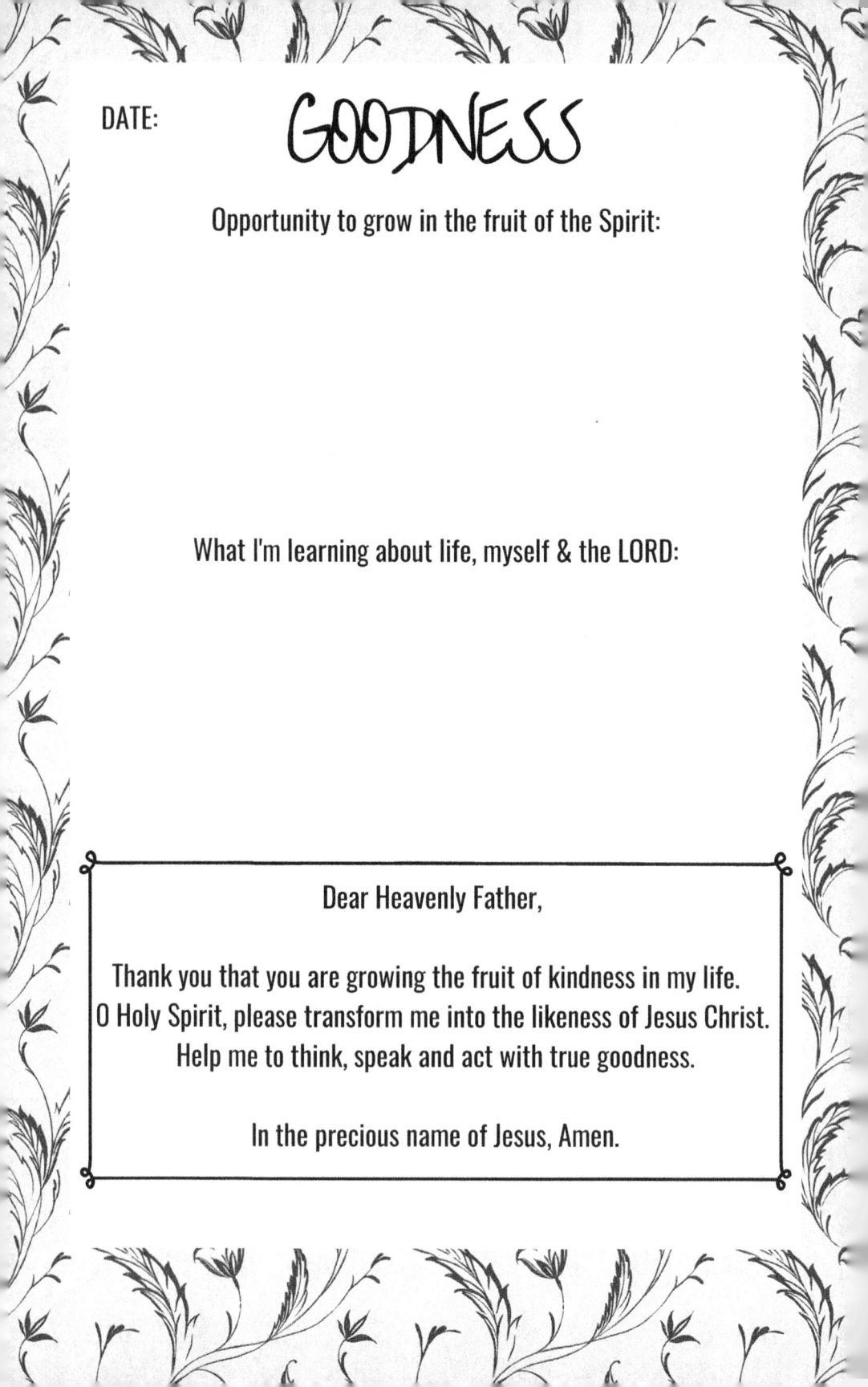

GOODNESS

Opportunity to grow in the fruit of the Spirit:

What I'm learning about life, myself & the LORD:

Dear Heavenly Father,

Thank you that you are growing the fruit of kindness in my life.
O Holy Spirit, please transform me into the likeness of Jesus Christ.
Help me to think, speak and act with true goodness.

In the precious name of Jesus, Amen.

DATE: # FAITHFULNESS

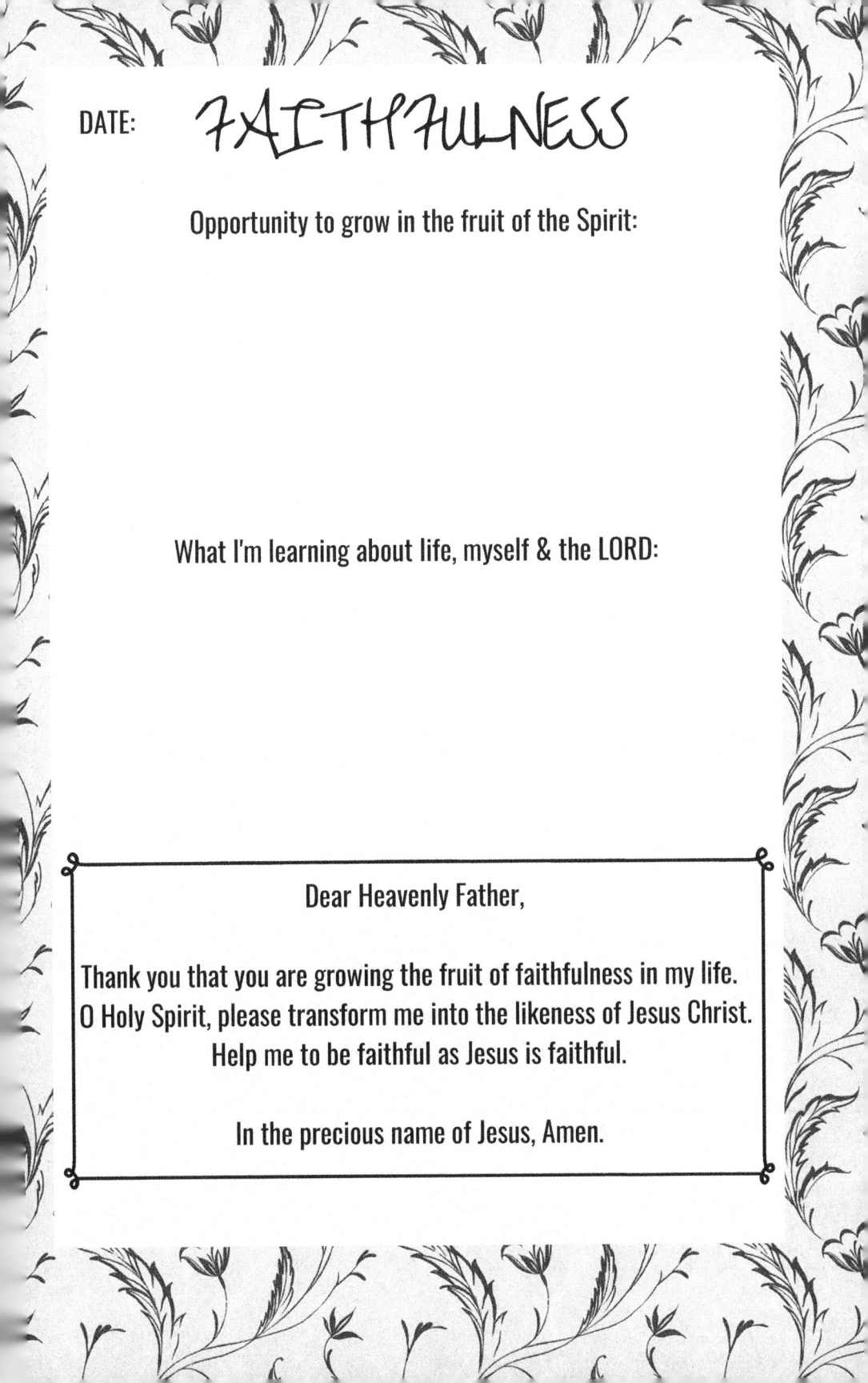

Opportunity to grow in the fruit of the Spirit:

What I'm learning about life, myself & the LORD:

Dear Heavenly Father,

Thank you that you are growing the fruit of faithfulness in my life. O Holy Spirit, please transform me into the likeness of Jesus Christ. Help me to be faithful as Jesus is faithful.

In the precious name of Jesus, Amen.

DATE:

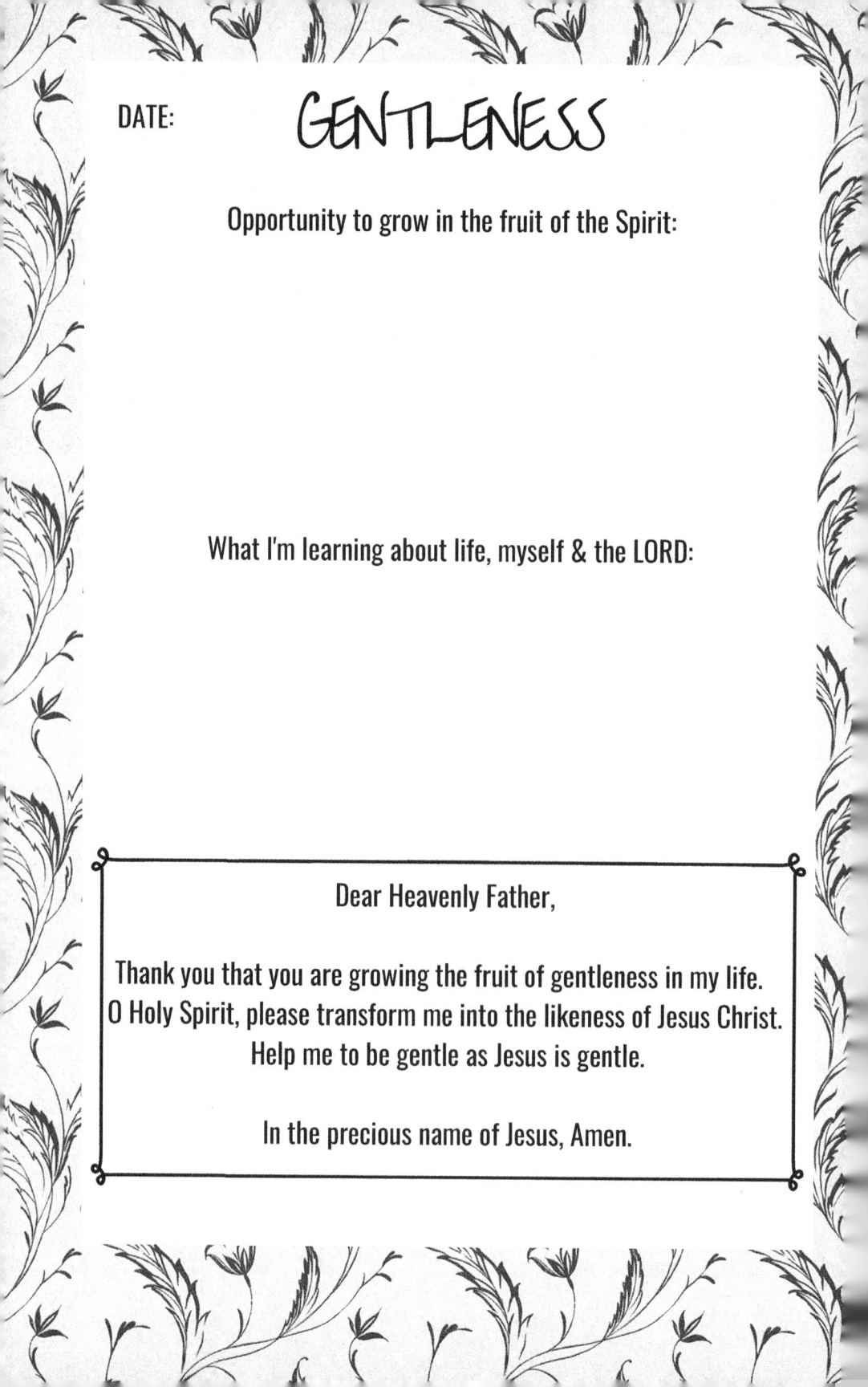

GENTLENESS

Opportunity to grow in the fruit of the Spirit:

What I'm learning about life, myself & the LORD:

Dear Heavenly Father,

Thank you that you are growing the fruit of gentleness in my life.
O Holy Spirit, please transform me into the likeness of Jesus Christ.
Help me to be gentle as Jesus is gentle.

In the precious name of Jesus, Amen.

DATE:

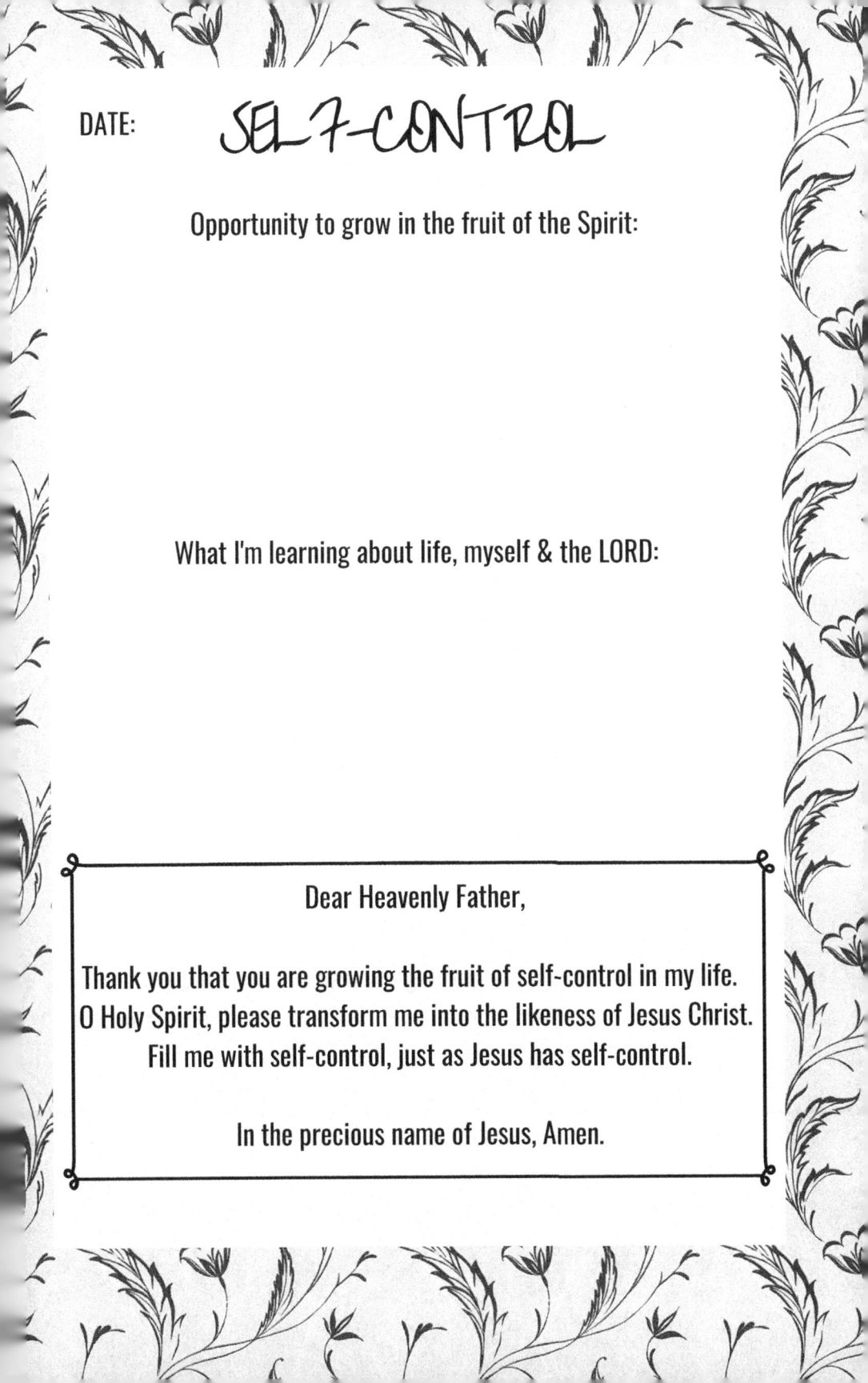

SELF-CONTROL

Opportunity to grow in the fruit of the Spirit:

What I'm learning about life, myself & the LORD:

Dear Heavenly Father,

Thank you that you are growing the fruit of self-control in my life. O Holy Spirit, please transform me into the likeness of Jesus Christ. Fill me with self-control, just as Jesus has self-control.

In the precious name of Jesus, Amen.

DATE:

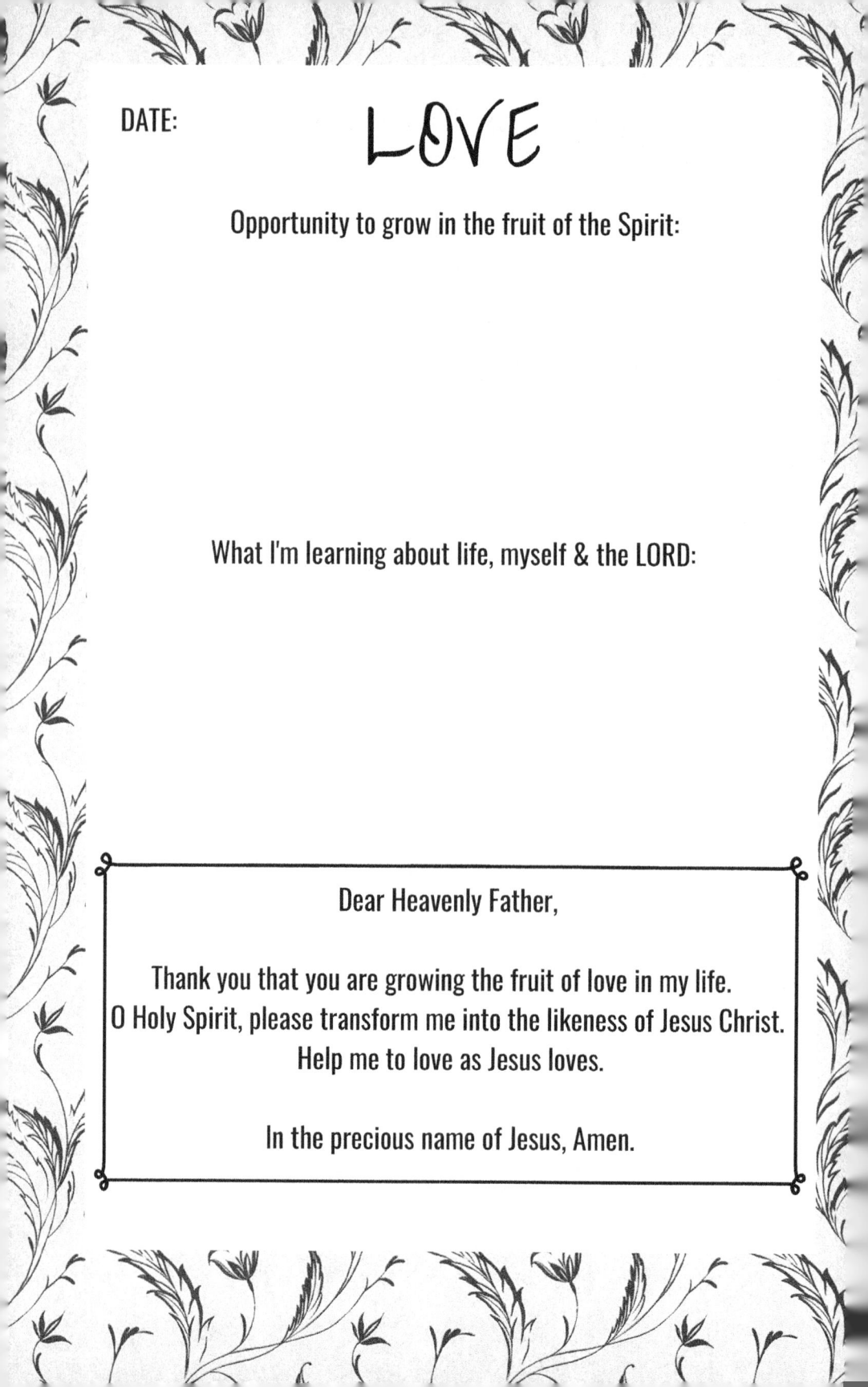

LOVE

Opportunity to grow in the fruit of the Spirit:

What I'm learning about life, myself & the LORD:

Dear Heavenly Father,

Thank you that you are growing the fruit of love in my life.
O Holy Spirit, please transform me into the likeness of Jesus Christ.
Help me to love as Jesus loves.

In the precious name of Jesus, Amen.

DATE:

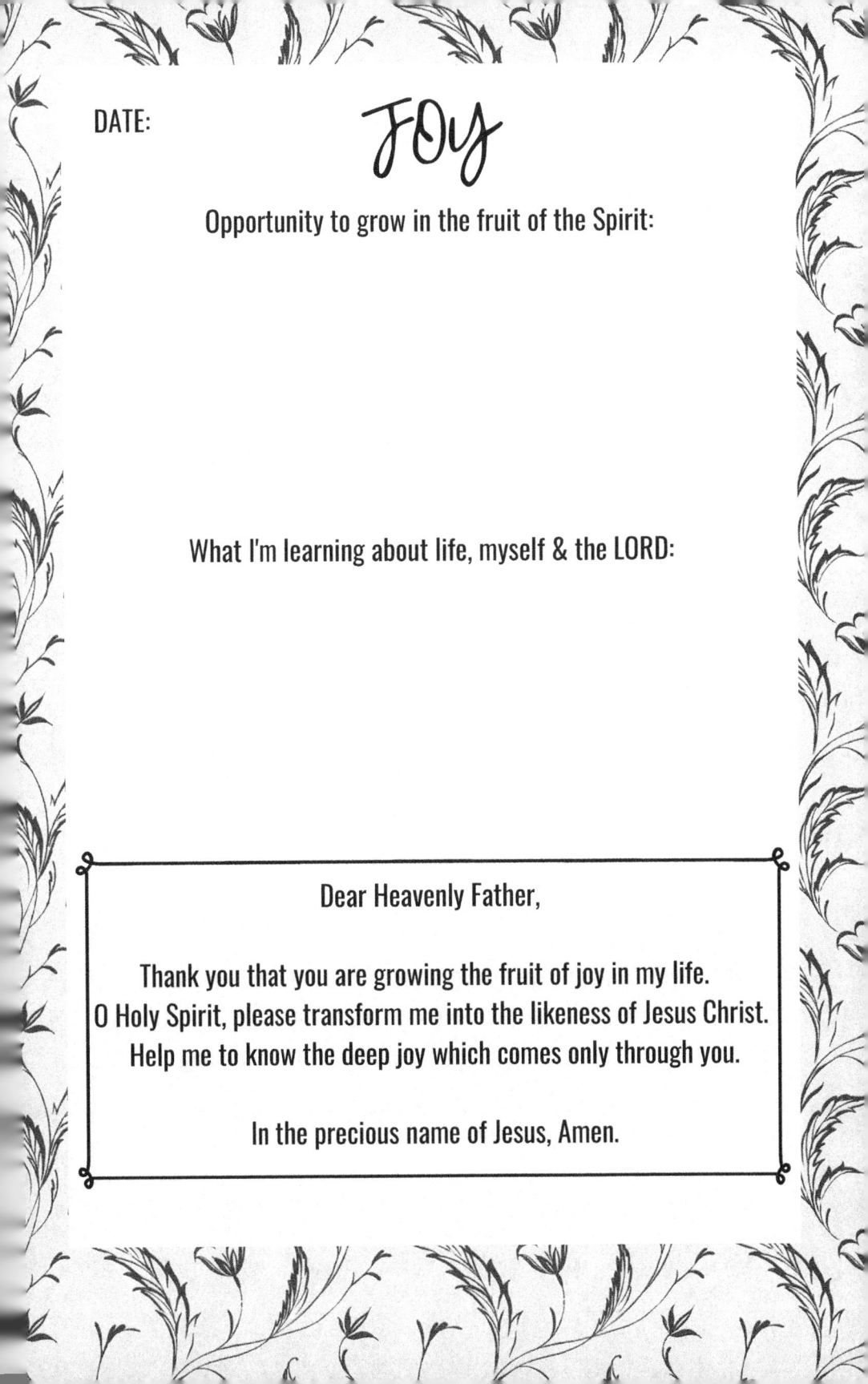

JOY

Opportunity to grow in the fruit of the Spirit:

What I'm learning about life, myself & the LORD:

Dear Heavenly Father,

Thank you that you are growing the fruit of joy in my life.
O Holy Spirit, please transform me into the likeness of Jesus Christ.
Help me to know the deep joy which comes only through you.

In the precious name of Jesus, Amen.

DATE:

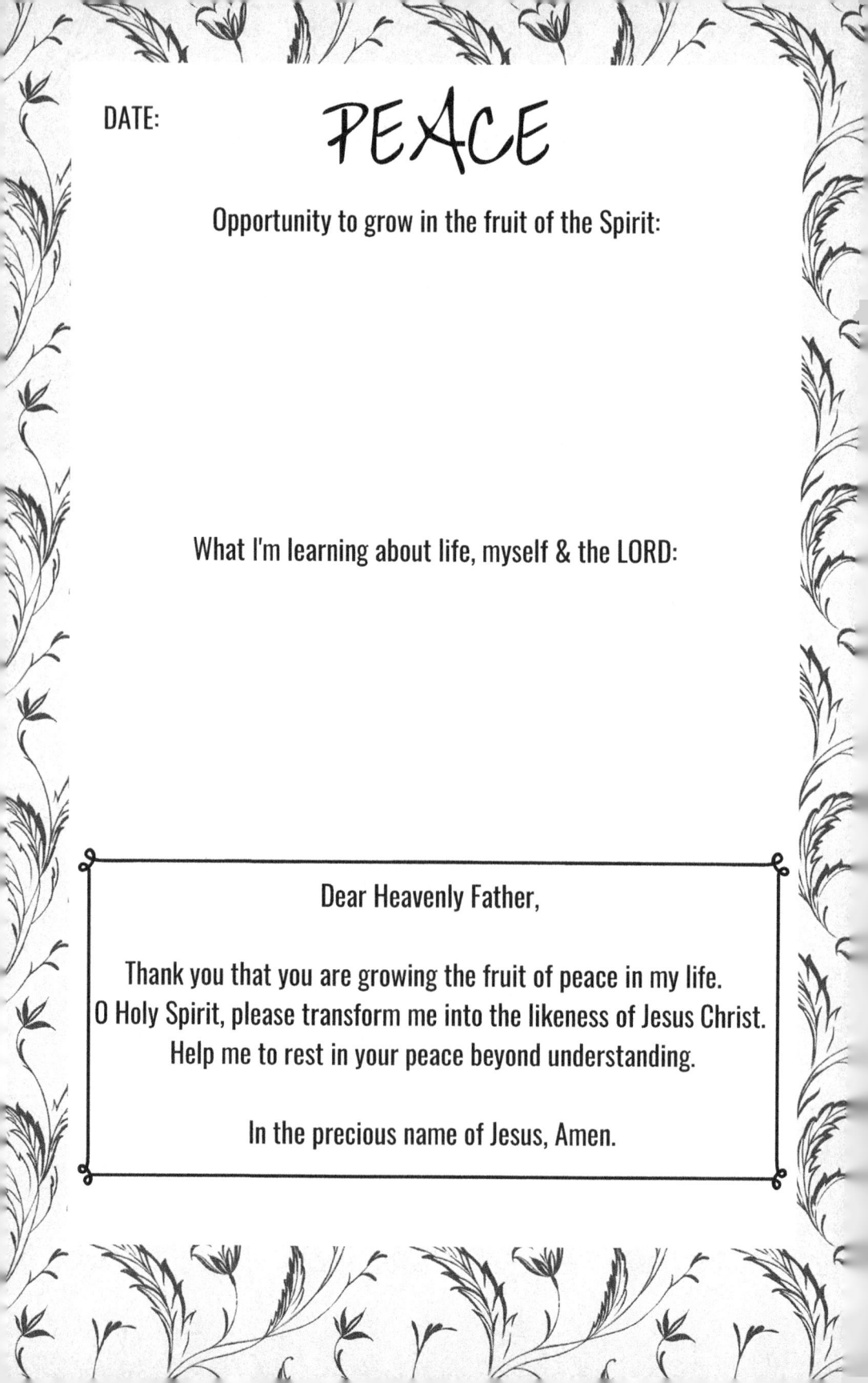

PEACE

Opportunity to grow in the fruit of the Spirit:

What I'm learning about life, myself & the LORD:

Dear Heavenly Father,

Thank you that you are growing the fruit of peace in my life.
O Holy Spirit, please transform me into the likeness of Jesus Christ.
Help me to rest in your peace beyond understanding.

In the precious name of Jesus, Amen.

DATE:

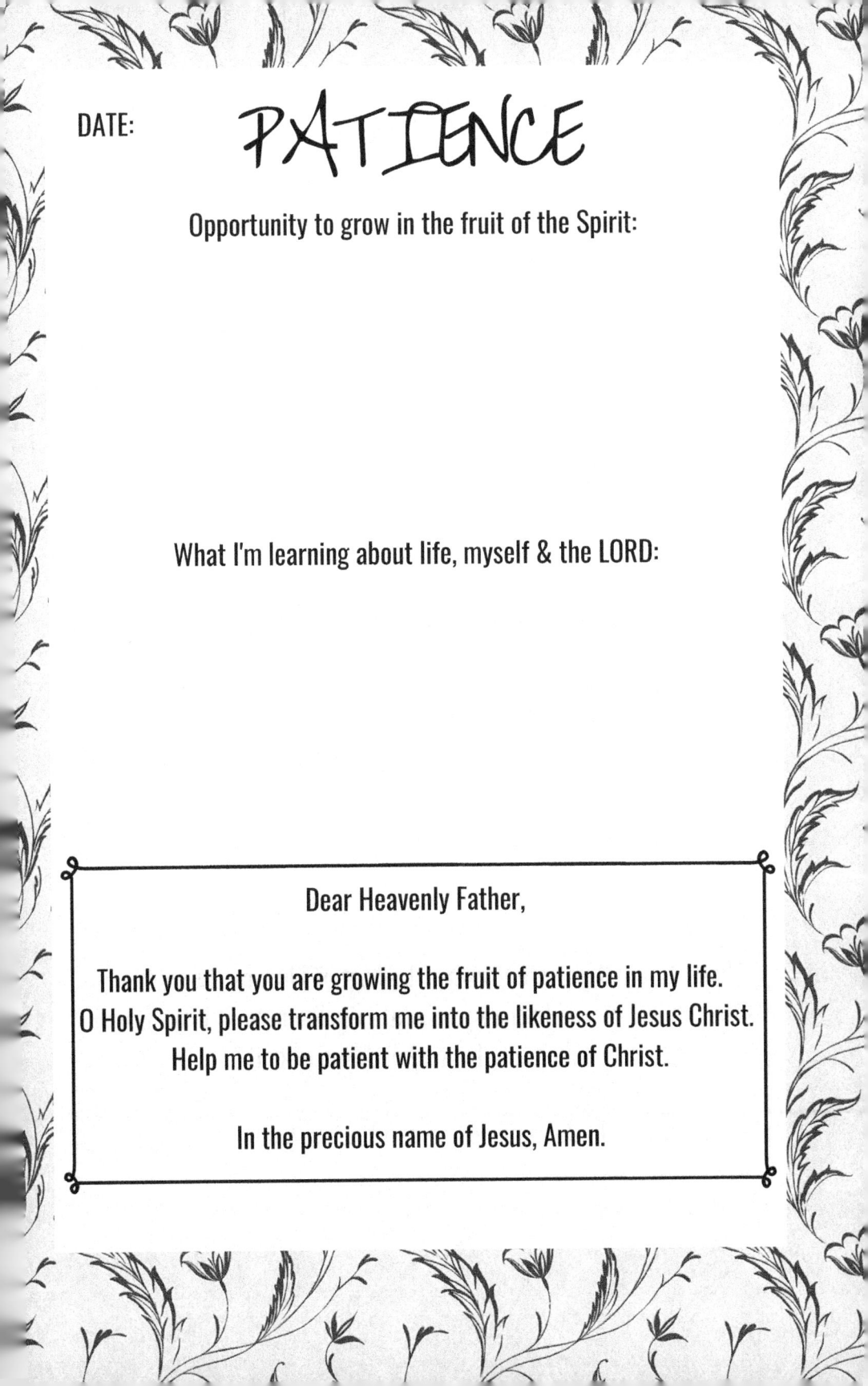

PATIENCE

Opportunity to grow in the fruit of the Spirit:

What I'm learning about life, myself & the LORD:

Dear Heavenly Father,

Thank you that you are growing the fruit of patience in my life.
O Holy Spirit, please transform me into the likeness of Jesus Christ.
Help me to be patient with the patience of Christ.

In the precious name of Jesus, Amen.

DATE:

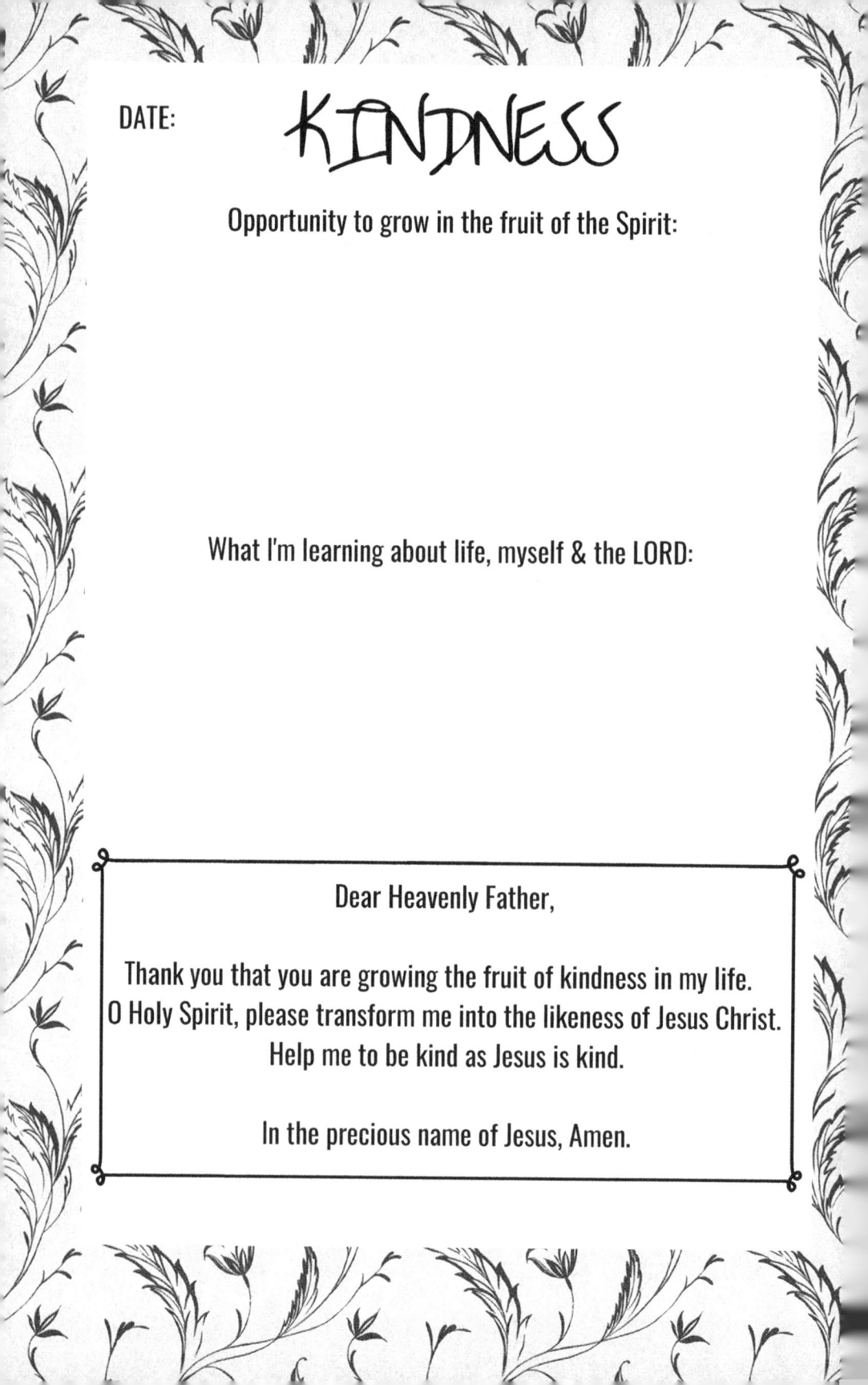

KINDNESS

Opportunity to grow in the fruit of the Spirit:

What I'm learning about life, myself & the LORD:

> Dear Heavenly Father,
>
> Thank you that you are growing the fruit of kindness in my life.
> O Holy Spirit, please transform me into the likeness of Jesus Christ.
> Help me to be kind as Jesus is kind.
>
> In the precious name of Jesus, Amen.

DATE:

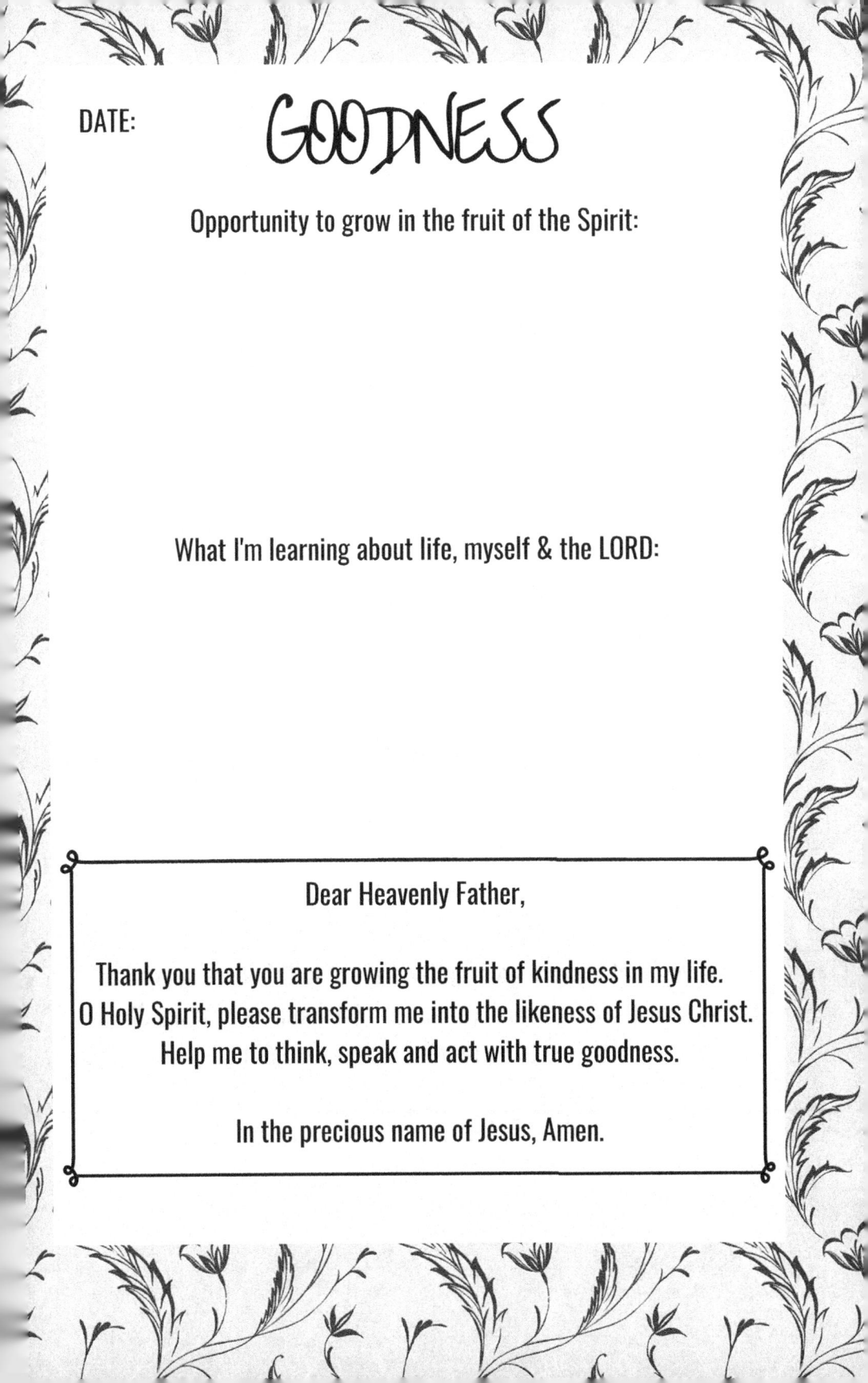

GOODNESS

Opportunity to grow in the fruit of the Spirit:

What I'm learning about life, myself & the LORD:

Dear Heavenly Father,

Thank you that you are growing the fruit of kindness in my life.
O Holy Spirit, please transform me into the likeness of Jesus Christ.
Help me to think, speak and act with true goodness.

In the precious name of Jesus, Amen.

DATE: # FAITHFULNESS

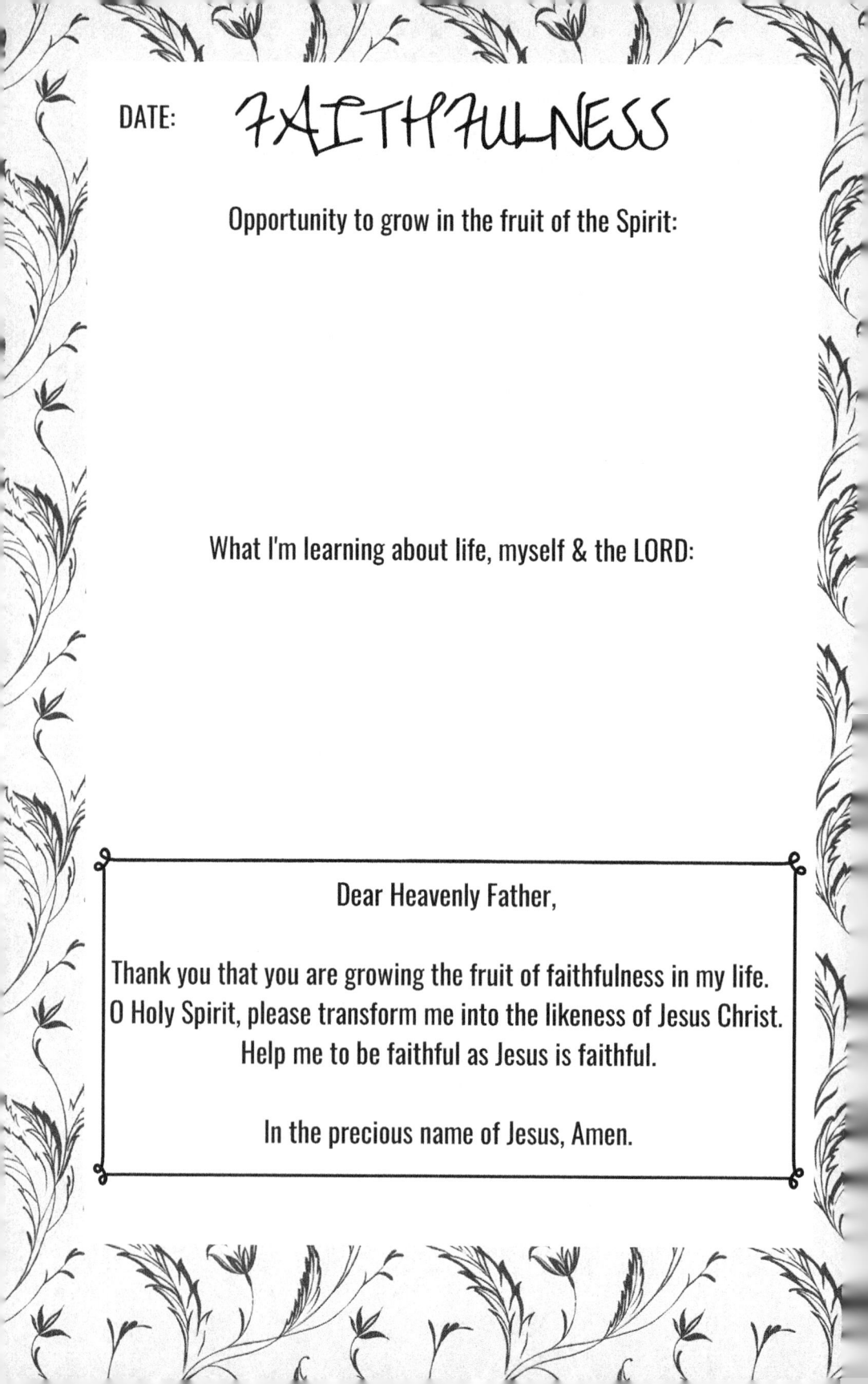

Opportunity to grow in the fruit of the Spirit:

What I'm learning about life, myself & the LORD:

Dear Heavenly Father,

Thank you that you are growing the fruit of faithfulness in my life.
O Holy Spirit, please transform me into the likeness of Jesus Christ.
Help me to be faithful as Jesus is faithful.

In the precious name of Jesus, Amen.

DATE: **GENTLENESS**

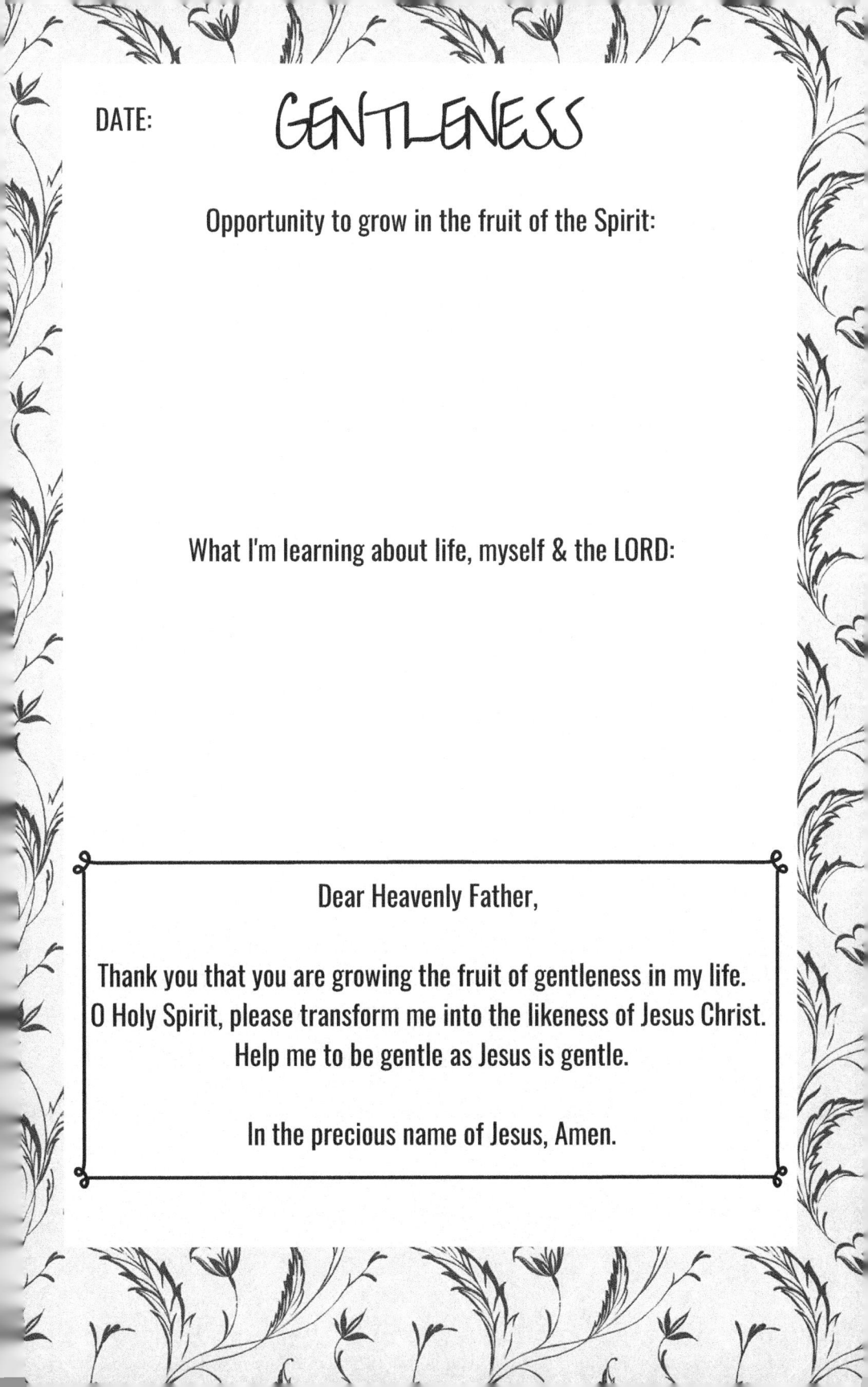

Opportunity to grow in the fruit of the Spirit:

What I'm learning about life, myself & the LORD:

Dear Heavenly Father,

Thank you that you are growing the fruit of gentleness in my life.
O Holy Spirit, please transform me into the likeness of Jesus Christ.
Help me to be gentle as Jesus is gentle.

In the precious name of Jesus, Amen.

DATE:

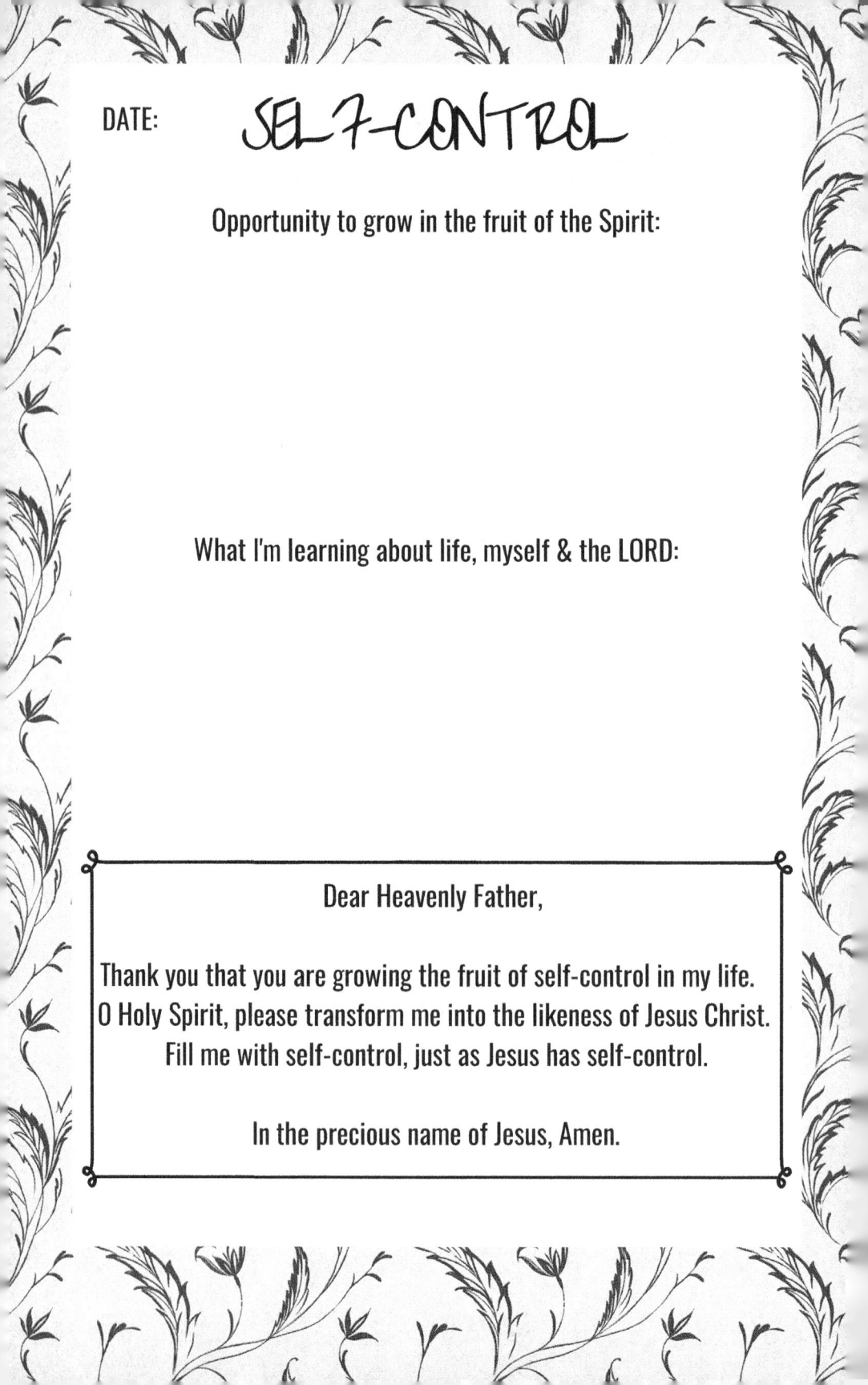

SELF-CONTROL

Opportunity to grow in the fruit of the Spirit:

What I'm learning about life, myself & the LORD:

Dear Heavenly Father,

Thank you that you are growing the fruit of self-control in my life. O Holy Spirit, please transform me into the likeness of Jesus Christ. Fill me with self-control, just as Jesus has self-control.

In the precious name of Jesus, Amen.

Against
these things
there is no law.

DATE:

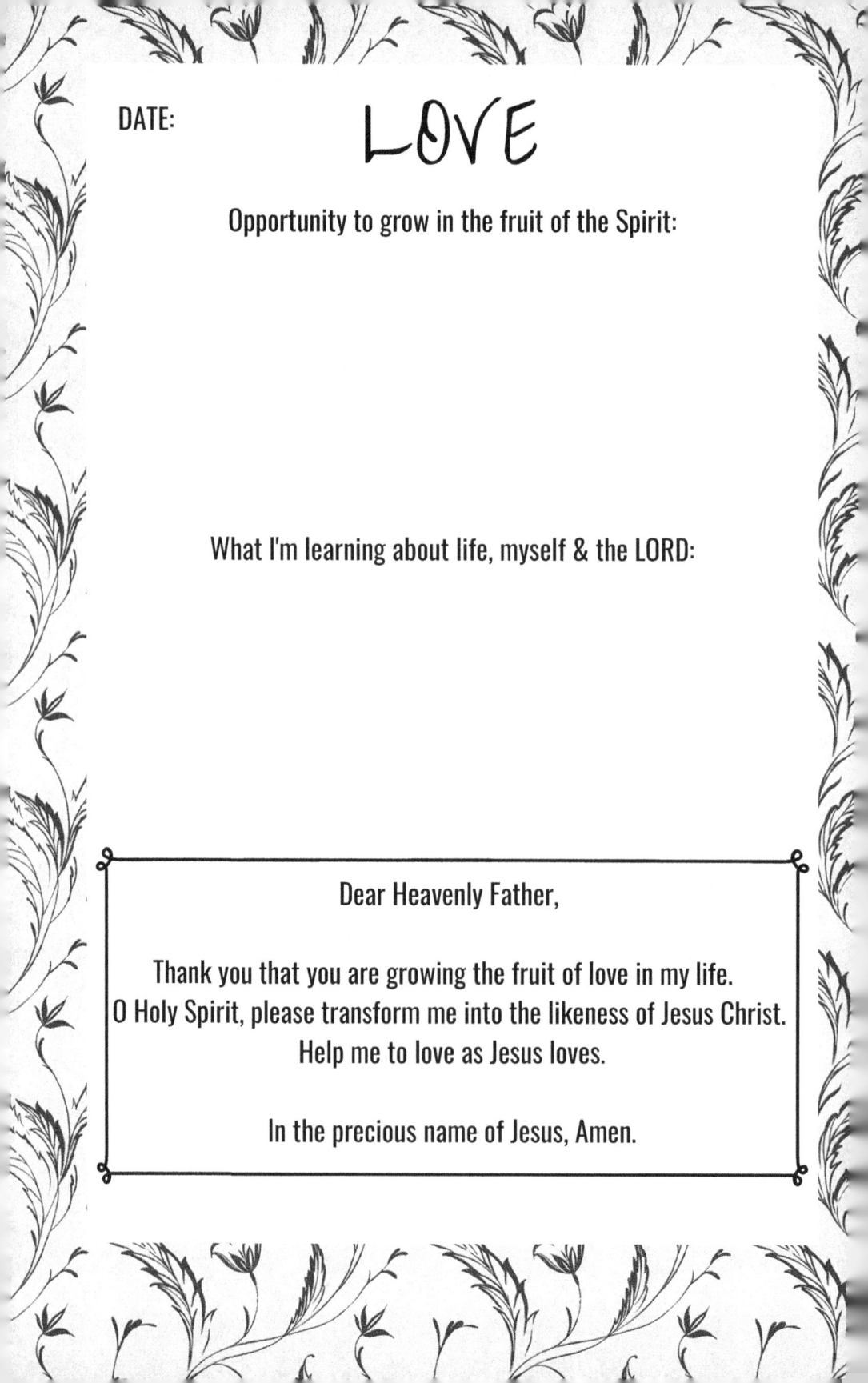

LOVE

Opportunity to grow in the fruit of the Spirit:

What I'm learning about life, myself & the LORD:

Dear Heavenly Father,

Thank you that you are growing the fruit of love in my life.
O Holy Spirit, please transform me into the likeness of Jesus Christ.
Help me to love as Jesus loves.

In the precious name of Jesus, Amen.

DATE:

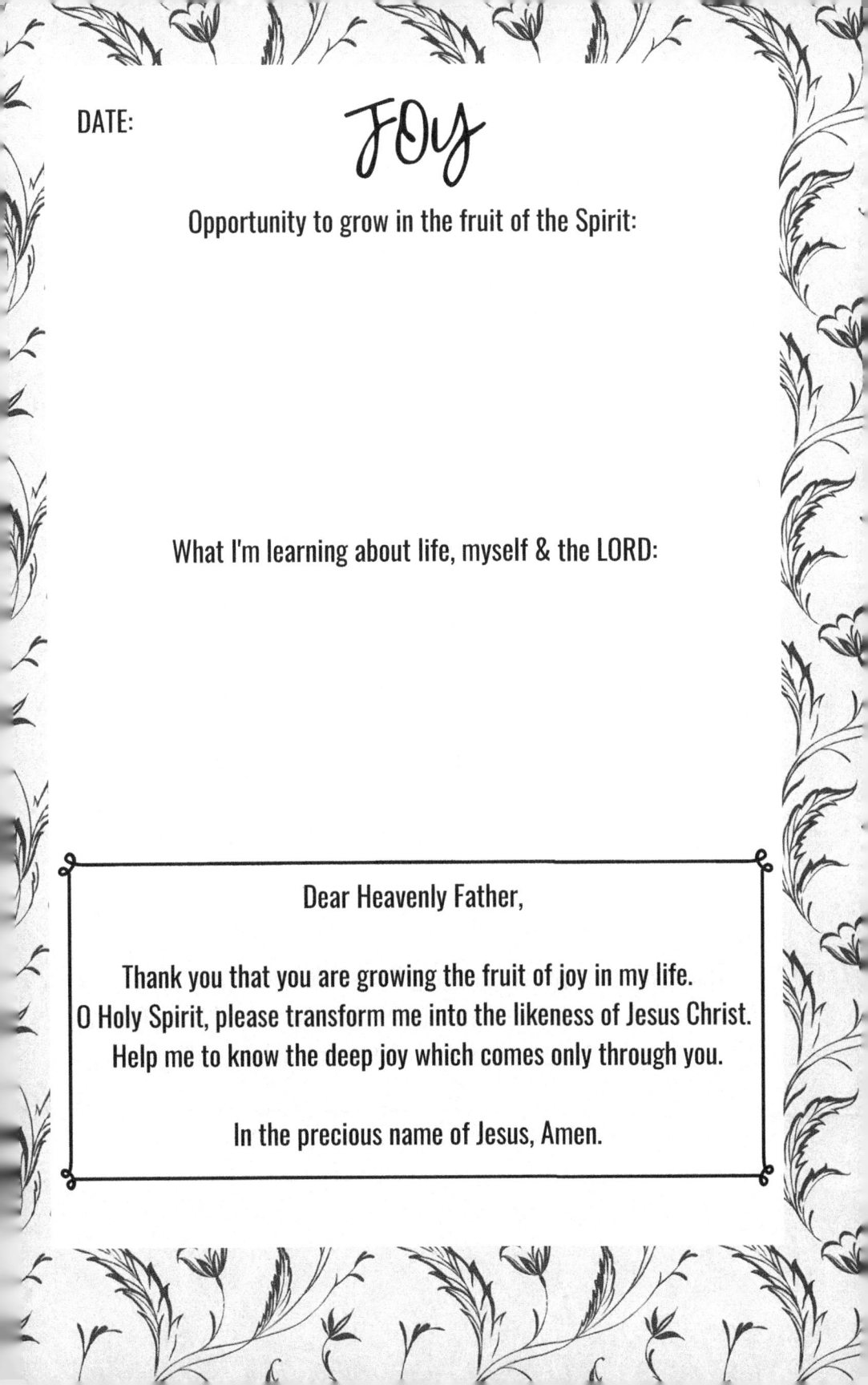

JOY

Opportunity to grow in the fruit of the Spirit:

What I'm learning about life, myself & the LORD:

Dear Heavenly Father,

Thank you that you are growing the fruit of joy in my life.
O Holy Spirit, please transform me into the likeness of Jesus Christ.
Help me to know the deep joy which comes only through you.

In the precious name of Jesus, Amen.

DATE:

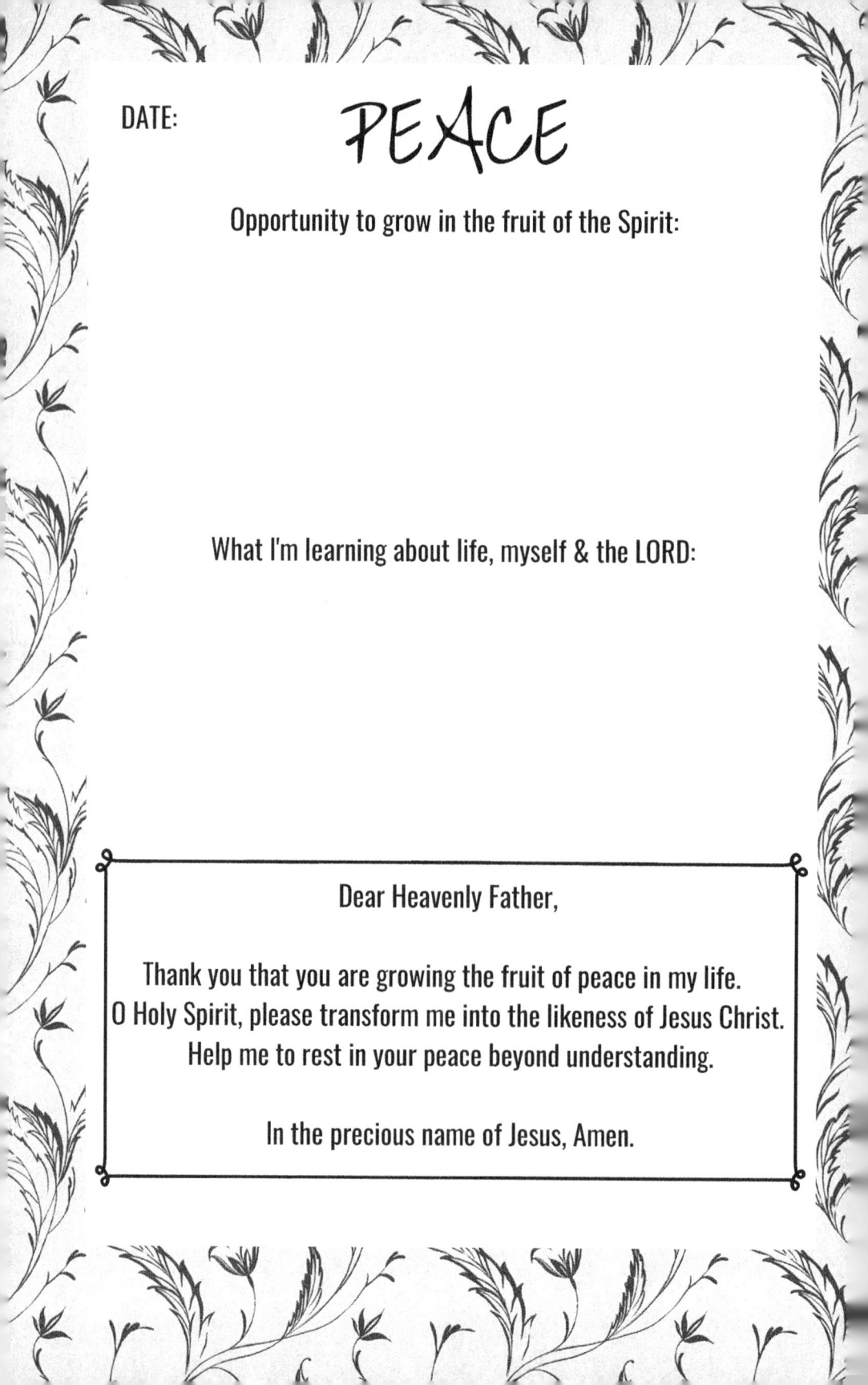

PEACE

Opportunity to grow in the fruit of the Spirit:

What I'm learning about life, myself & the LORD:

Dear Heavenly Father,

Thank you that you are growing the fruit of peace in my life.
O Holy Spirit, please transform me into the likeness of Jesus Christ.
Help me to rest in your peace beyond understanding.

In the precious name of Jesus, Amen.

DATE:

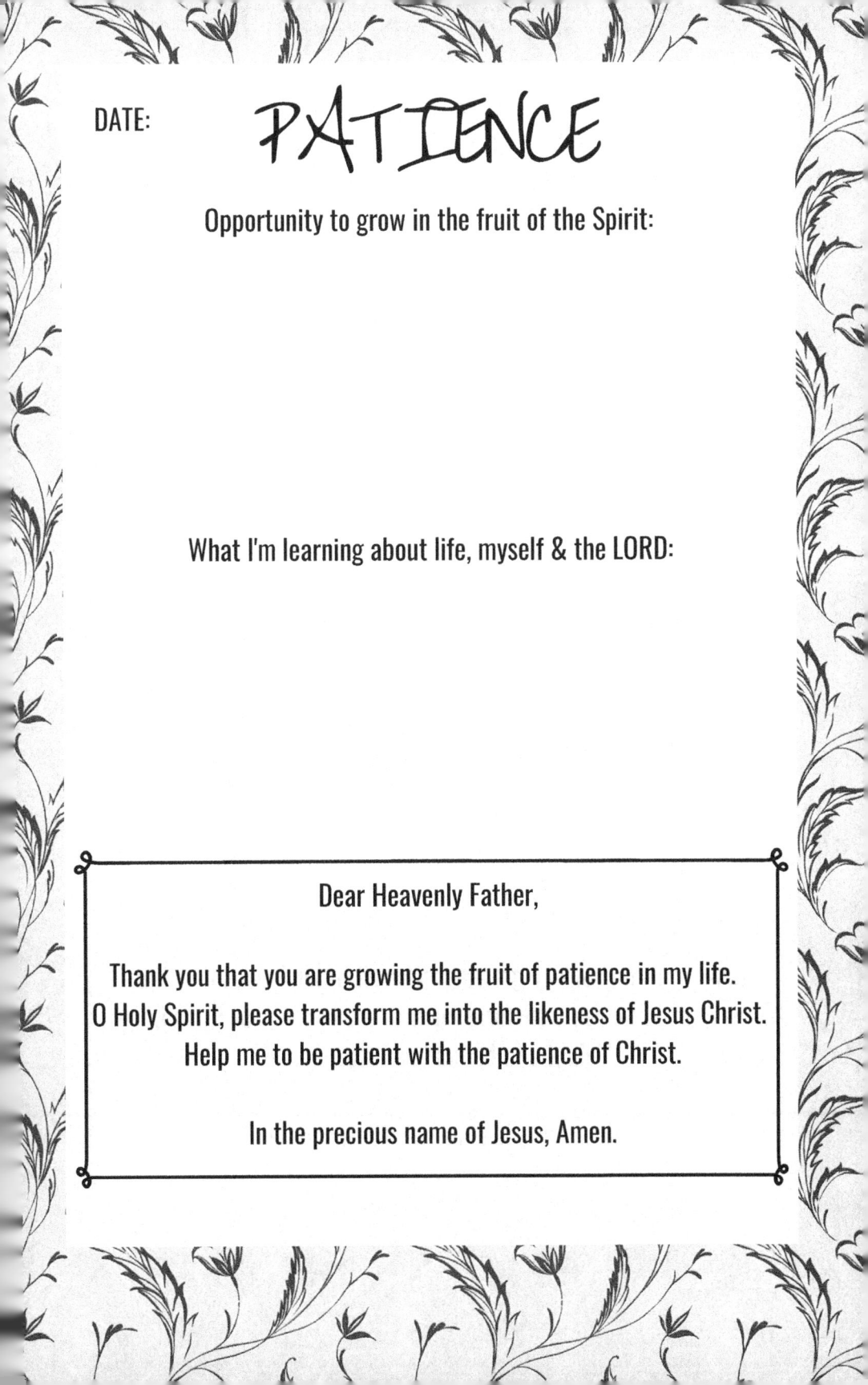

PATIENCE

Opportunity to grow in the fruit of the Spirit:

What I'm learning about life, myself & the LORD:

Dear Heavenly Father,

Thank you that you are growing the fruit of patience in my life.
O Holy Spirit, please transform me into the likeness of Jesus Christ.
Help me to be patient with the patience of Christ.

In the precious name of Jesus, Amen.

DATE:

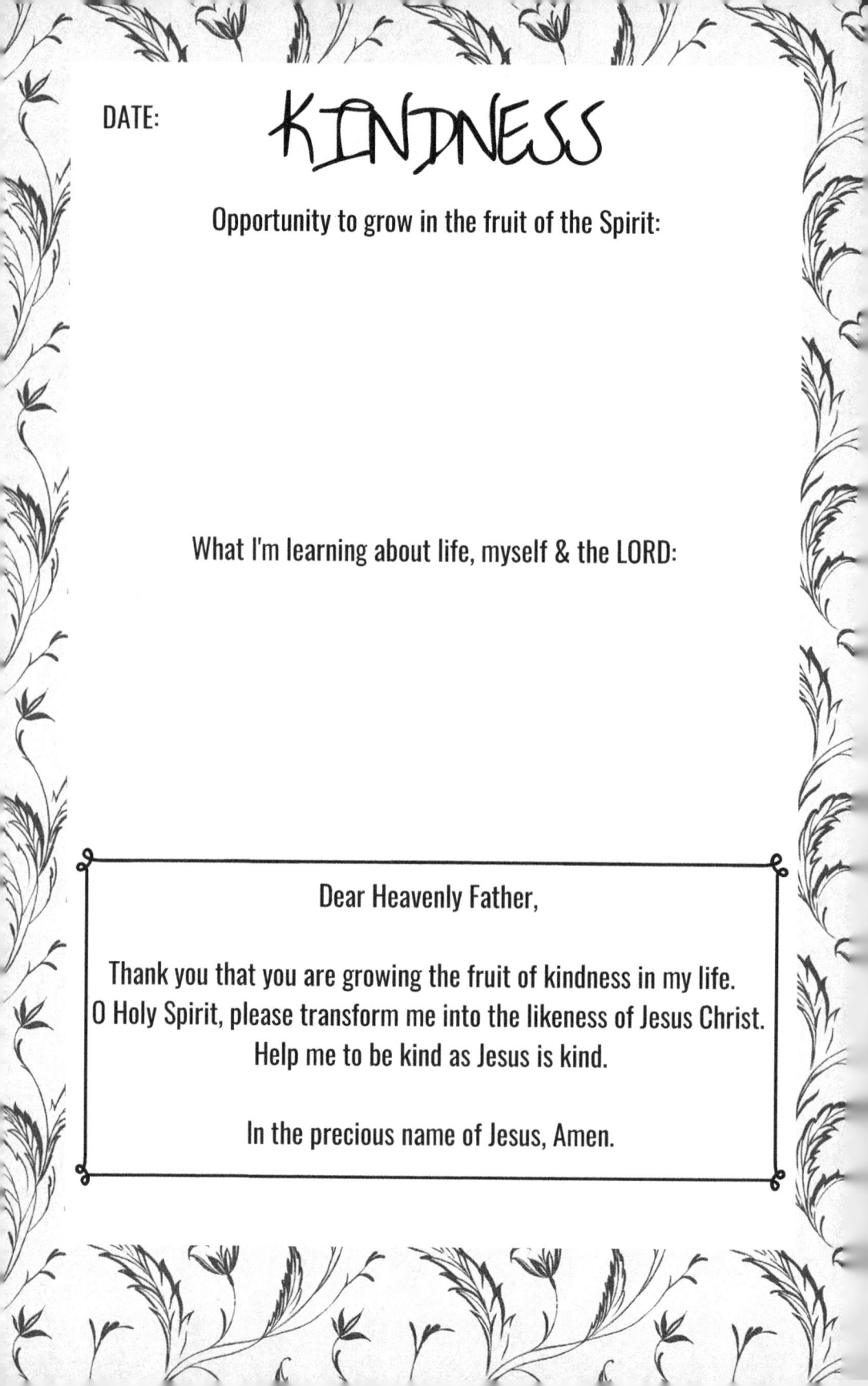

KINDNESS

Opportunity to grow in the fruit of the Spirit:

What I'm learning about life, myself & the LORD:

Dear Heavenly Father,

Thank you that you are growing the fruit of kindness in my life.
O Holy Spirit, please transform me into the likeness of Jesus Christ.
Help me to be kind as Jesus is kind.

In the precious name of Jesus, Amen.

DATE:

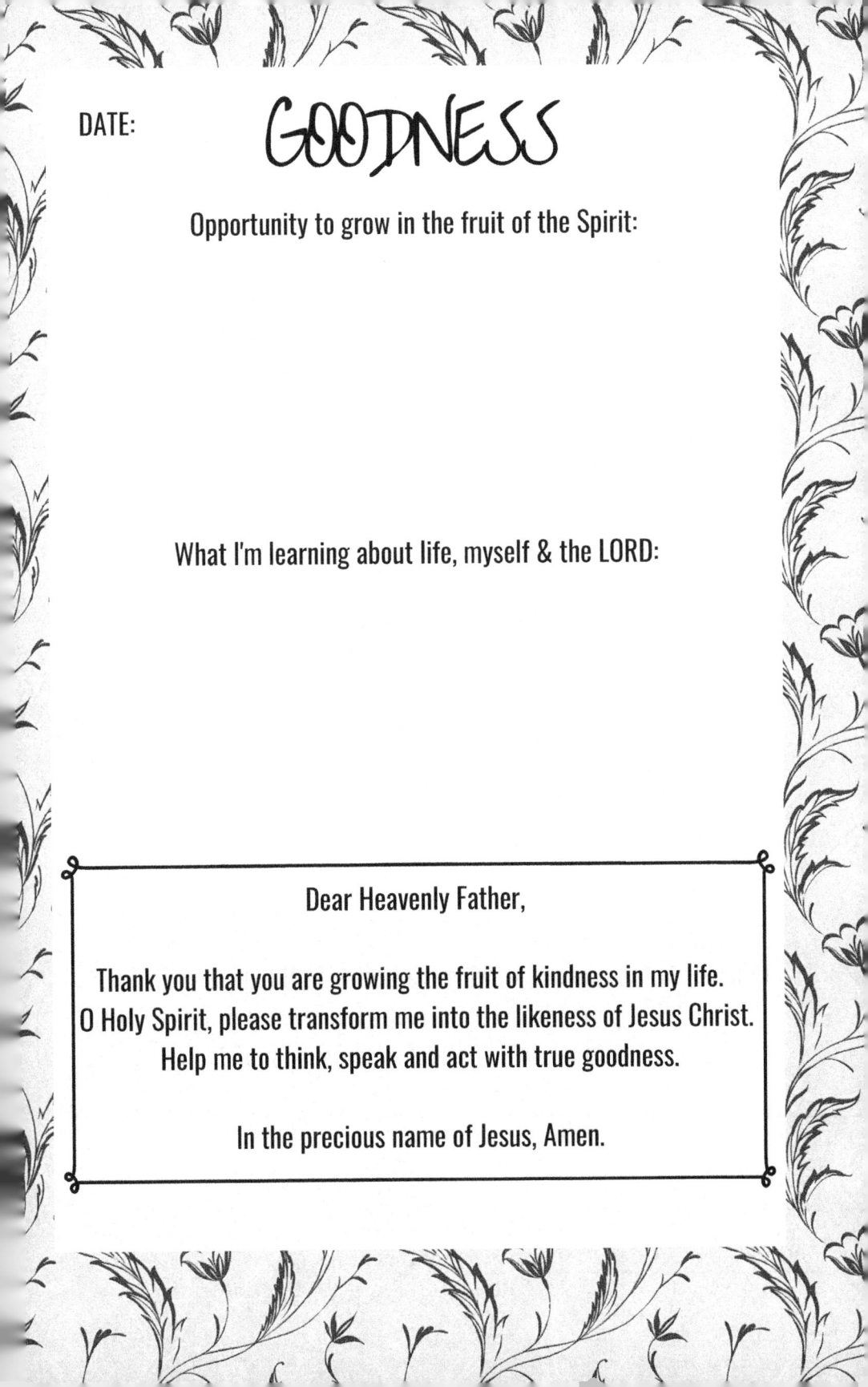

GOODNESS

Opportunity to grow in the fruit of the Spirit:

What I'm learning about life, myself & the LORD:

Dear Heavenly Father,

Thank you that you are growing the fruit of kindness in my life.
O Holy Spirit, please transform me into the likeness of Jesus Christ.
Help me to think, speak and act with true goodness.

In the precious name of Jesus, Amen.

DATE: # FAITHFULNESS

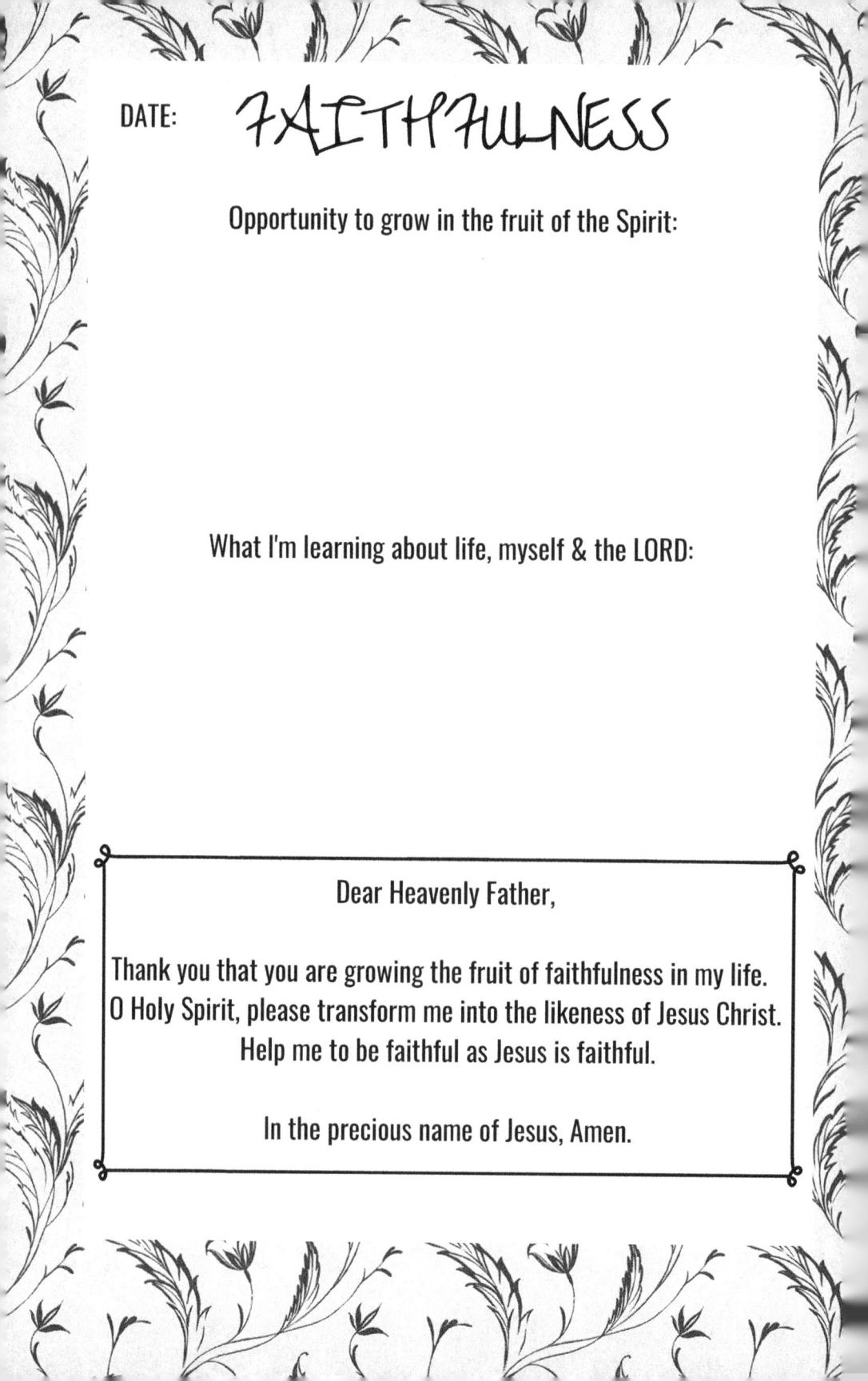

Opportunity to grow in the fruit of the Spirit:

What I'm learning about life, myself & the LORD:

Dear Heavenly Father,

Thank you that you are growing the fruit of faithfulness in my life.
O Holy Spirit, please transform me into the likeness of Jesus Christ.
Help me to be faithful as Jesus is faithful.

In the precious name of Jesus, Amen.

DATE:

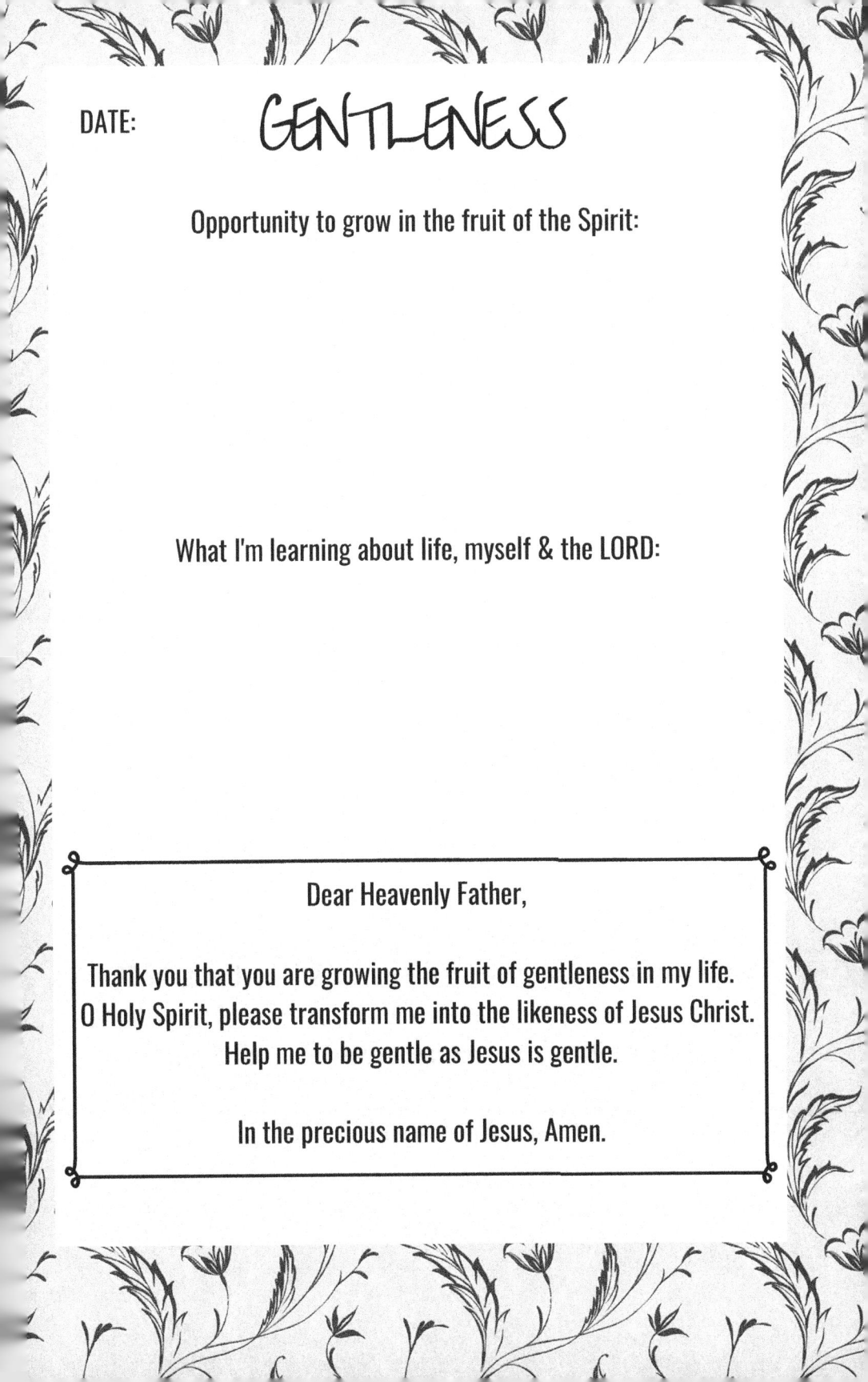

GENTLENESS

Opportunity to grow in the fruit of the Spirit:

What I'm learning about life, myself & the LORD:

Dear Heavenly Father,

Thank you that you are growing the fruit of gentleness in my life.
O Holy Spirit, please transform me into the likeness of Jesus Christ.
Help me to be gentle as Jesus is gentle.

In the precious name of Jesus, Amen.

DATE: **SELF-CONTROL**

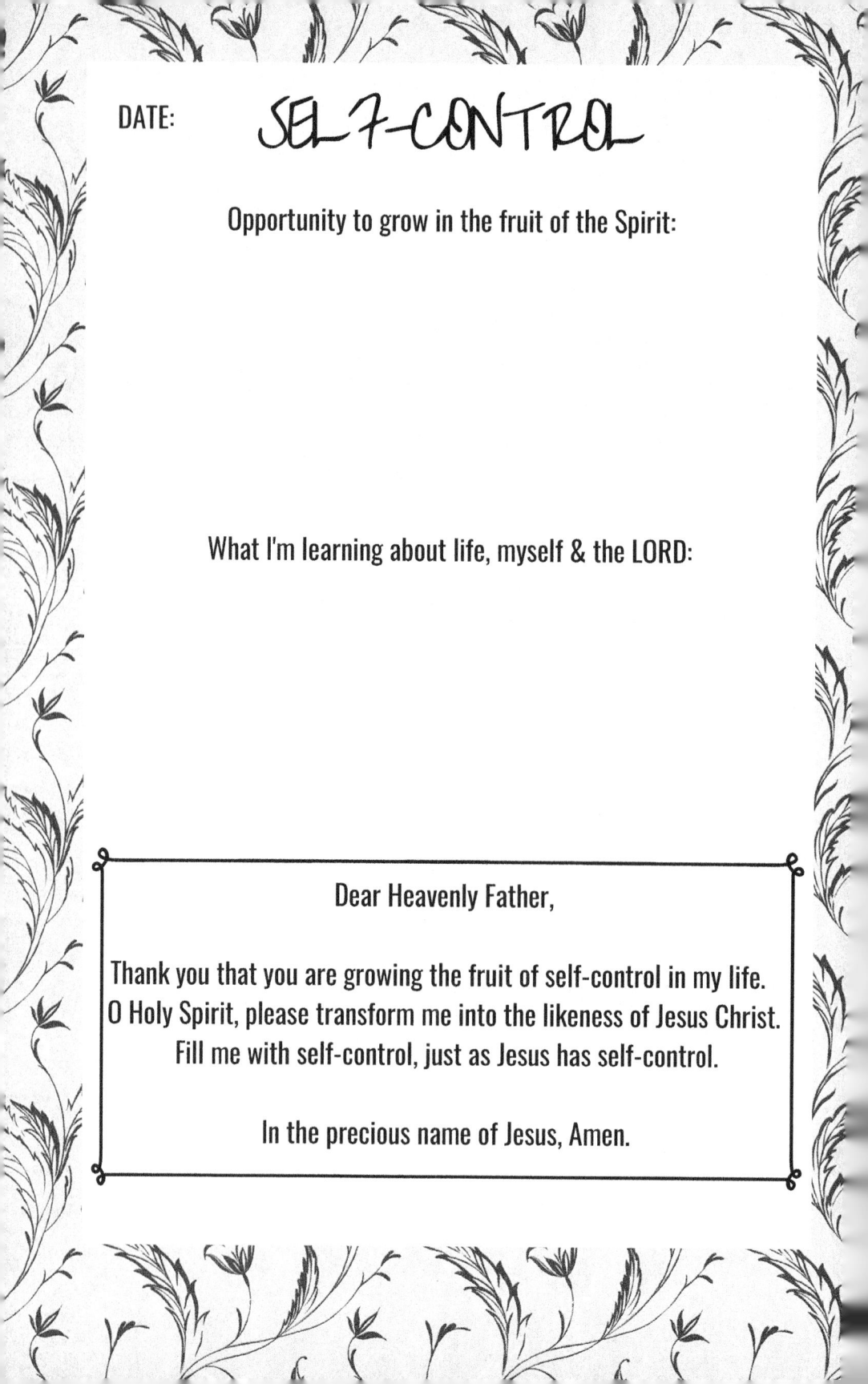

Opportunity to grow in the fruit of the Spirit:

What I'm learning about life, myself & the LORD:

Dear Heavenly Father,

Thank you that you are growing the fruit of self-control in my life. O Holy Spirit, please transform me into the likeness of Jesus Christ. Fill me with self-control, just as Jesus has self-control.

In the precious name of Jesus, Amen.

love,
joy,
peace,
patience,
kindness,
goodness,
faithfulness,
gentleness,
self-control

DATE:

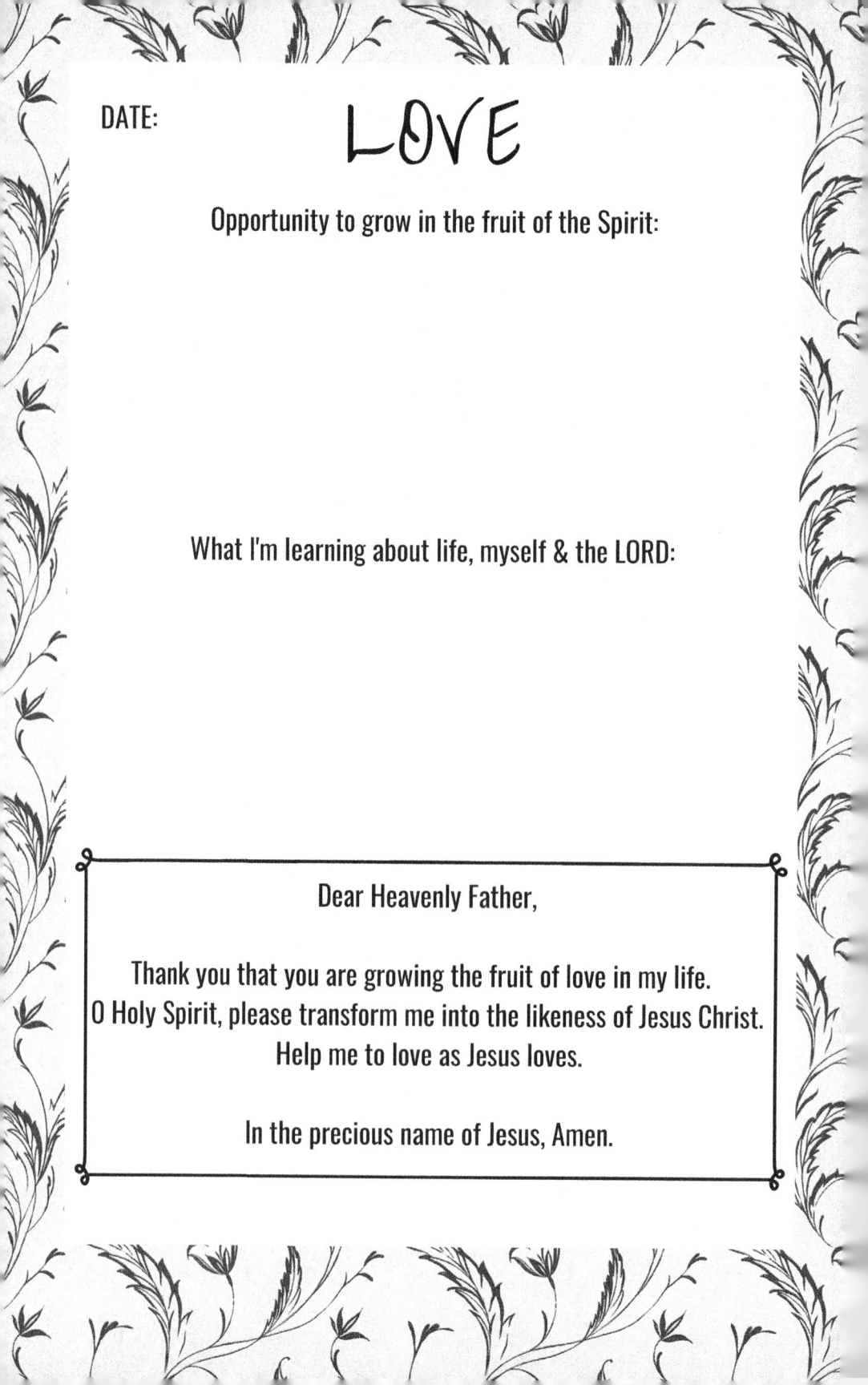

LOVE

Opportunity to grow in the fruit of the Spirit:

What I'm learning about life, myself & the LORD:

Dear Heavenly Father,

Thank you that you are growing the fruit of love in my life.
O Holy Spirit, please transform me into the likeness of Jesus Christ.
Help me to love as Jesus loves.

In the precious name of Jesus, Amen.

DATE:

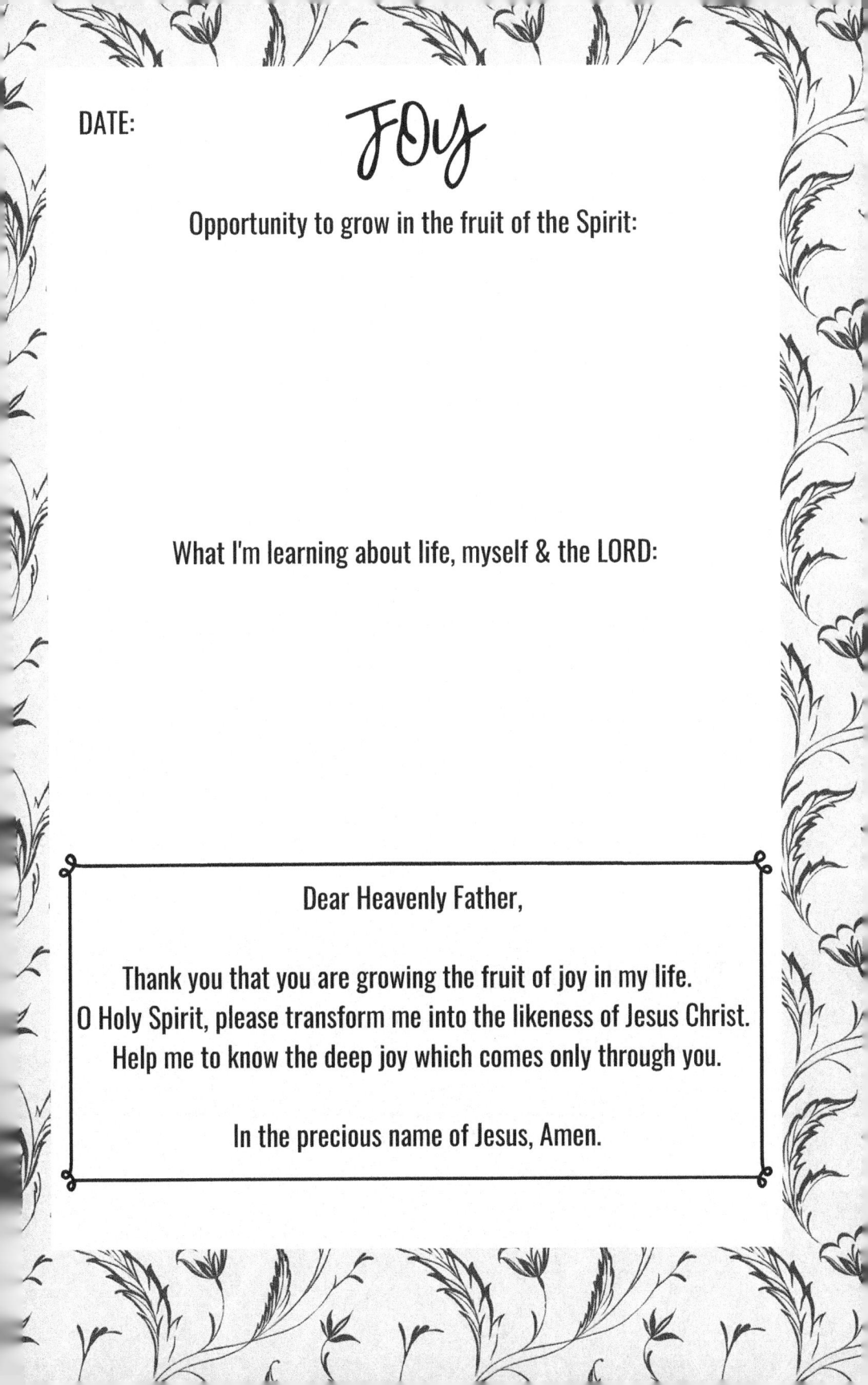

JOY

Opportunity to grow in the fruit of the Spirit:

What I'm learning about life, myself & the LORD:

Dear Heavenly Father,

Thank you that you are growing the fruit of joy in my life.
O Holy Spirit, please transform me into the likeness of Jesus Christ.
Help me to know the deep joy which comes only through you.

In the precious name of Jesus, Amen.

DATE:

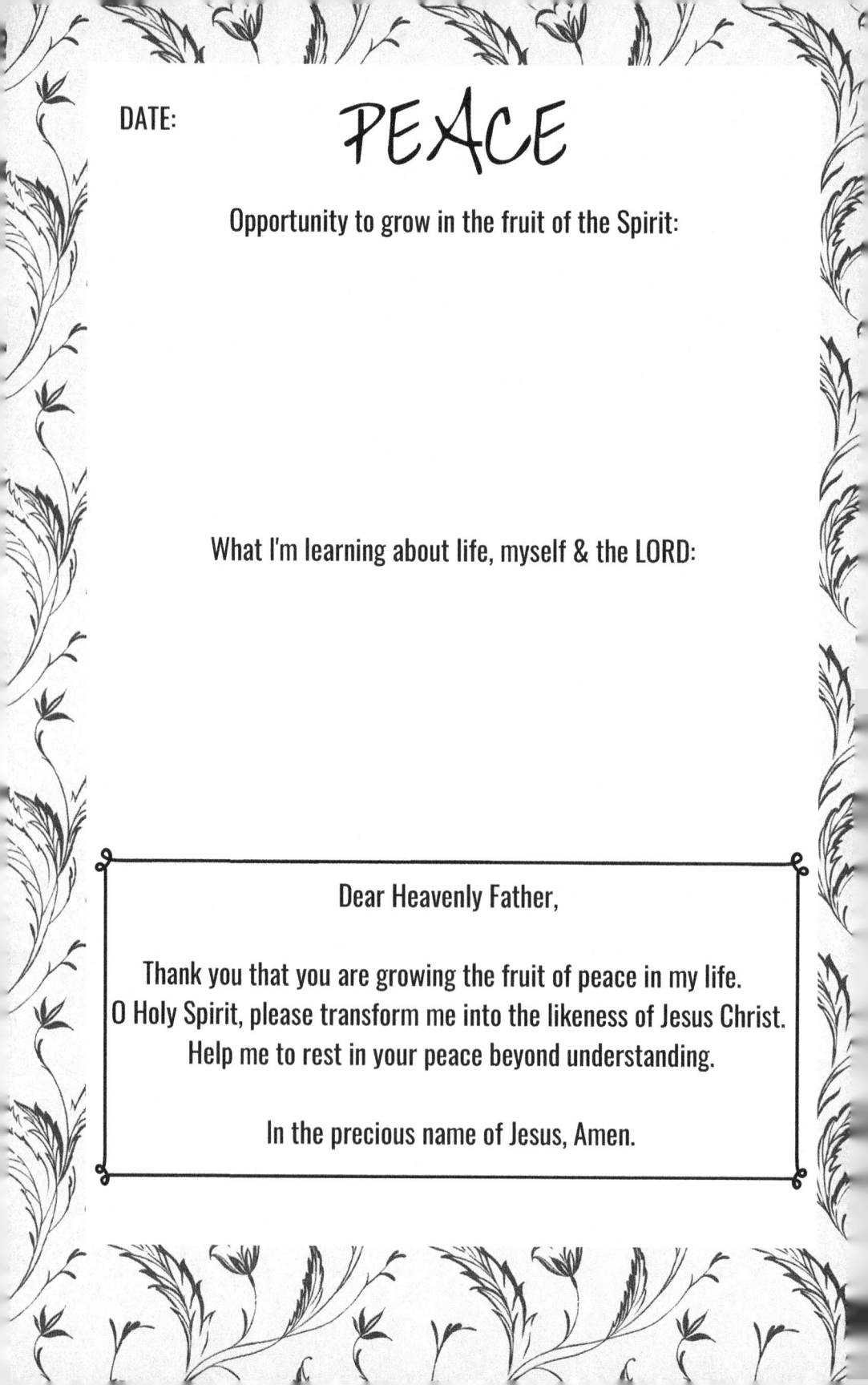

PEACE

Opportunity to grow in the fruit of the Spirit:

What I'm learning about life, myself & the LORD:

Dear Heavenly Father,

Thank you that you are growing the fruit of peace in my life.
O Holy Spirit, please transform me into the likeness of Jesus Christ.
Help me to rest in your peace beyond understanding.

In the precious name of Jesus, Amen.

DATE:

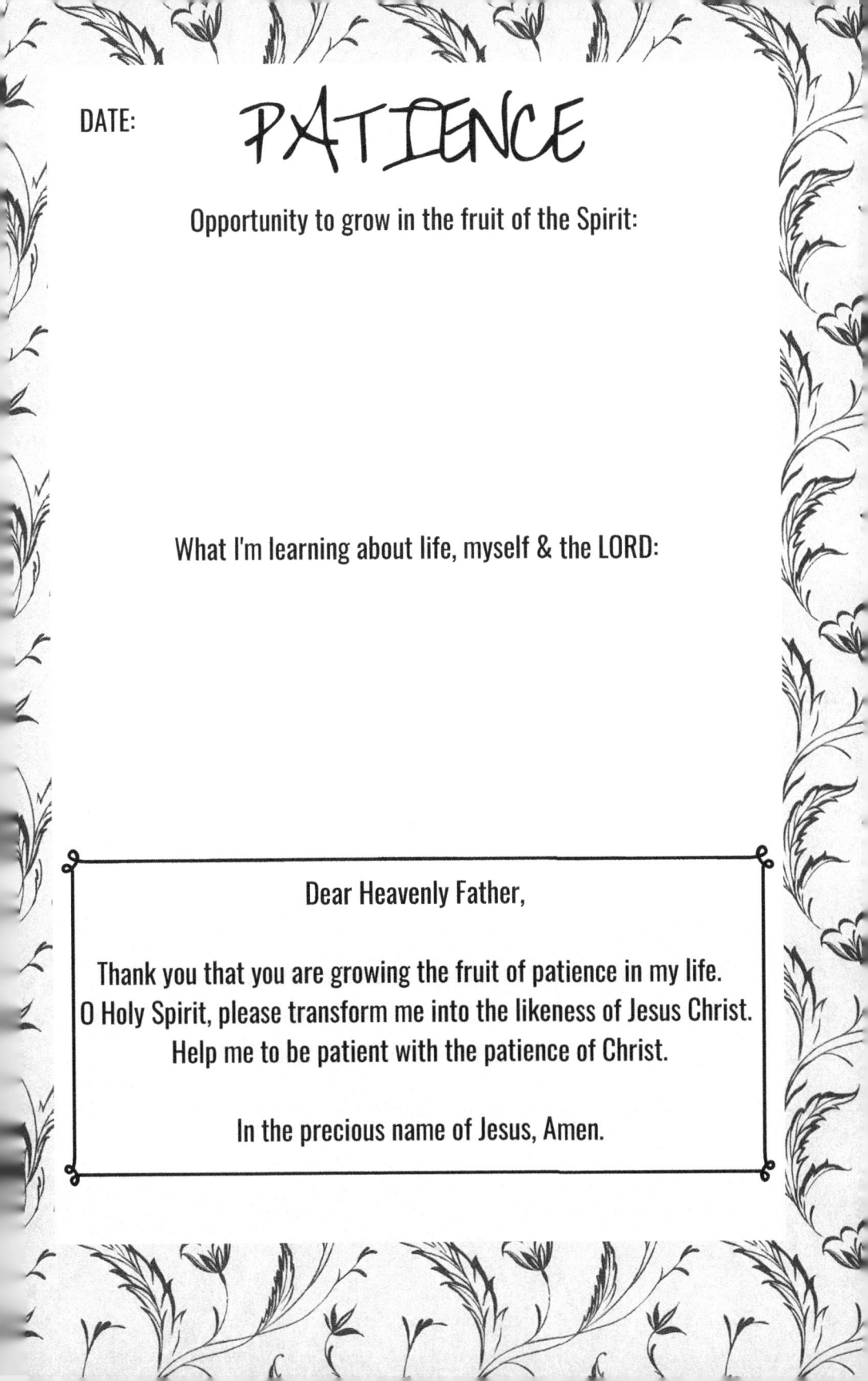

PATIENCE

Opportunity to grow in the fruit of the Spirit:

What I'm learning about life, myself & the LORD:

Dear Heavenly Father,

Thank you that you are growing the fruit of patience in my life.
O Holy Spirit, please transform me into the likeness of Jesus Christ.
Help me to be patient with the patience of Christ.

In the precious name of Jesus, Amen.

DATE:

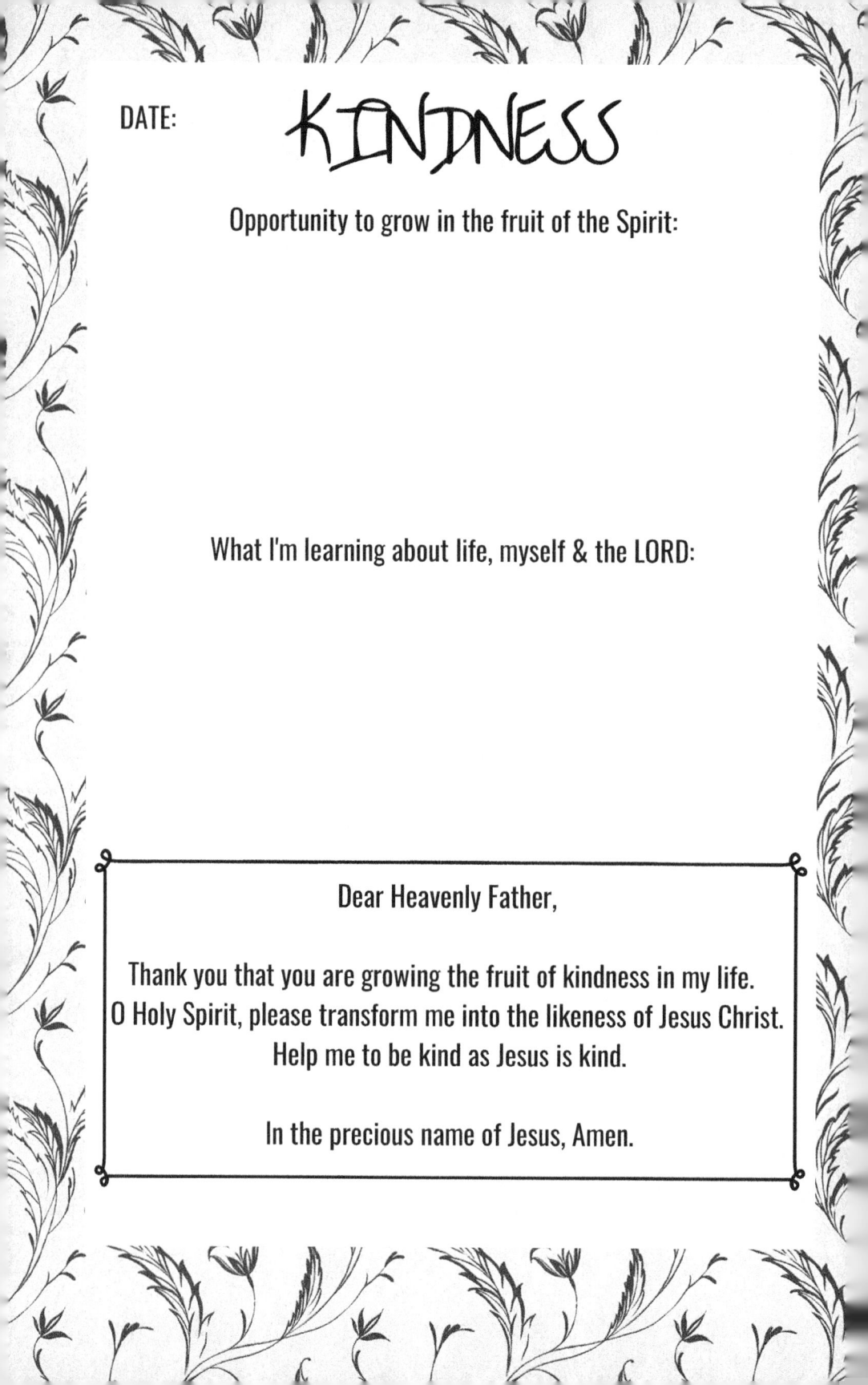

KINDNESS

Opportunity to grow in the fruit of the Spirit:

What I'm learning about life, myself & the LORD:

Dear Heavenly Father,

Thank you that you are growing the fruit of kindness in my life.
O Holy Spirit, please transform me into the likeness of Jesus Christ.
Help me to be kind as Jesus is kind.

In the precious name of Jesus, Amen.

DATE:

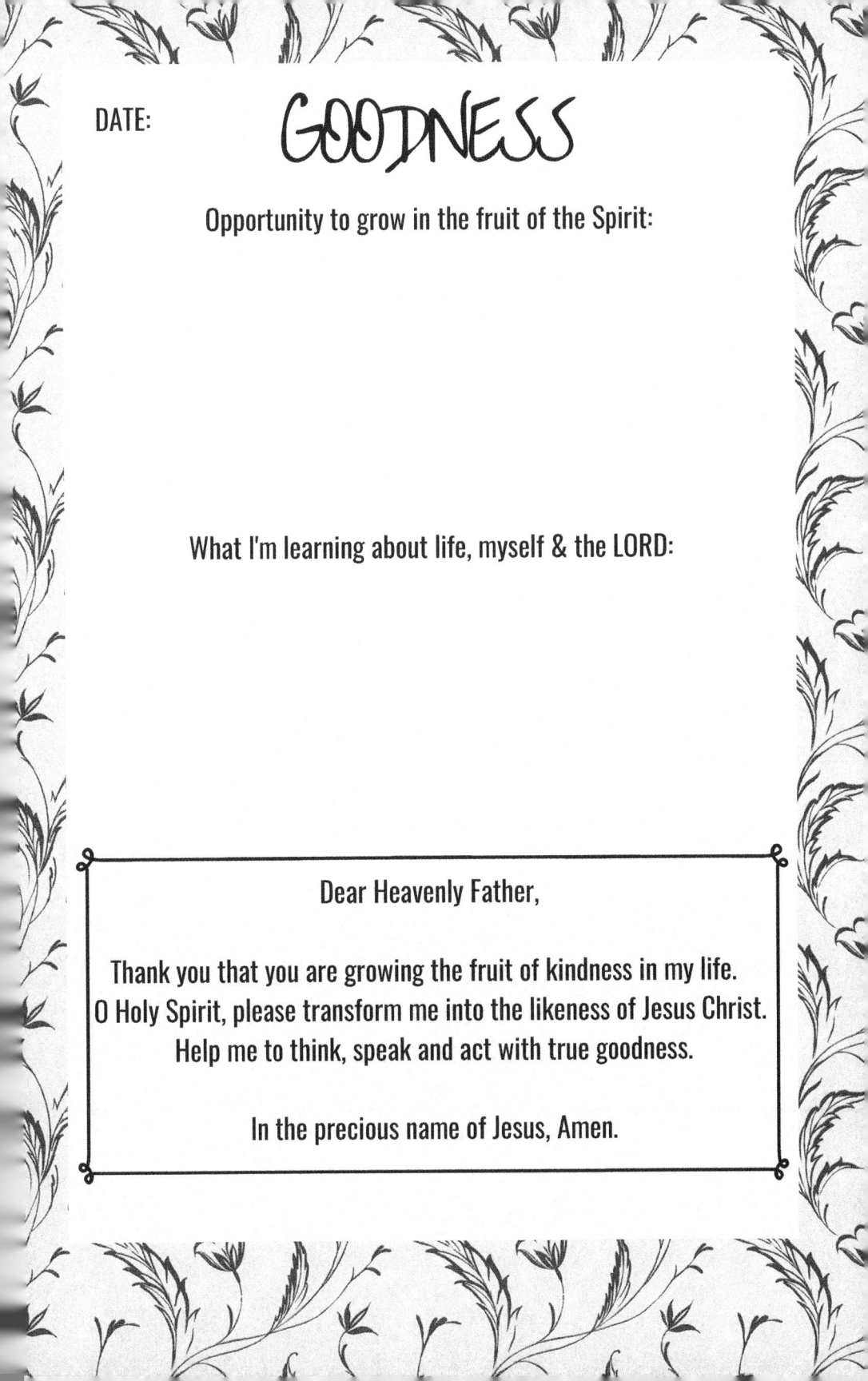

GOODNESS

Opportunity to grow in the fruit of the Spirit:

What I'm learning about life, myself & the LORD:

Dear Heavenly Father,

Thank you that you are growing the fruit of kindness in my life.
O Holy Spirit, please transform me into the likeness of Jesus Christ.
Help me to think, speak and act with true goodness.

In the precious name of Jesus, Amen.

DATE: _____ # FAITHFULNESS

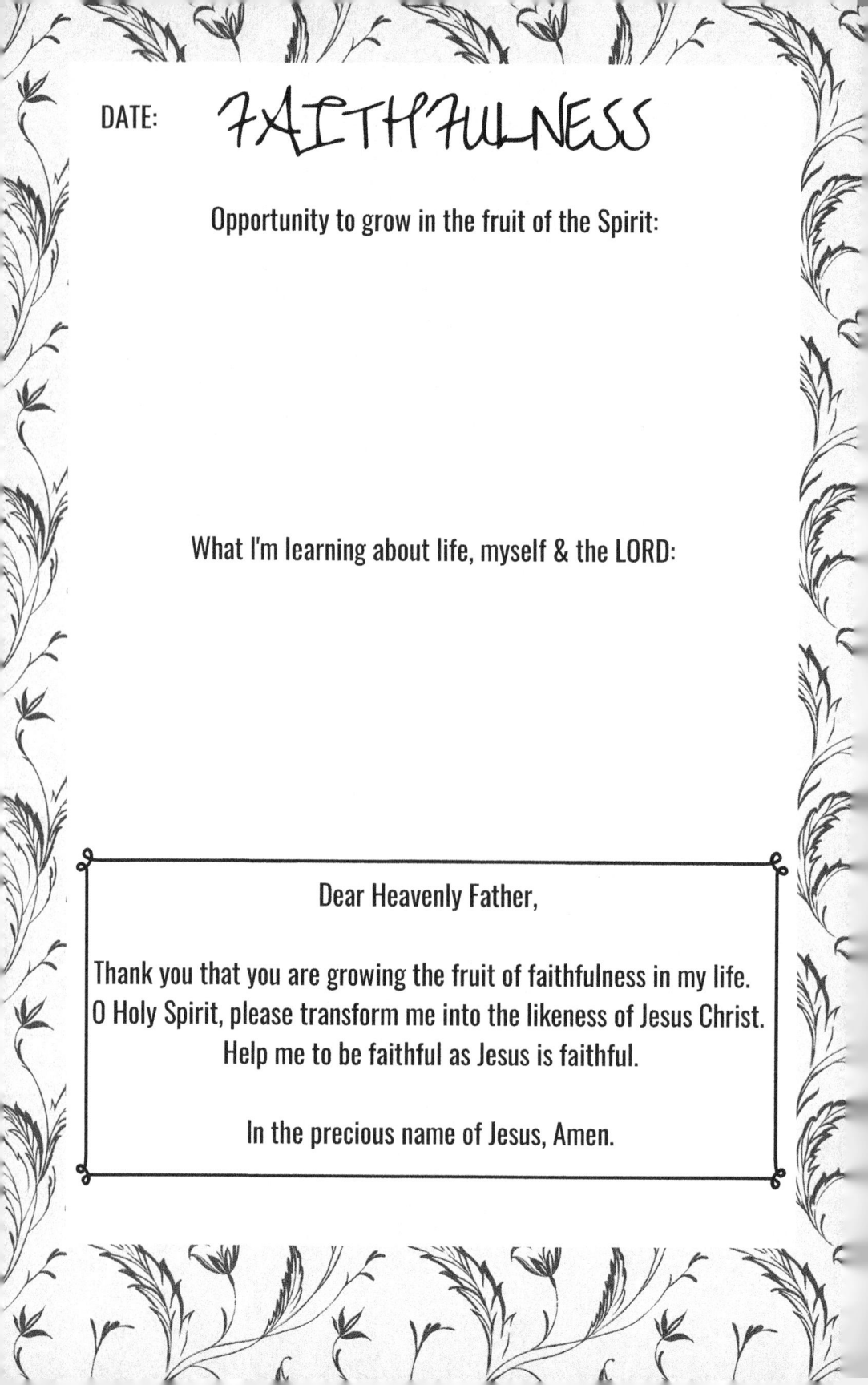

Opportunity to grow in the fruit of the Spirit:

What I'm learning about life, myself & the LORD:

> Dear Heavenly Father,
>
> Thank you that you are growing the fruit of faithfulness in my life. O Holy Spirit, please transform me into the likeness of Jesus Christ. Help me to be faithful as Jesus is faithful.
>
> In the precious name of Jesus, Amen.

DATE:

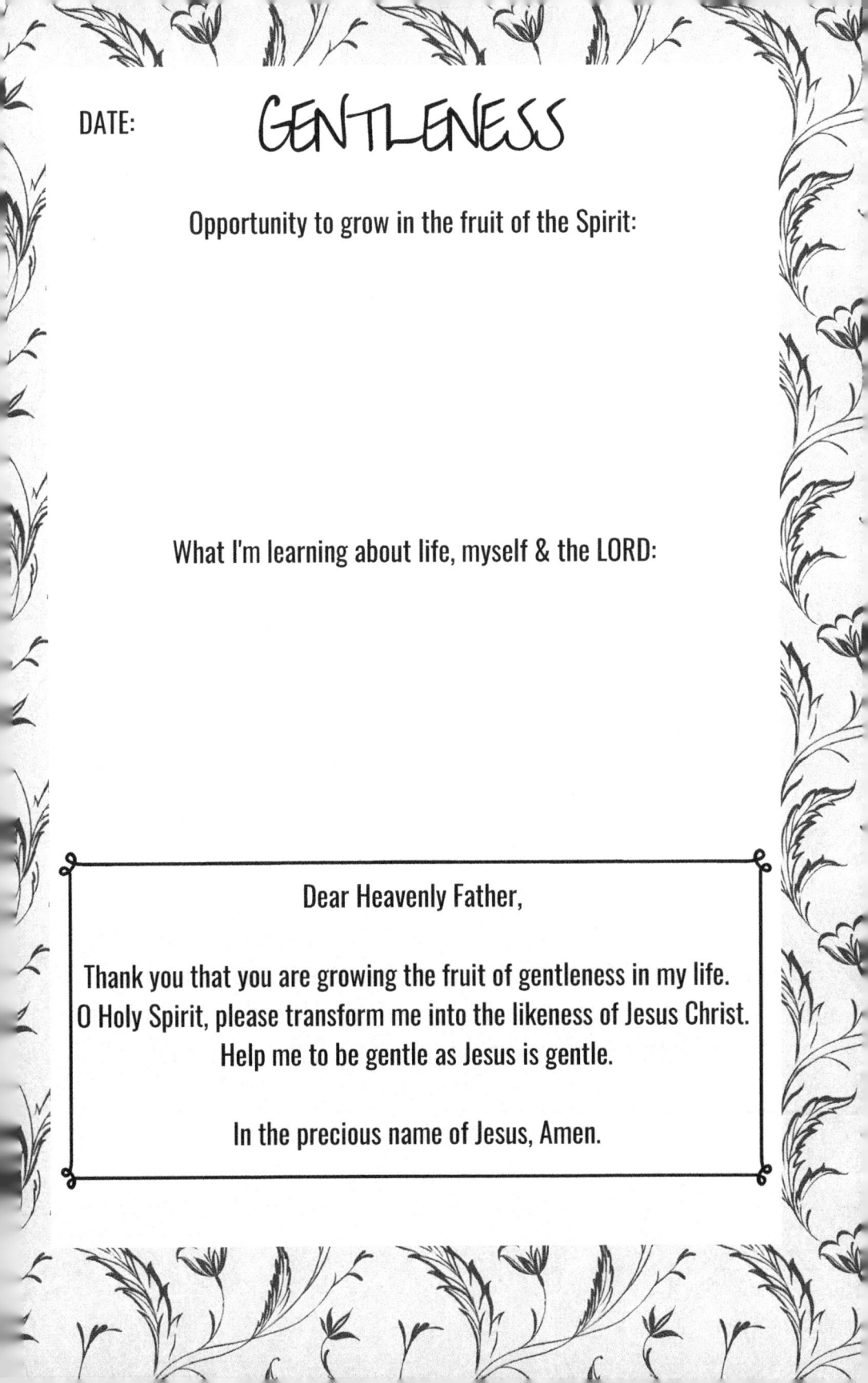

GENTLENESS

Opportunity to grow in the fruit of the Spirit:

What I'm learning about life, myself & the LORD:

Dear Heavenly Father,

Thank you that you are growing the fruit of gentleness in my life.
O Holy Spirit, please transform me into the likeness of Jesus Christ.
Help me to be gentle as Jesus is gentle.

In the precious name of Jesus, Amen.

DATE: SELF-CONTROL

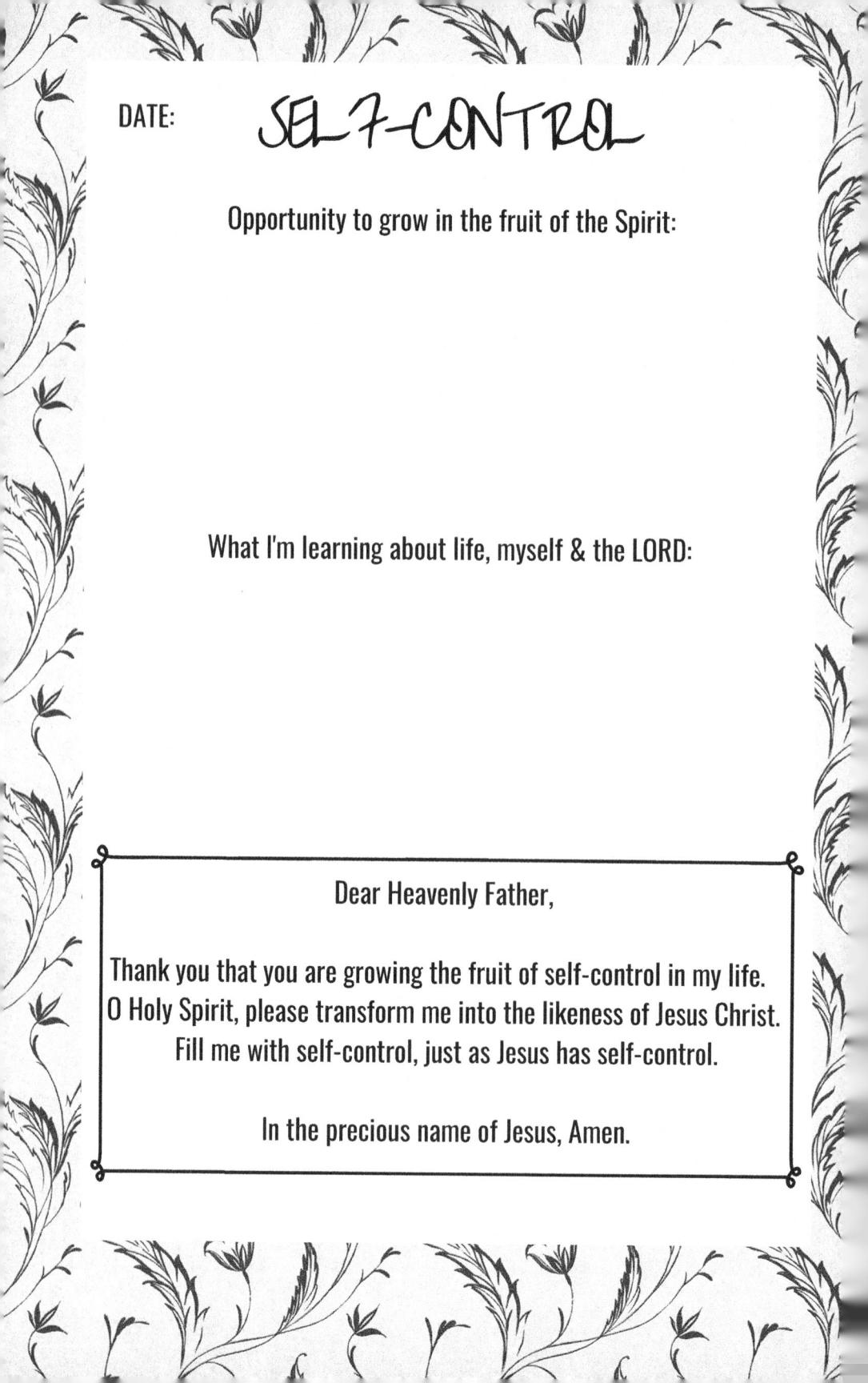

Opportunity to grow in the fruit of the Spirit:

What I'm learning about life, myself & the LORD:

Dear Heavenly Father,

Thank you that you are growing the fruit of self-control in my life. O Holy Spirit, please transform me into the likeness of Jesus Christ. Fill me with self-control, just as Jesus has self-control.

In the precious name of Jesus, Amen.

Against
these things
there is no law.

DATE:

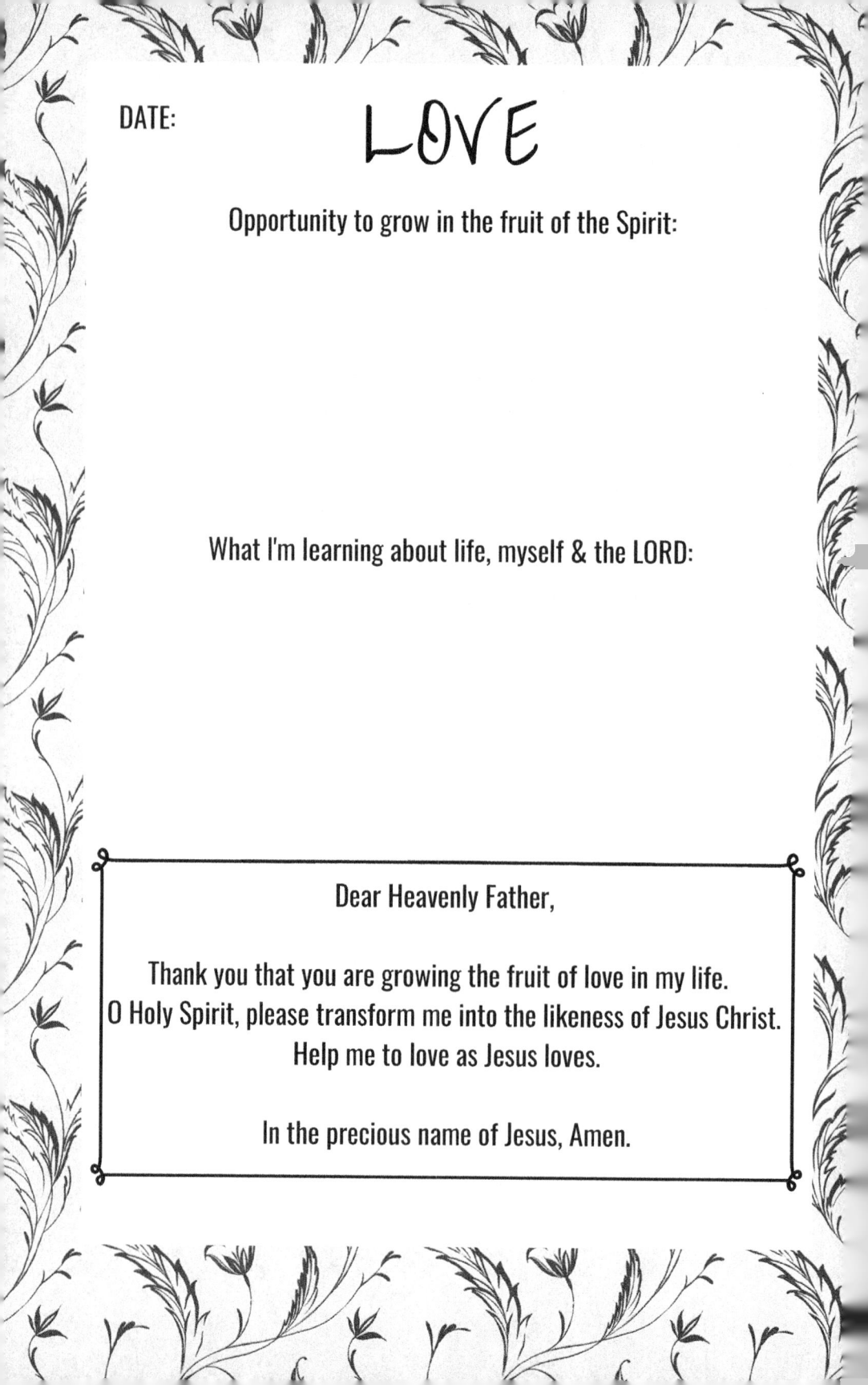

LOVE

Opportunity to grow in the fruit of the Spirit:

What I'm learning about life, myself & the LORD:

Dear Heavenly Father,

Thank you that you are growing the fruit of love in my life.
O Holy Spirit, please transform me into the likeness of Jesus Christ.
Help me to love as Jesus loves.

In the precious name of Jesus, Amen.

DATE:

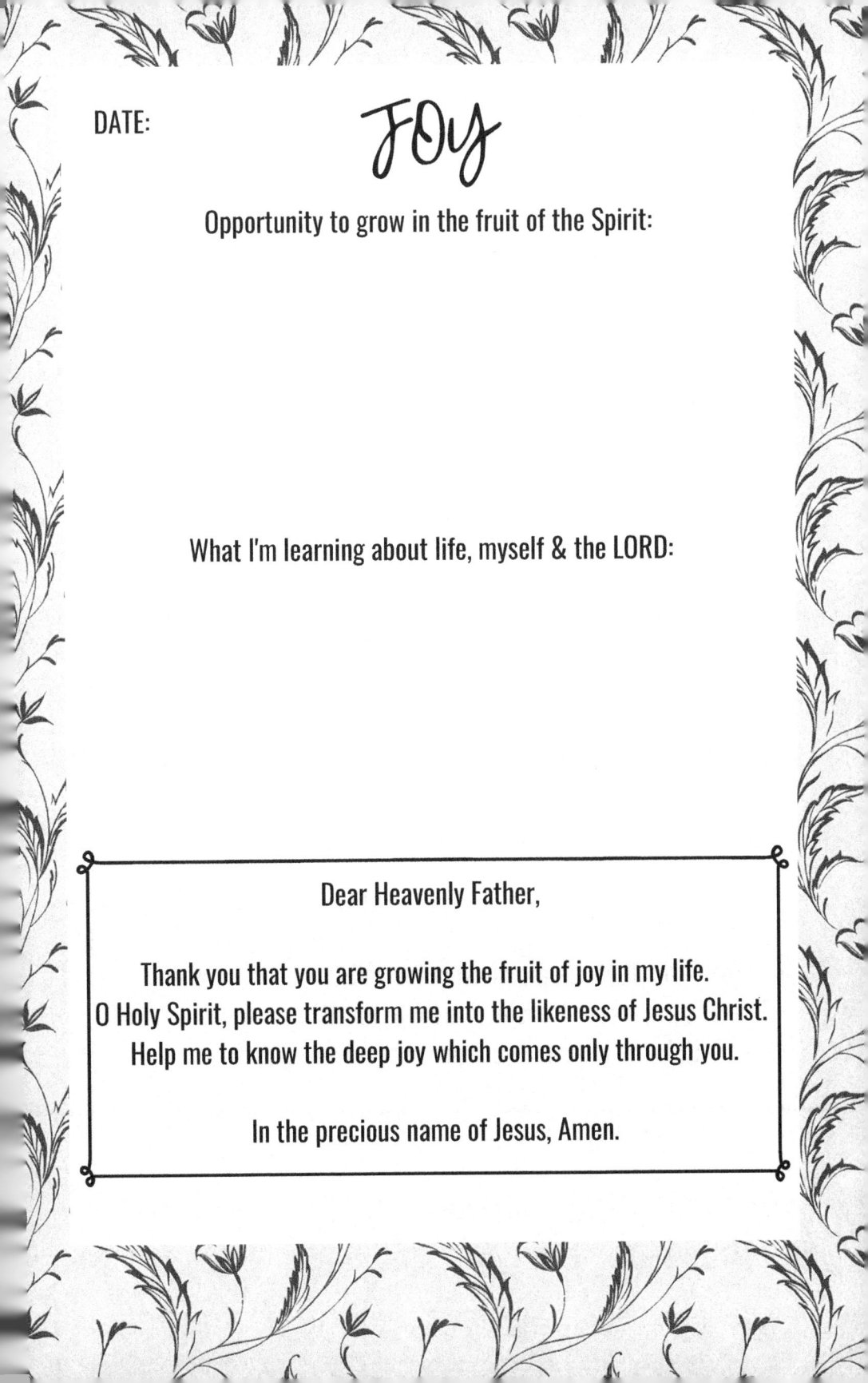

JOY

Opportunity to grow in the fruit of the Spirit:

What I'm learning about life, myself & the LORD:

Dear Heavenly Father,

Thank you that you are growing the fruit of joy in my life.
O Holy Spirit, please transform me into the likeness of Jesus Christ.
Help me to know the deep joy which comes only through you.

In the precious name of Jesus, Amen.

DATE:

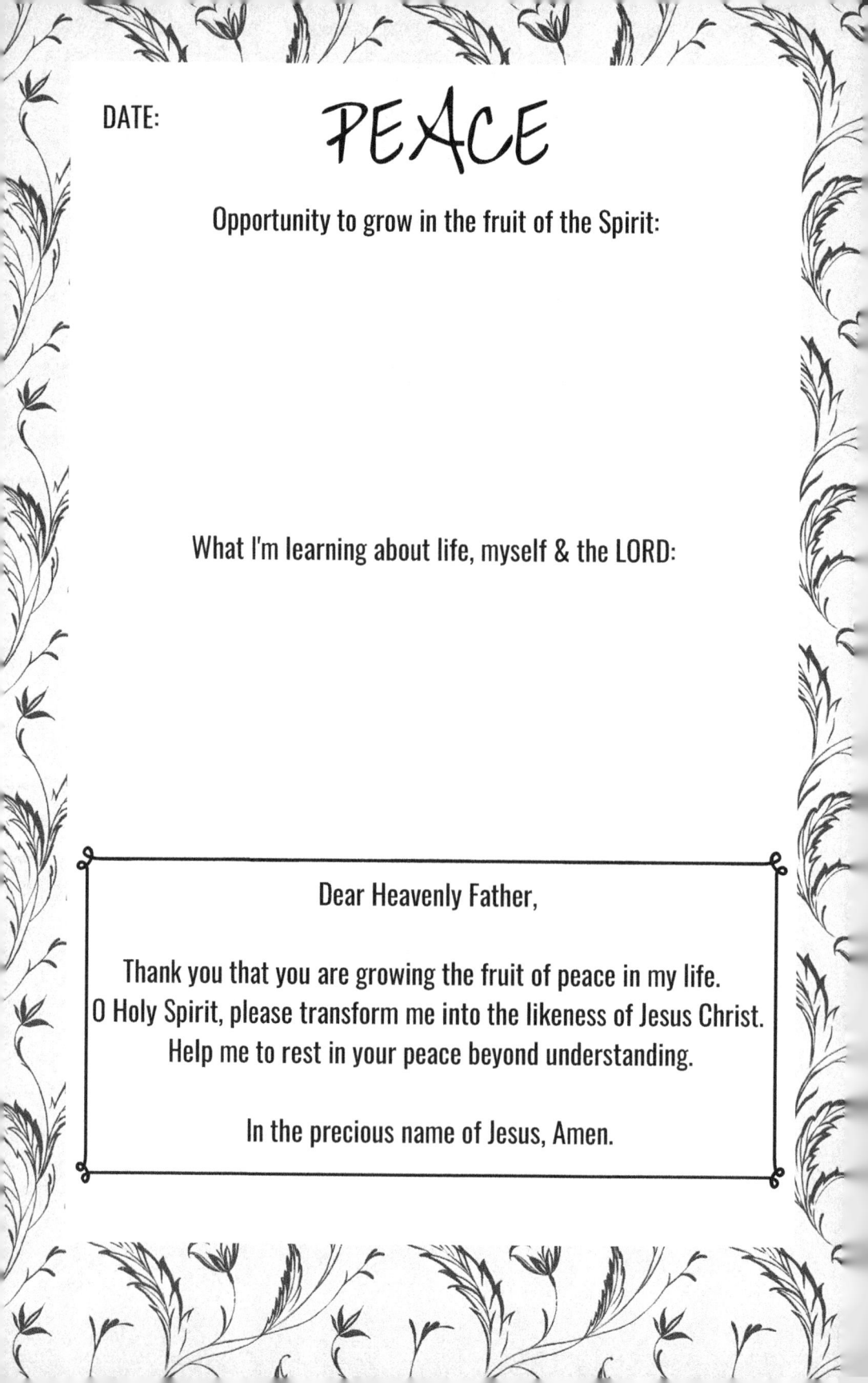

PEACE

Opportunity to grow in the fruit of the Spirit:

What I'm learning about life, myself & the LORD:

Dear Heavenly Father,

Thank you that you are growing the fruit of peace in my life.
O Holy Spirit, please transform me into the likeness of Jesus Christ.
Help me to rest in your peace beyond understanding.

In the precious name of Jesus, Amen.

DATE:

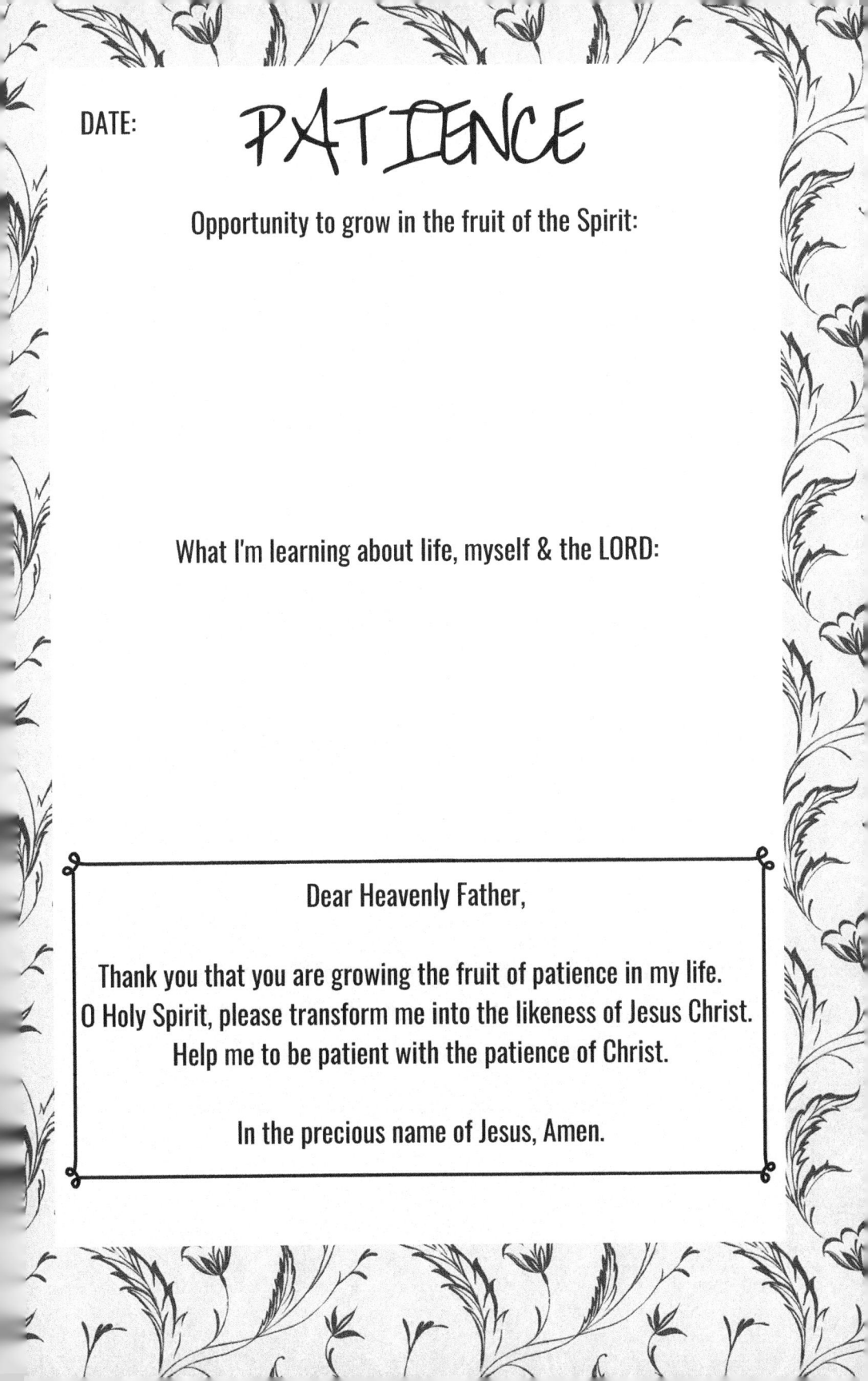

PATIENCE

Opportunity to grow in the fruit of the Spirit:

What I'm learning about life, myself & the LORD:

Dear Heavenly Father,

Thank you that you are growing the fruit of patience in my life.
O Holy Spirit, please transform me into the likeness of Jesus Christ.
Help me to be patient with the patience of Christ.

In the precious name of Jesus, Amen.

DATE:

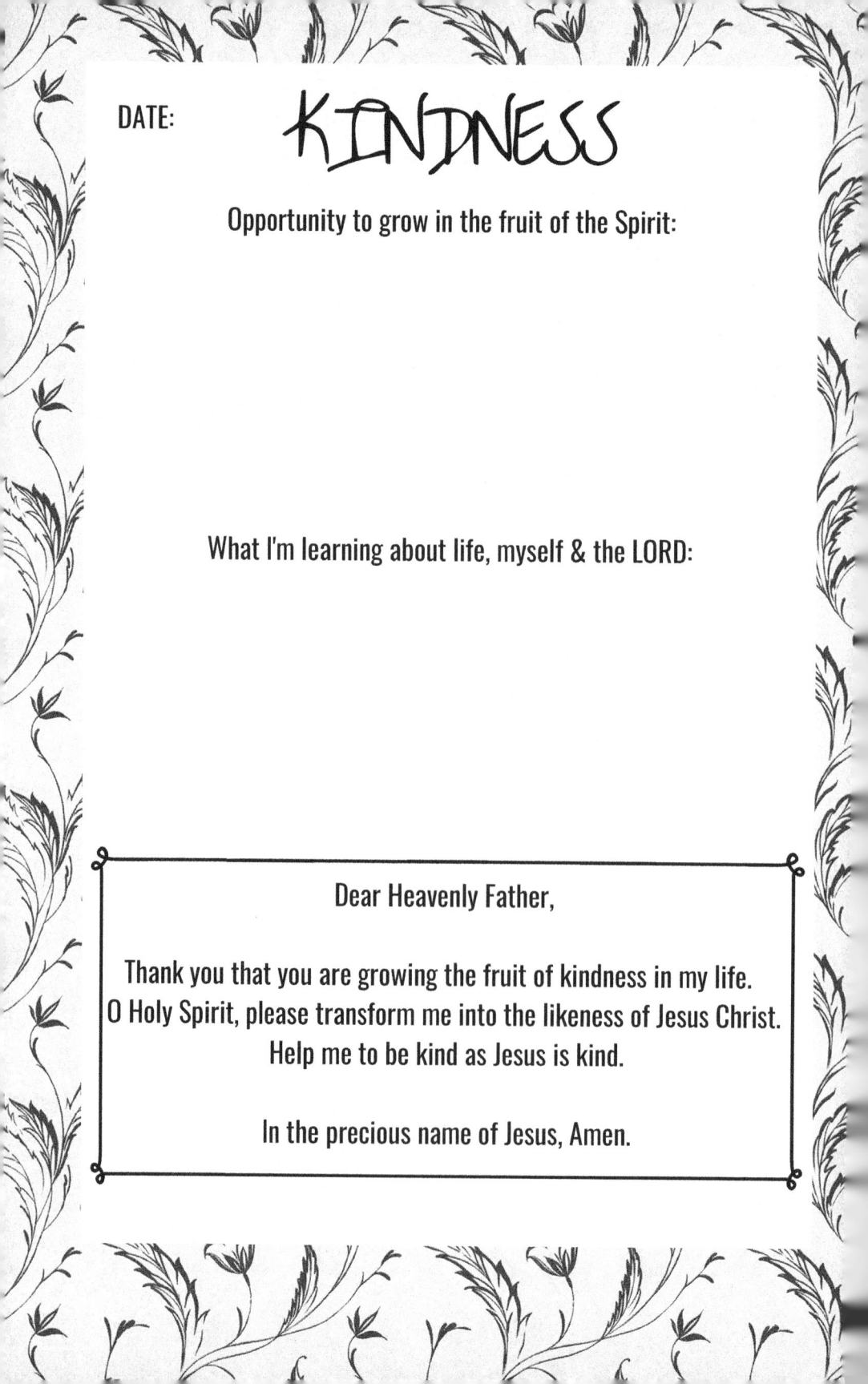

KINDNESS

Opportunity to grow in the fruit of the Spirit:

What I'm learning about life, myself & the LORD:

Dear Heavenly Father,

Thank you that you are growing the fruit of kindness in my life.
O Holy Spirit, please transform me into the likeness of Jesus Christ.
Help me to be kind as Jesus is kind.

In the precious name of Jesus, Amen.

DATE:

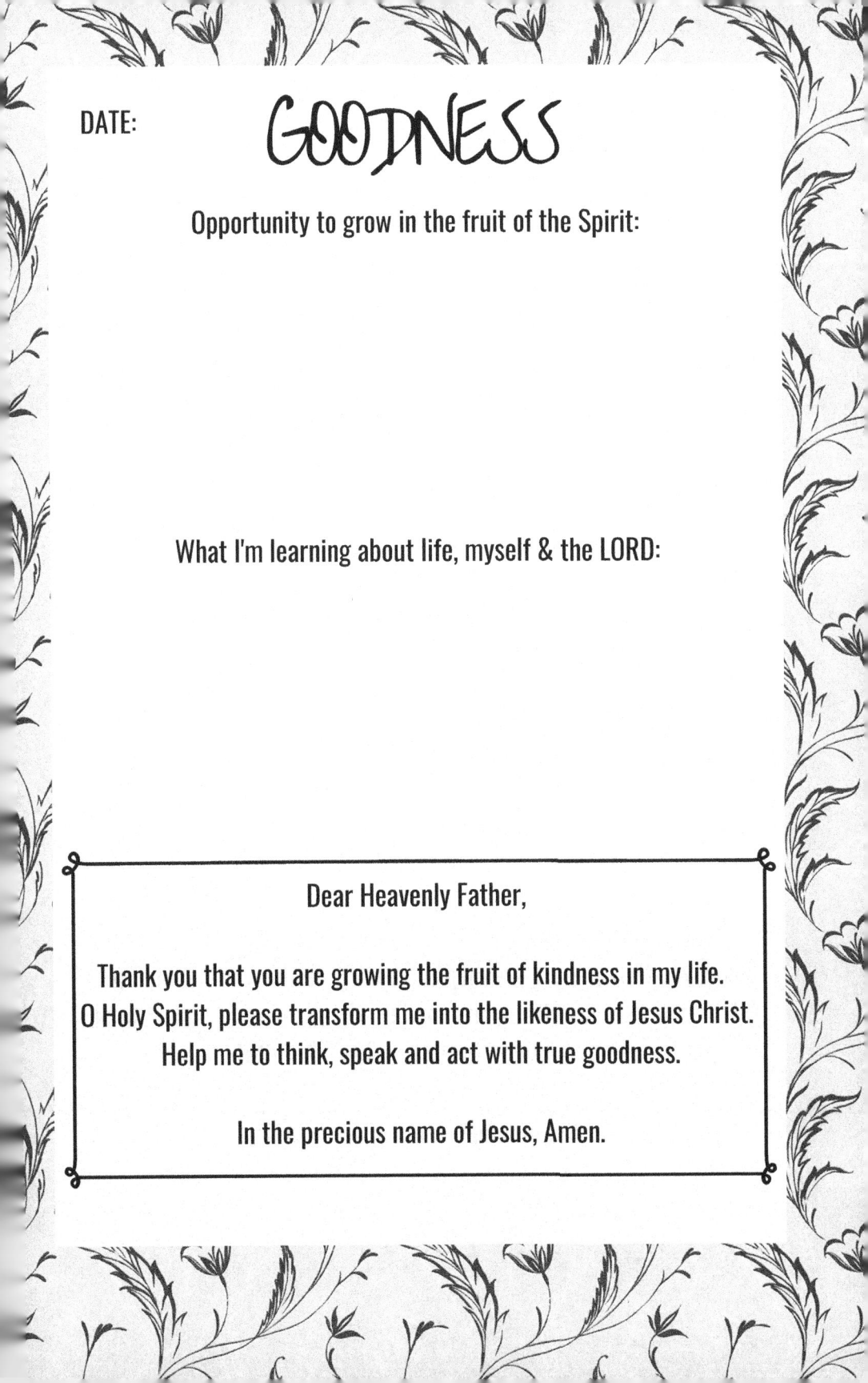

GOODNESS

Opportunity to grow in the fruit of the Spirit:

What I'm learning about life, myself & the LORD:

Dear Heavenly Father,

Thank you that you are growing the fruit of kindness in my life.
O Holy Spirit, please transform me into the likeness of Jesus Christ.
Help me to think, speak and act with true goodness.

In the precious name of Jesus, Amen.

DATE: # FAITHFULNESS

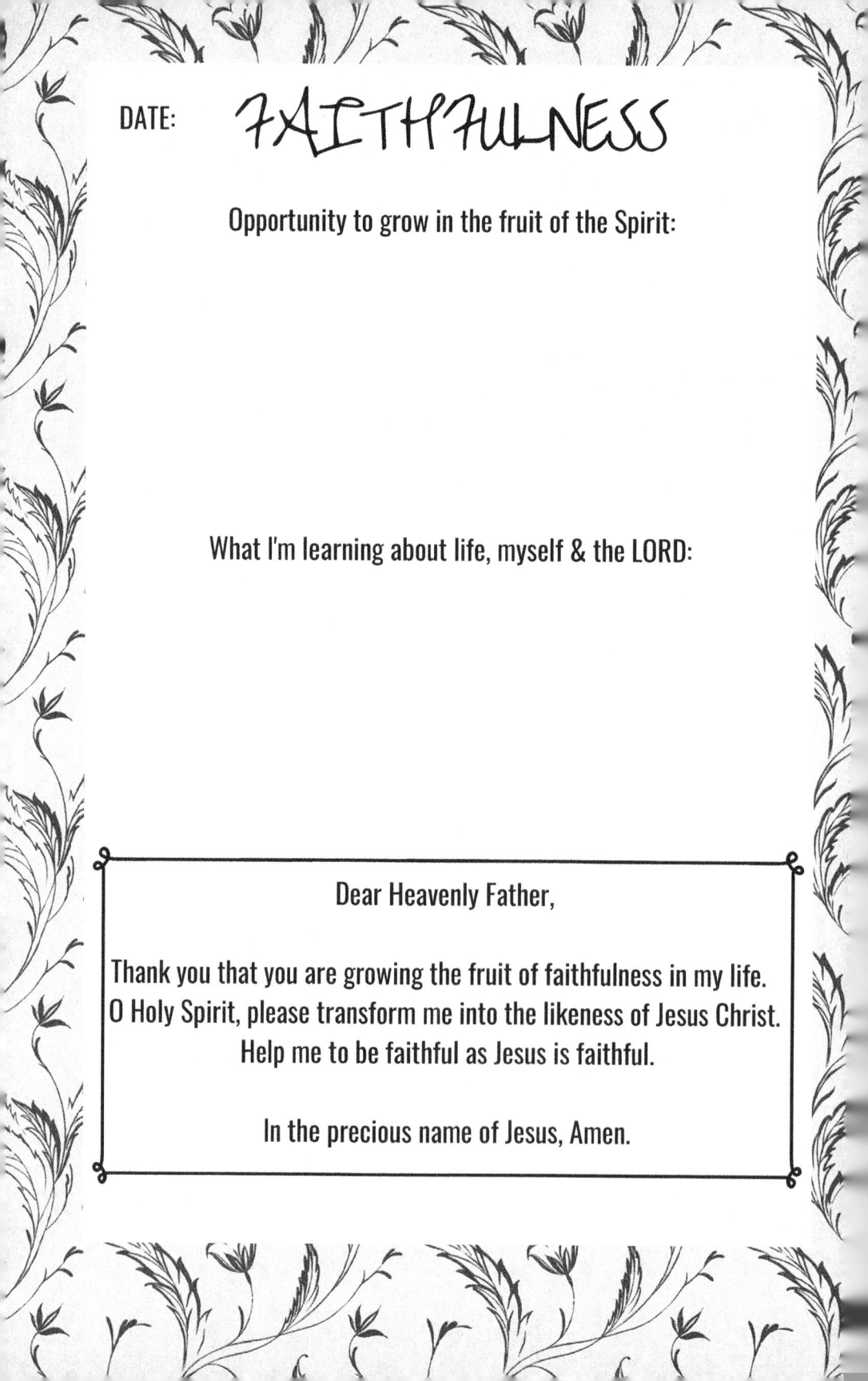

Opportunity to grow in the fruit of the Spirit:

What I'm learning about life, myself & the LORD:

Dear Heavenly Father,

Thank you that you are growing the fruit of faithfulness in my life.
O Holy Spirit, please transform me into the likeness of Jesus Christ.
Help me to be faithful as Jesus is faithful.

In the precious name of Jesus, Amen.

DATE:

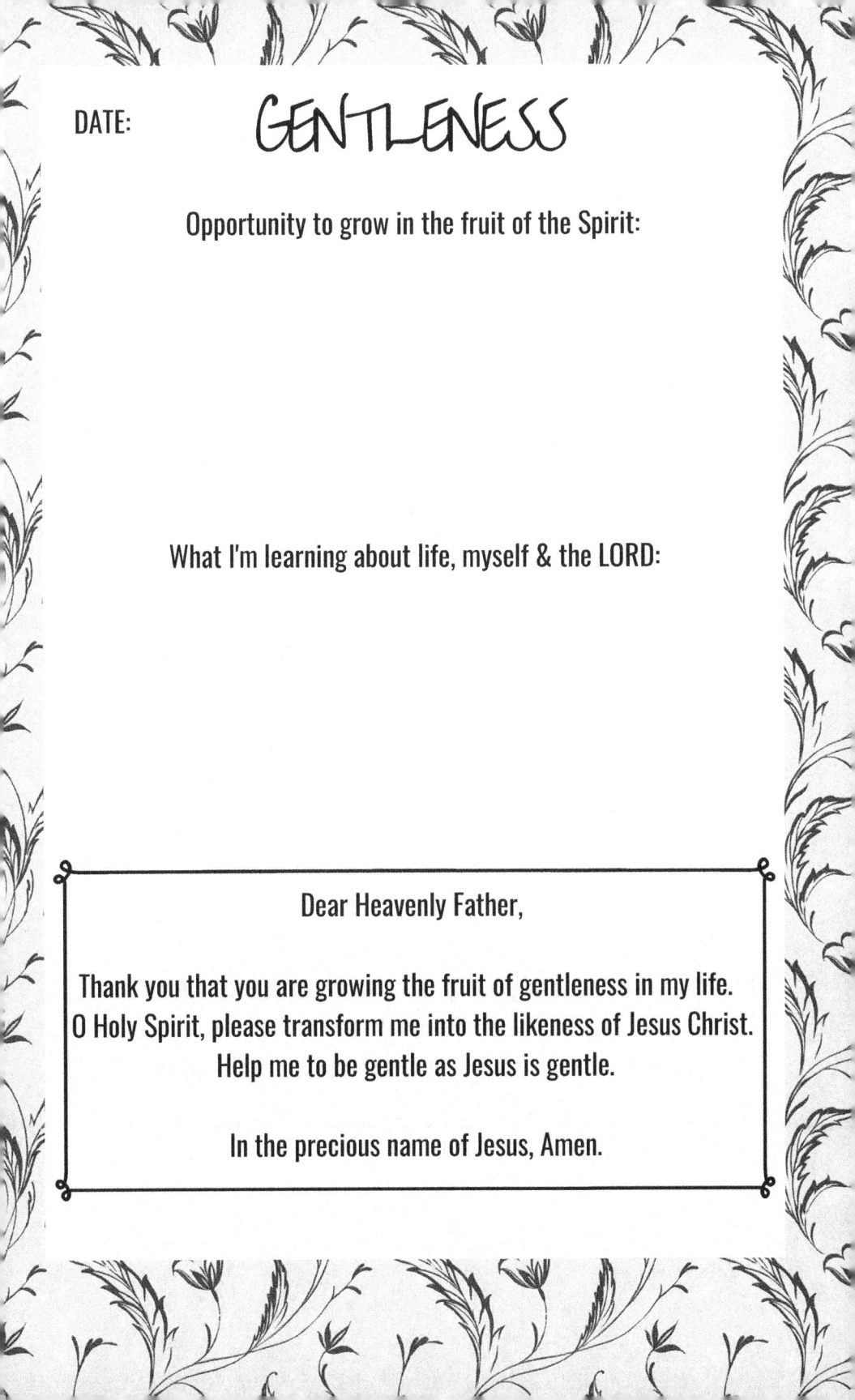

GENTLENESS

Opportunity to grow in the fruit of the Spirit:

What I'm learning about life, myself & the LORD:

> Dear Heavenly Father,
>
> Thank you that you are growing the fruit of gentleness in my life. O Holy Spirit, please transform me into the likeness of Jesus Christ. Help me to be gentle as Jesus is gentle.
>
> In the precious name of Jesus, Amen.

DATE:

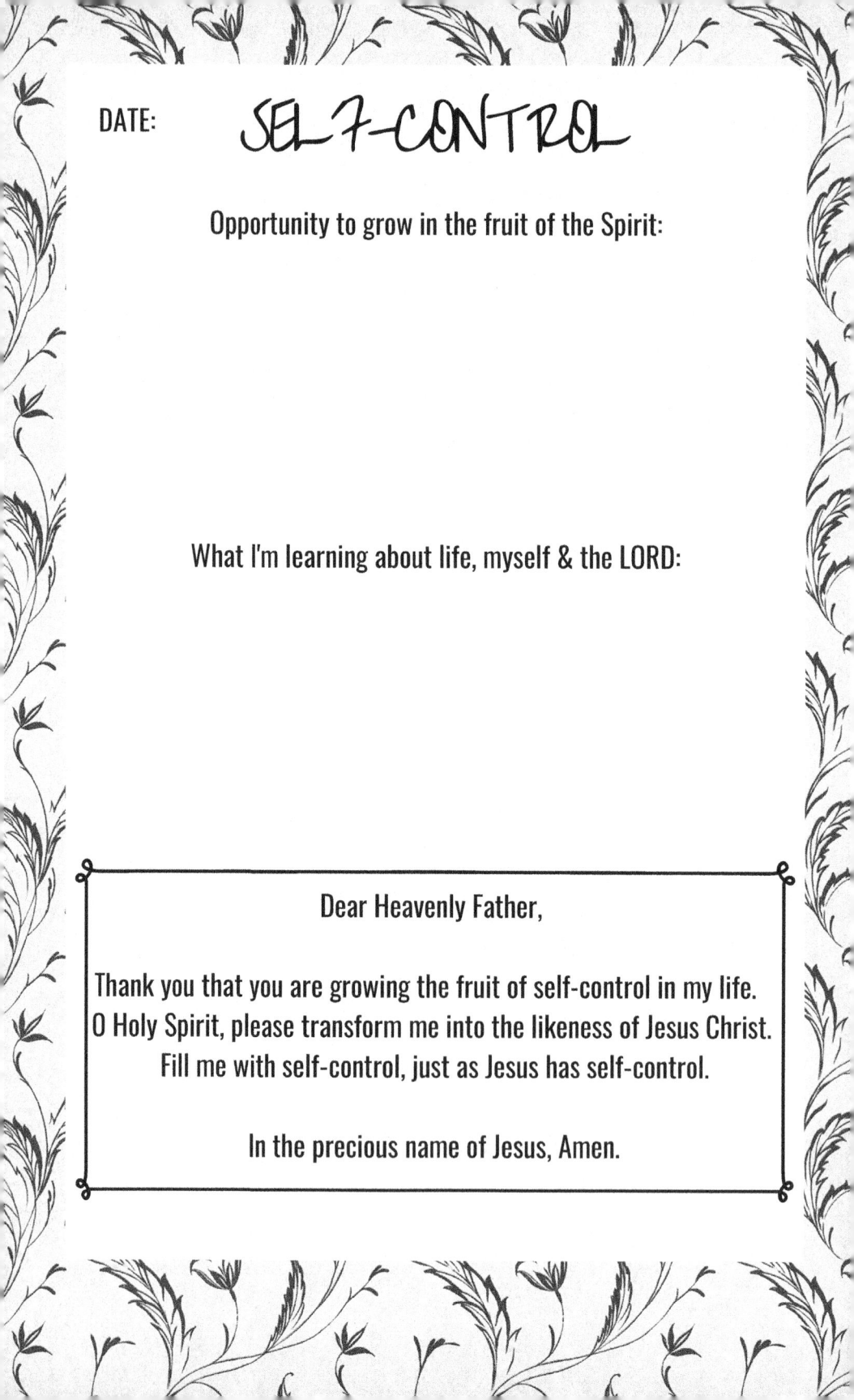

SELF-CONTROL

Opportunity to grow in the fruit of the Spirit:

What I'm learning about life, myself & the LORD:

Dear Heavenly Father,

Thank you that you are growing the fruit of self-control in my life. O Holy Spirit, please transform me into the likeness of Jesus Christ. Fill me with self-control, just as Jesus has self-control.

In the precious name of Jesus, Amen.

DATE:

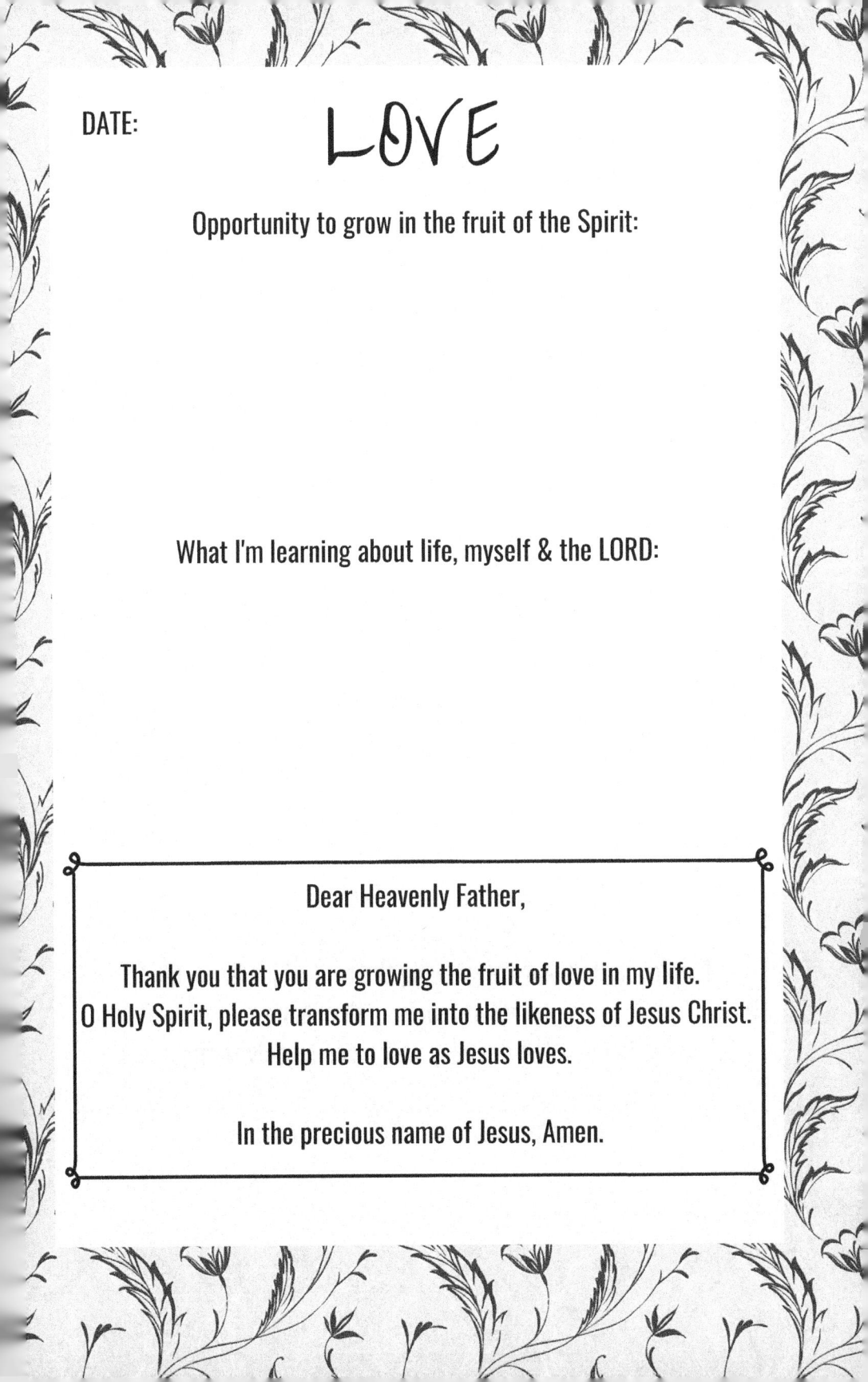

LOVE

Opportunity to grow in the fruit of the Spirit:

What I'm learning about life, myself & the LORD:

Dear Heavenly Father,

Thank you that you are growing the fruit of love in my life.
O Holy Spirit, please transform me into the likeness of Jesus Christ.
Help me to love as Jesus loves.

In the precious name of Jesus, Amen.

DATE:

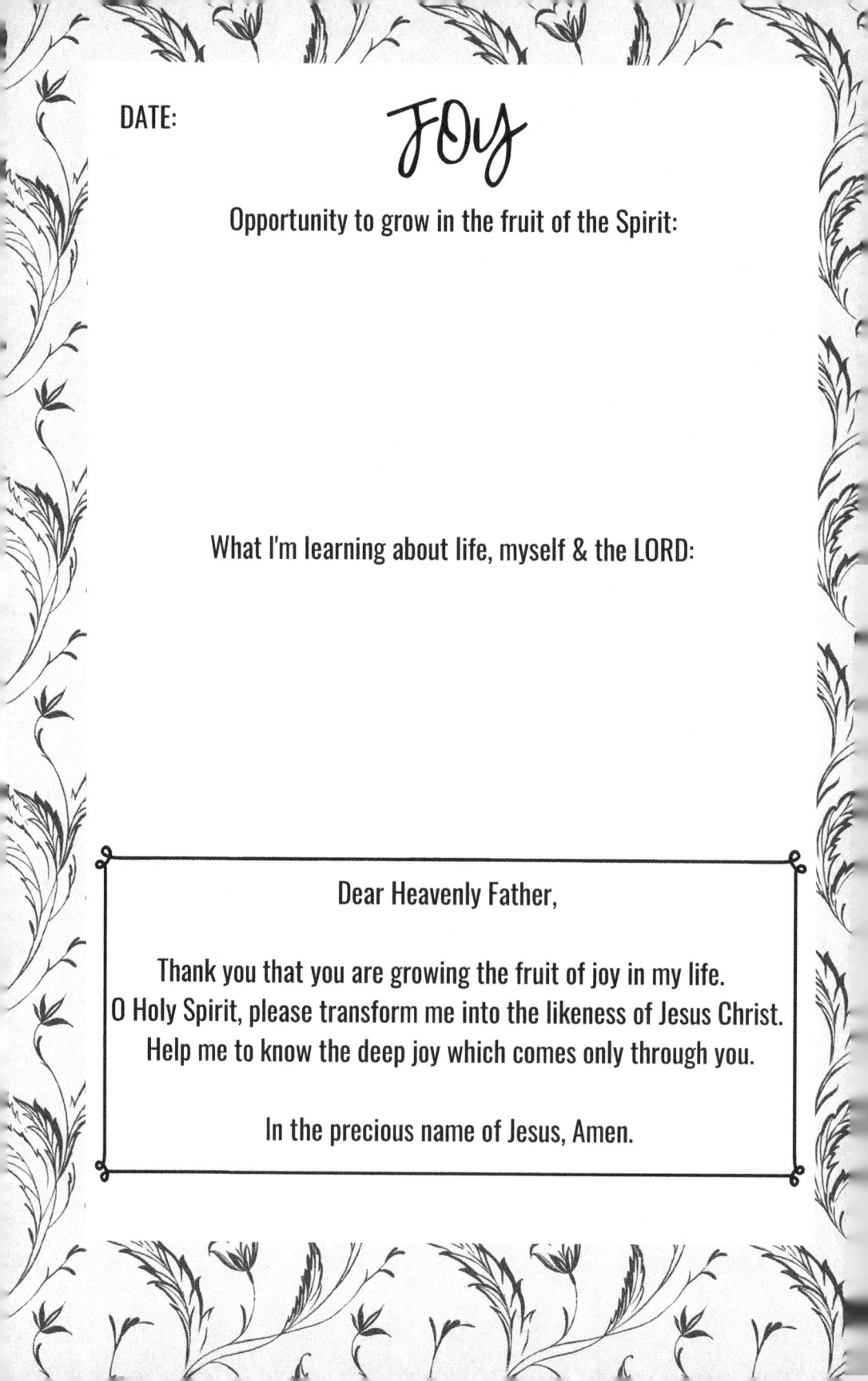

JOY

Opportunity to grow in the fruit of the Spirit:

What I'm learning about life, myself & the LORD:

Dear Heavenly Father,

Thank you that you are growing the fruit of joy in my life.
O Holy Spirit, please transform me into the likeness of Jesus Christ.
Help me to know the deep joy which comes only through you.

In the precious name of Jesus, Amen.

DATE:

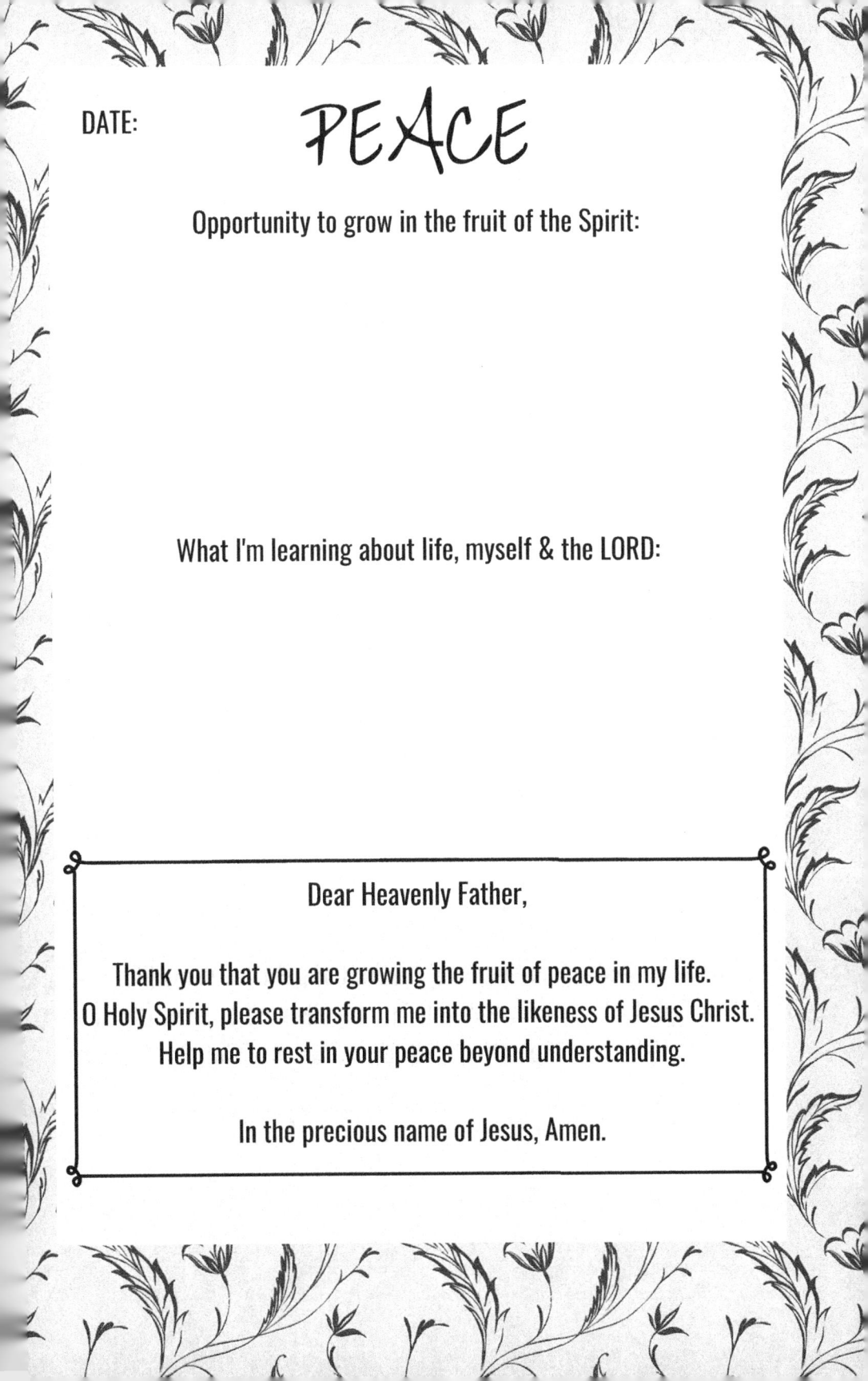

PEACE

Opportunity to grow in the fruit of the Spirit:

What I'm learning about life, myself & the LORD:

Dear Heavenly Father,

Thank you that you are growing the fruit of peace in my life.
O Holy Spirit, please transform me into the likeness of Jesus Christ.
Help me to rest in your peace beyond understanding.

In the precious name of Jesus, Amen.

DATE:

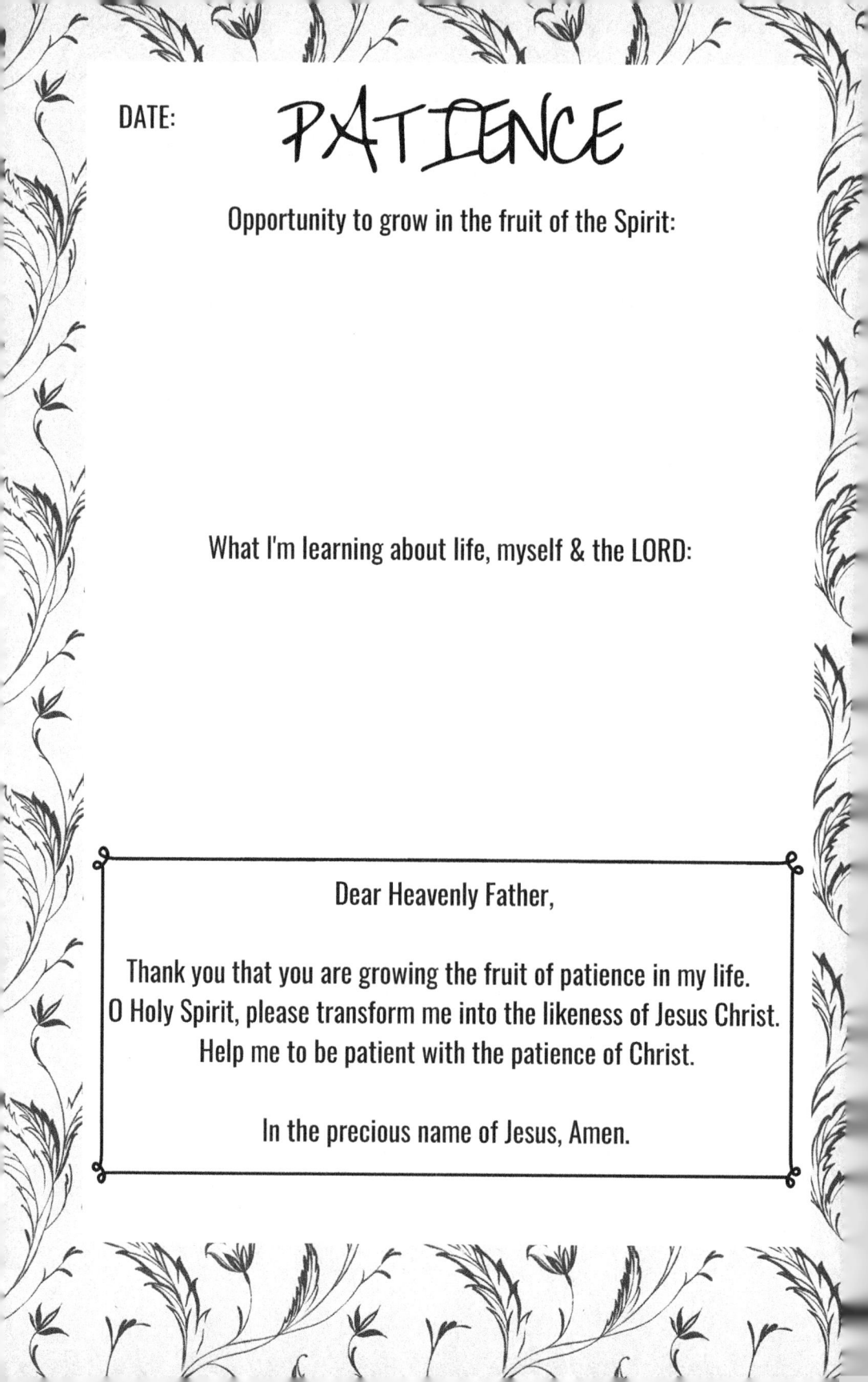

PATIENCE

Opportunity to grow in the fruit of the Spirit:

What I'm learning about life, myself & the LORD:

Dear Heavenly Father,

Thank you that you are growing the fruit of patience in my life.
O Holy Spirit, please transform me into the likeness of Jesus Christ.
Help me to be patient with the patience of Christ.

In the precious name of Jesus, Amen.

DATE:

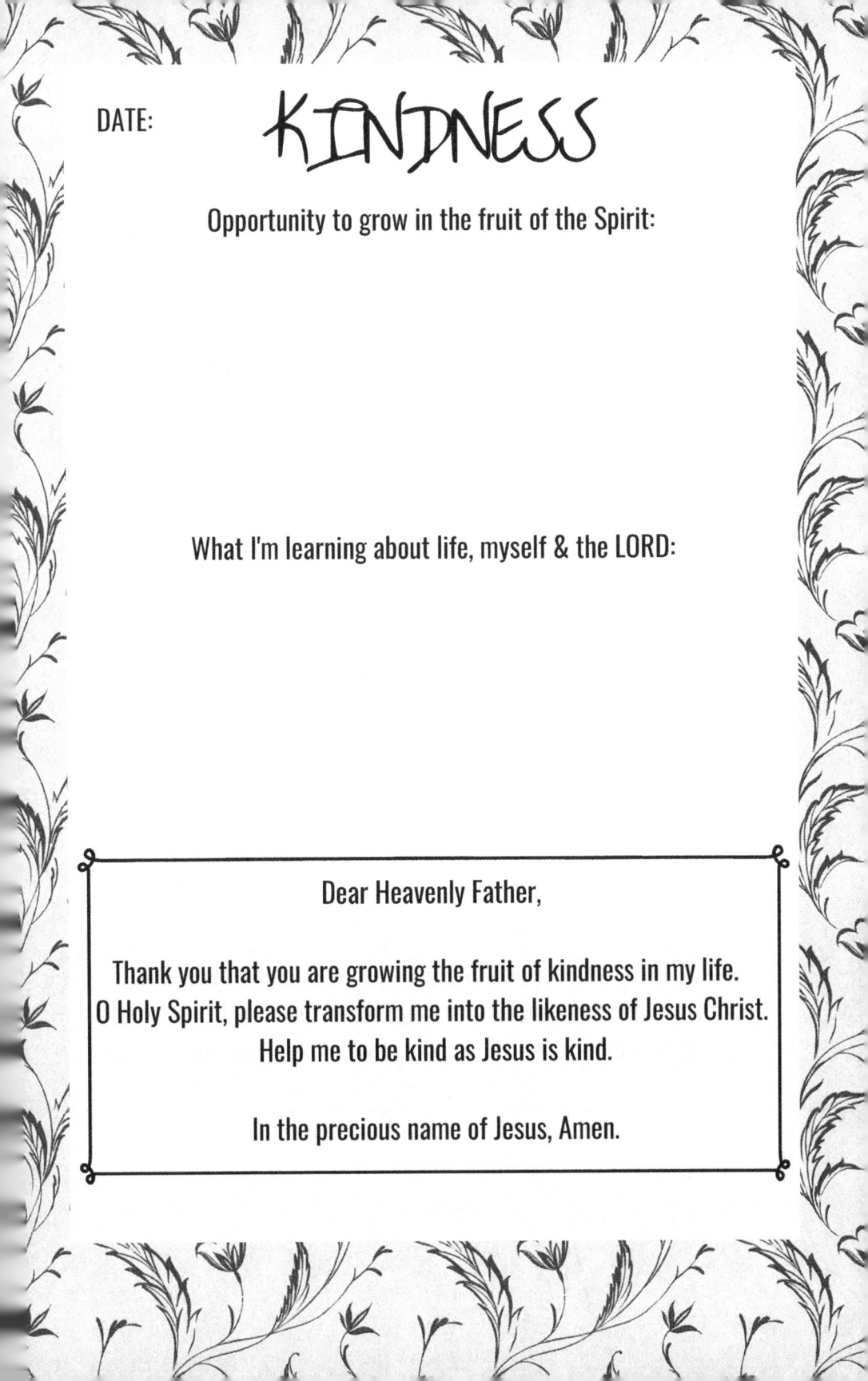

KINDNESS

Opportunity to grow in the fruit of the Spirit:

What I'm learning about life, myself & the LORD:

Dear Heavenly Father,

Thank you that you are growing the fruit of kindness in my life.
O Holy Spirit, please transform me into the likeness of Jesus Christ.
Help me to be kind as Jesus is kind.

In the precious name of Jesus, Amen.

DATE:

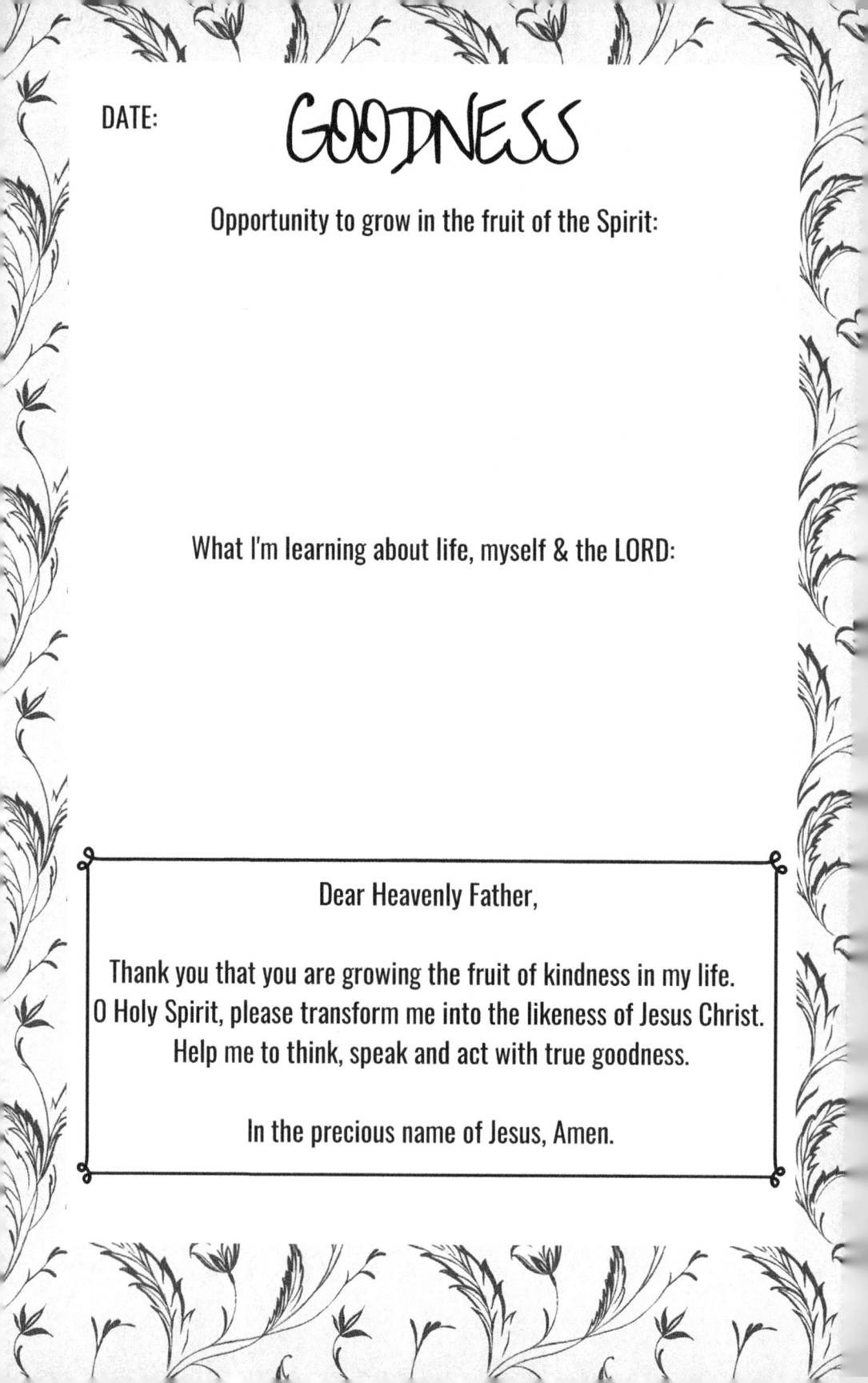

GOODNESS

Opportunity to grow in the fruit of the Spirit:

What I'm learning about life, myself & the LORD:

Dear Heavenly Father,

Thank you that you are growing the fruit of kindness in my life.
O Holy Spirit, please transform me into the likeness of Jesus Christ.
Help me to think, speak and act with true goodness.

In the precious name of Jesus, Amen.

DATE:

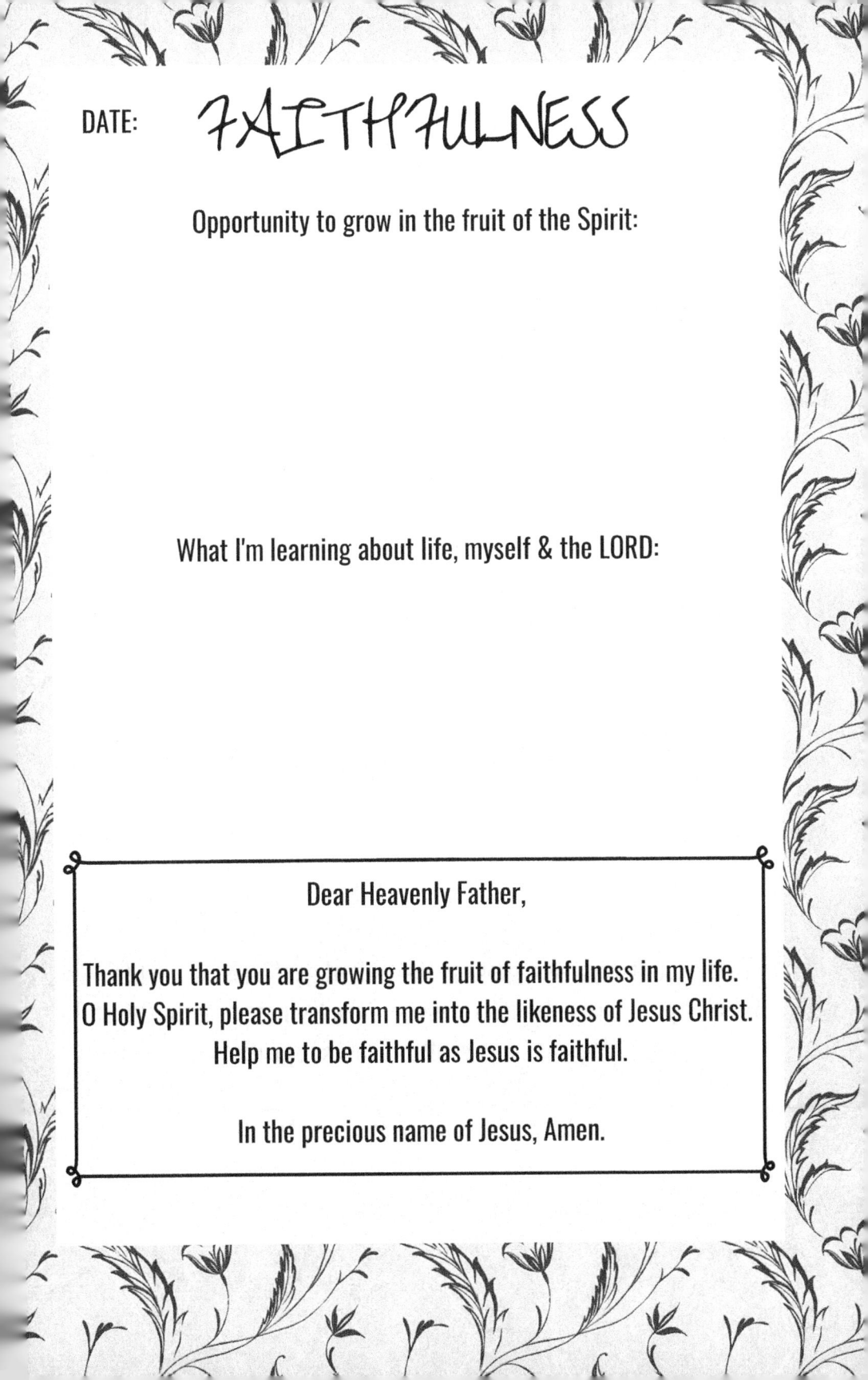

FAITHFULNESS

Opportunity to grow in the fruit of the Spirit:

What I'm learning about life, myself & the LORD:

Dear Heavenly Father,

Thank you that you are growing the fruit of faithfulness in my life. O Holy Spirit, please transform me into the likeness of Jesus Christ. Help me to be faithful as Jesus is faithful.

In the precious name of Jesus, Amen.

DATE:

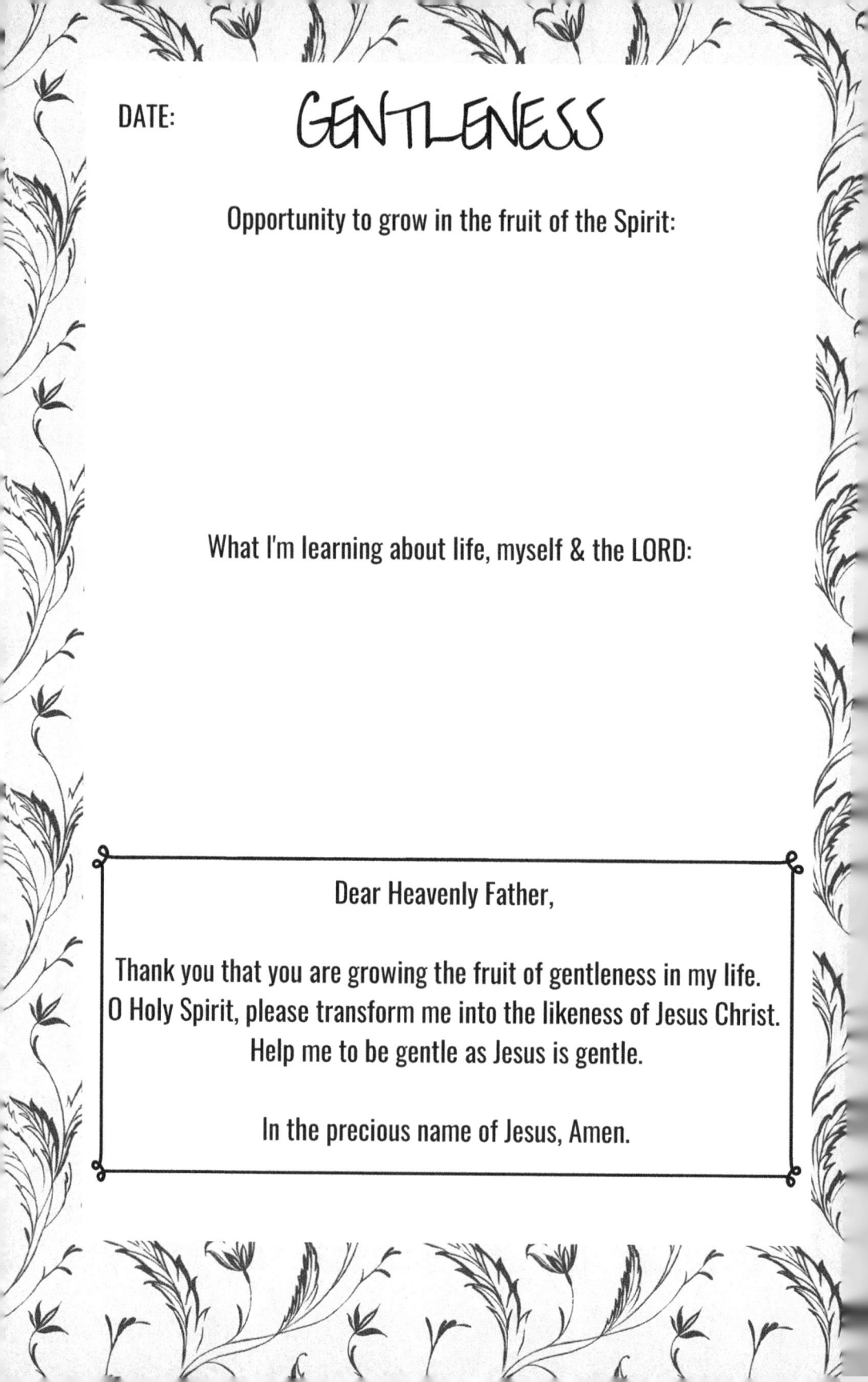

GENTLENESS

Opportunity to grow in the fruit of the Spirit:

What I'm learning about life, myself & the LORD:

Dear Heavenly Father,

Thank you that you are growing the fruit of gentleness in my life.
O Holy Spirit, please transform me into the likeness of Jesus Christ.
Help me to be gentle as Jesus is gentle.

In the precious name of Jesus, Amen.

DATE: _____   # SELF-CONTROL

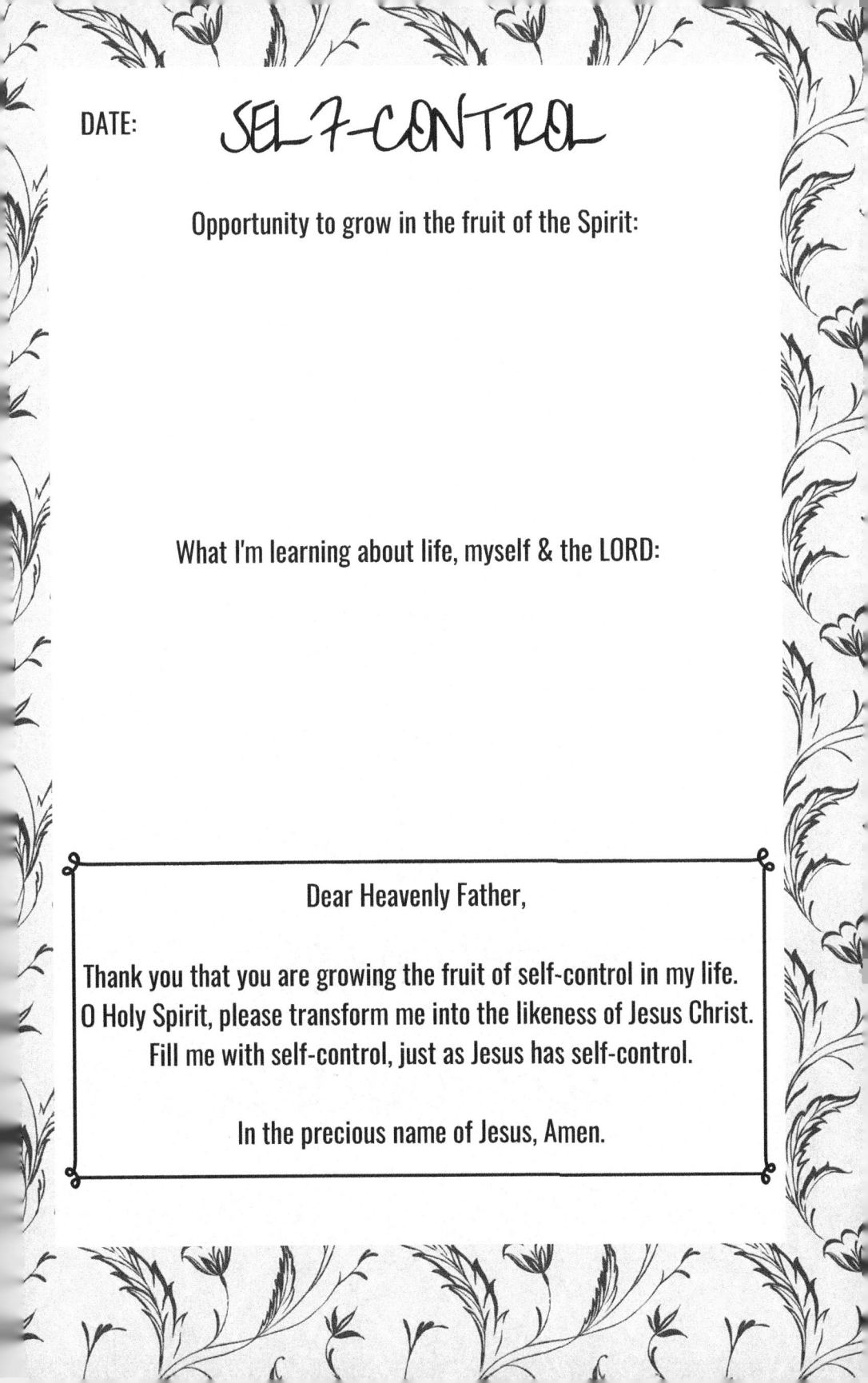

Opportunity to grow in the fruit of the Spirit:

What I'm learning about life, myself & the LORD:

Dear Heavenly Father,

Thank you that you are growing the fruit of self-control in my life.
O Holy Spirit, please transform me into the likeness of Jesus Christ.
Fill me with self-control, just as Jesus has self-control.

In the precious name of Jesus, Amen.

love,
joy,
peace,
patience,
kindness,
goodness,
faithfulness,
gentleness,
self-control